Grammar Builder

A grammar guidebook for students of English

2

A. Amin

R. Eravelly

F.J. Ibrahim

CAMBRIDGE
UNIVERSITY PRESS

PUBLISHED BY THE PRESS SYNDICATE OF THE UNIVERSITY OF CAMBRIDGE
The Pitt Building, Trumpington Street, Cambridge, United Kingdom

CAMBRIDGE UNIVERSITY PRESS
The Edinburgh Building, Cambridge CB2 2RU, UK
40 West 20th Street, New York, NY 10011–4211, USA
477 Williamstown Road, Port Melbourne, VIC 3207, Australia
Ruiz de Alarcón 13, 28014 Madrid, Spain
Dock House, The Waterfront, Cape Town 8001, South Africa
43-45 Kreta Ayer Road, Singapore 089004

http://www.cambridge.org

First published 2004

Printed in Singapore

Typeface Utopia. *System* QuarkXPress®

ISBN 0 521 54859 4 Grammar Builder Book 1
ISBN 0 521 54860 8 Grammar Builder Book 2
ISBN 0 521 54861 6 Grammar Builder Book 3
ISBN 0 521 54862 4 Grammar Builder Book 4
ISBN 0 521 54863 2 Grammar Builder Book 5

• • INTRODUCTION • • •

To the student

This book is designed to help you master key concepts in English grammar easily and quickly. Students who need to take written exams as well as those who wish to write well will find the *Grammar Builder* series helpful.

You may use this book for self-study and practice. An Answers section is located at the back of the book.

To the teacher

The *Grammar Builder* series is a useful supplement to any main English language course and is suitable for both classroom teaching and self-study. The series focuses on written grammar and the key grammar concepts that students need to know for written exercises.

How the book is organised

The *Grammar Builder* series comprises five books for beginner to upper-intermediate level learners of British English. Books 1 and 2 are intended for learners who need to acquire the basics of grammar. Books 3 to 5 are for learners who need to strengthen their proficiency in grammar and improve their written English.

Each book is made up of 42 to 56 units, and units dealing with related topics (e.g. prepositions) are grouped together for ease of use.

A unit covers three to five grammar concepts and includes four to six different types of exercises. Key grammar concepts (e.g. tenses) taught in the lower level books are re-visited and expanded upon in the other books of this series. For a list of units, refer to the *Contents* at the beginning of each book.

The books use a simple but effective three-step approach (error identification, correction, and practice) to help learners master English grammar.

There are four pages per unit, and each unit is divided into three sections: *Checkpoint, Grammar Points*, and *Practice*.

All units begin with a *Checkpoint* section containing several pairs of numbered examples that show common grammatical errors and then their corrected forms. These examples of correct and incorrect usage demonstrate to the student how slight differences in expression can result in grammatical errors.

The students can then refer to the corresponding *Grammar Points* in the next section which explain the grammar concepts highlighted under *Checkpoint*, show how to apply the grammar concepts correctly, and provide more examples.

In the third section, *Practice*, students revise the grammar concepts they have learned by completing a group of exercises. (The answers can be found at the back of the book.) This enables quick revision of each concept, and allows students to see if there are any aspects that they do not fully comprehend. Students may review what they have learned by going through the *Grammar Points* again after completing each exercise. The *Grammar Points* can also be used for quick reference purposes.

There are six revision and evaluation tests towards the back of every book. These tests deal with most of the *Grammar Points* covered in each book.

CONTENTS

· · · · · · · · · **CONTENTS** · · · · · · · · ·

UNIT 1.1 **ARTICLES**

a and **an** with singular nouns

Look at the **A** and **B** sentences below. Find out why **B** is correct and **A** is wrong in the **Grammar Points** section.

CHECKPOINT

			GRAMMAR POINTS
1A	Eric has a **guitars**.	✗	
1B	Eric has a **guitar**.	✓	1
2A	I wear **an** uniform to school.	✗	
2B	I wear **a** uniform to school.	✓	2
3A	I have **a** eraser.	✗	
3B	I have **an** eraser.	✓	3
4A	She is **a** intelligent girl.	✗	
4B	She is **an** intelligent girl.	✓	4

GRAMMAR POINTS

1 We use **a** or **an** with singular nouns only.

  EXAMPLES: Singular nouns: a girl, an orange ✓

  Plural nouns: a girls, an oranges ✗

2 We use **a** with singular nouns which begin with consonant sounds.
(Consonants: b, c, d, f, g, h, j, k, l, m, n, p, q, r, s, t, v, w, x, y, z)
  EXAMPLES: **a** computer
  a town
  a unit (sounds like 'yu-nit')

3 We use **an** with singular nouns which begin with vowel sounds.
(Vowels: a, e, i, o, u)
  EXAMPLES: **an** orchid
  an examination
  an heiress (sounds like '-eiress')

4 We also use **a** before adjectives with consonant sounds and **an** before adjectives with vowel sounds.

  a/an + adjective + singular noun

  EXAMPLES: **a** shopkeeper ✓   **an** artist ✓

  a honest shopkeeper ✗   **an** wonderful artist ✗

  an honest shopkeeper ✓   **a w**onderful artist ✓

> **REMEMBER!**
> - The words **a**, **an** and **the** are called articles.
> - A noun is the name of a person, an animal, a plant, a place or a thing.
>   **EXAMPLES:** student
>   cat
>   rose
>   farm
>   diskette

> **REMEMBER!**
> - An adjective is a word that describes a noun.
>   **EXAMPLES:**
>
> | Adjective | Noun |
> |---|---|
> | friendly | boy |
> | interesting | story |

PRACTICE $\boxed{A}$ Complete columns A and B with the correct nouns in the box.

arrangements	audience	conductor
entrance	flute	groups
harps	instrument	musician
orchestra	pianist	sounds
trumpets	usher	violin

A
a

1 _____
2 _____
3 _____
4 _____
5 _____

B
an

1 _____
2 _____
3 _____
4 _____
5 _____

YOUR SCORE
10

PRACTICE $\boxed{B}$ Fill in the blanks with **a** or **an**.

1   Mr Micawber is _____ unrealistic person.

2   Elizabeth Bennet is _____ bright woman.

3   Jane Bennet is _____ sweet-natured lady.

4   Huck Finn is _____ adventurous boy.

5   Jo March is _____ enthusiastic girl.

6   Uriah Heep is _____ evil man.

7   Mr Darcy is _____ arrogant man.

8   Mr Wickham is _____ irresponsible person.

9   Mr Collins is _____ conceited bore.

10   Miss Havisham is _____ bitter woman.

YOUR SCORE
10

Rewrite the sentences. Put in **a** or **an** where necessary.

1 Alan sat on buffalo and I sat on elephant at the zoo.
   Alan sat on a buffalo and I sat on an elephant at the zoo.

2 We gave Mum anklet and bracelet for her birthday.

3 This is egg, not ping-pong ball.

4 My cousin is engineer and his wife is architect.

5 A pilot flies aeroplane or helicopter.

6 Marina lives in village and Shan lives in city.

YOUR SCORE
10

PRACTICE *D* Fill in the blanks with the correct adjectives in the boxes.

1 She is an _____ secretary. | efficient / hardworking |

2 I would like an _____ mirror for my bathroom. | oval / round |

3 This is a _____ armchair. | unique / unusual |

4 Spain is a _____ country. | exciting / fascinating |

5 He is an _____ man. | honourable / humble |

6 Brenda has an _____ bicycle. | black / orange |

7 That is a _____ house. | enormous / huge |

8 Let's have a _____ meal tonight. | ordinary / simple |

9 I saw a _____ dress in the shop window. | attractive / beautiful |

10 Miss Jones read us an _____ essay by Christy. | delightful / excellent |

YOUR SCORE
10

4

PRACTICE *E*   Tick the correct words to complete the sentences.

1 I have an _____ .
   - [ ] ring
   - [ ] opal ring

2 Joe is drawing a _____ .
   - [ ] octagon
   - [ ] large octagon

3 Mr Lee had a _____ just now.
   - [ ] meal
   - [ ] enormous meal

4 Ken and Mary want to live in a _____ .
   - [ ] area
   - [ ] quiet area

5 We heard an _____ in the lab.
   - [ ] explosion
   - [ ] terrible explosion

6 There is an _____ to Bangkok tomorrow.
   - [ ] train
   - [ ] express train

7 They are going to join a _____ .
   - [ ] club
   - [ ] adventure club

8 This house has an _____ .
   - [ ] attic
   - [ ] tiny attic

9 Mrs Hall is a _____ .
   - [ ] editor
   - [ ] patient editor

10 I usually write an_____ in my desk diary.
   - [ ] address
   - [ ] new address

YOUR SCORE
10

PRACTICE *F*   Circle **a**, **an** or **–** (no article) to complete the paragraph.

Last month I had **1** (a   an   –) experience I will remember for the rest of my life. I attended **2** (a   an   –) five-day camp in Selangor, Malaysia. It was **3** (a   an   –) international event. I met youths from Britain, Canada, Fiji, Japan and other **4** (a   an   –) countries. We had **5** (a   an   –) wonderful time getting to know one another. We went hiking, climbed **6** (a   an   –) rocks, jungle-trekked and played games. On the fourth day, we held **7** (a   an   –) exhibition and treated guests to **8** (a   an   –) cultural performance.

We spent the last day in groups. We gave reports, shared our experiences and exchanged **9** (a   an   –) addresses. All of us felt sad that we had to part. I had **10** (a   an   –) autograph book with me and I got all the other participants to sign in it.

YOUR SCORE
10

5

UNIT 1.2 ARTICLES

a, an, the with singular nouns

Look at the **A** and **B** sentences below. Find out why **B** is correct and **A** is wrong in the **Grammar Points** section.

CHECKPOINT

			GRAMMAR POINTS
1A	Julia spent $200 on a dress yesterday. She wants to show off **a dress** at this weekend's party.	✗	
1B	Julia spent $200 on a dress yesterday. She wants to show off **the dress** at this weekend's party.	✓	1
2A	You look very ill. I think you should go to **clinic**.	✗	
2B	You look very ill. I think you should go to **the clinic**.	✓	2
3A	Sit on **ground** and rest.	✗	
3B	Sit on **the ground** and rest.	✓	3
4A	I was born on **12th of May**, 1985.	✗	
4B	I was born on **the 12th of May**, 1985.	✓	4

GRAMMAR POINTS

1 We use **a** or **an** when we speak of someone or something for the first time. We use **the** when we mention that person or thing a second time.
EXAMPLES: I found **a** purse just now. I believe that **the** purse belongs to Emily.
John's favourite pet is **a** parrot. He talks to **the** parrot every day.

2 We use **the** when it is clear to the listener or reader which person or thing we are referring to.
EXAMPLES: My car is at **the** workshop on Campbell Road.
Serene lives opposite **the** museum. (= the museum in this town)

3 We use **the** when there is only one such thing.
EXAMPLES: Look! There's a rainbow in **the** sky.
The air is fresh this evening.

4 We usually use **the** before ordinal numbers.
EXAMPLES: Joseph won **the** first prize in the competition.
Today is **the** 30th of January.

REMEMBER!
- An ordinal number is a number like **first**, **second**, **third** or **fourth** which shows the position of something in a list of items.

6

PRACTICE A Fill in the blanks with **a**, **an** or **the**.

1 I can see _____ aeroplane on the runway. _____ aeroplane is going to take off.

2 Mr Paulson has _____ new house. _____ house is on Green Street.

3 Our ship crossed _____ equator at 3 p.m. today.

4 I have to go to _____ post office on Birch Road to post _____ parcel.

5 Salim is going to Sri Lanka on _____ 22nd of February. He will attend _____ art conference there.

6 Mr Gibson plans to travel around _____ world in his hot-air balloon.

YOUR SCORE
10

PRACTICE B Rewrite the sentences. Put in **a**, **an** or **the** where necessary.

1 Wind is blowing gently.

_____

2 Our Sports Day is on fourth of May.

_____

3 Patrick chopped some firewood with big axe. He piled firewood behind his house.

_____

4 I need taxi because I am going to train station now.

_____

5 Dina has pictures of ape and panda. She likes picture of panda.

_____

YOUR SCORE
10

PRACTICE C Tick the correct articles to complete the paragraph.

Yoghurt is **1** [a | an] type of food. It is used as **2** [an | the] aid to digestion.

It is said that **3** [a | the] people of Turkey eat more than **4** [a | an] million tons

of yoghurt **5** [a | an] year.

The story goes that in 1526, Suleiman the Magnificent sent **6** [a | the] doctor and

7 [a | the] goat to France. Each day **8** [a | the] doctor prepared yoghurt from

fresh goat's milk for **9** [a | the] ailing king of France. What was **10** [a | the]

result? Francis I of France was cured.

YOUR SCORE
10

7

PRACTICE **D** Underline the correct articles to complete the paragraph.

In **1** (a / an) quiet residential area, I saw **2** (a / an) old house. The handle on **3** (a / the) front door came off at the slightest touch. **4** (A / The) living room was musty and damp. **5** (An / The) attic had a mountain of rubbish. Everything was in **6** (a / the) mess.

Then I walked into **7** (a / the) kitchen. It had **8** (an / the) interesting bay window where **9** (a / the) sun's rays filtered through. I knew then that I had found **10** (a / the) house of my dreams.

YOUR SCORE
/10

PRACTICE **E** Mark with ⟨ wherever the article **the** is missing.

I brought in a contractor to renovate ⟨house. He walked around place and turned me down. Second contractor began work on house but never returned after first day. Fortunately for me, third contractor stayed and finished job. He pulled down several walls, he redid staircase and turned patio into an office for me. He was expensive but excellent. As he stood at gleaming white gate he had fixed for me, ready to leave, he waved cheque in his hand and said, "Enjoy your castle."

YOUR SCORE
/10

PRACTICE **F** Rewrite the paragraph. Put in **a**, **an** or **the** where necessary.

You can make food cover for picnics using empty ice-cream container without its lid. You just need to buy door knob, a washer and a screw. Turn container upside down and make small hole in the base of the container. Hole should be at the centre of the base. Place door knob above the hole and fix it using washer and screw. Food cover is ready.

_____

_____

_____

_____

_____

_____

_____

_____

YOUR SCORE
/10

PRACTICE *G* Circle the letters of the sentences that are correct. There may be more than one answer for each question.

1 A Cambridge University was founded in the 13th century.
   B Cambridge University was founded in 13th century.
   C Cambridge University was founded in a 13th century.
   D Cambridge University was founded in 13th a century.

2 A I need a taxi to take me to a airport.
   B I need a taxi to take me to the airport.
   C I need the taxi to take me to a airport.
   D I need the taxi to take me to the airport.

3 A Do you always read a newspapers while having your breakfast?
   B Do you always read newspapers while having your breakfast?
   C Do you always read the newspaper while having your breakfast?
   D Do you always read newspaper while having your breakfast?

4 A Yesterday I finished a book about animals and the book was very interesting.
   B Yesterday I finished the book about animal and the book was very interesting.
   C Yesterday I finished a book about an animal and the book was very interesting.
   D Yesterday I finished a book about animals and book was very interesting.

5 A Walt Disney opened first amusement park in 1955. He named park 'Disneyland'.
   B Walt Disney opened the first amusement park in 1955. He named the park 'Disneyland'.
   C Walt Disney opened the first amusement park in 1955. He named a park 'Disneyland'.
   D Walt Disney opened a first amusement park in 1955. He named the park 'Disneyland'.

6 A A moon is illuminated by a sun and reflects some of a light to an Earth.
   B The moon is illuminated by a sun and reflects some of light to Earth.
   C The moon is illuminated by the sun and reflects some of the light to the Earth.
   D A moon is illuminated the sun and reflects some of the light to a Earth.

7 A There's the travel agency a block away from a hospital.
   B There's a travel agency a block away from hospital.
   C There's the travel agency block away from the hospital.
   D There's a travel agency a block away from the hospital.

YOUR SCORE
10

UNIT 1.3 ARTICLES

the with proper nouns

Look at the **A** and **B** sentences below. Find out why **B** is correct and **A** is wrong in the **Grammar Points** section.

				GRAMMAR POINTS
1A	We flew over **Yangtze River**.	✗		
1B	We flew over **the Yangtze River**.	✓	1a	
2A	He photographed **Empire State Building**.	✗		
2B	He photographed **the Empire State Building**.	✓	1b	
3A	That is **President of India**.	✗		
3B	That is **the President of India**.	✓	1c	
4A	**Himalayas** are the highest mountain range in the world.	✗		
4B	**The Himalayas** are the highest mountain range in the world.	✓	1d	

GRAMMAR POINTS

1 We use **the** before some proper nouns such as:

(a) the names of oceans, rivers, seas and straits
   EXAMPLES: **the** Atlantic Ocean
         the (River) Rhine
         the Sargasso Sea

(b) the names of most buildings, landmarks, monuments and natural wonders
   EXAMPLES: **the** National Museum
         the Star Cinema
         the Great Barrier Reef

(c) the names of places containing **of** and people's titles containing **of**
   EXAMPLES: **the** State **of** New York
         the General Manager **of** Global Bank

(d) the names of places ending in plural 's'
   EXAMPLES: **the** Marshall Islands
         the United States

REMEMBER!

■ A proper noun is the special name given to one particular person, animal, plant, place or thing. It begins with a capital letter.

■ The following are some proper nouns which do not use **the**:
   (a) the names of continents
      EXAMPLES: Australia, Europe
   (b) the names of most countries
      EXAMPLES: Egypt, Switzerland
   (c) the names of most towns and cities
      EXAMPLES: Colombo, London
   (d) the names of streets
      EXAMPLES: Avery Road
            Raffles Boulevard
   (e) the names of people
      EXAMPLES: George
            Sharon

10

PRACTICE $\boxed{A}$ Tick the correct boxes to complete the sentences.

1 ☐ Chongqing Tower in China is 460m tall.
  ☐ The Chongqing Tower

2 ☐ Mississippi is a river in ☐ America.
  ☐ The Mississippi ☐ the America.

3 ☐ Republic of Pakistan became an independent nation in 1947.
  ☐ The Republic of Pakistan

4 ☐ Berlin Wall was a man-made barrier between East and West Berlin that was
  ☐ The Berlin Wall
  dismantled in 1989.

5 Eisaku Sato was ☐ Prime Minister of Japan from 1964 to 1972.
                  ☐ the Prime Minister of Japan

6 The main newspaper offices in London were once located on ☐ Fleet Street.
                                                            ☐ the Fleet Street.

7 ☐ Carribean Sea is a part of ☐ Atlantic Ocean.
  ☐ The Carribean Sea ☐ the Atlantic Ocean.

8 The headquarters of ☐ United Nations is in New York.
                      ☐ the United Nations

PRACTICE $\boxed{B}$ Fill in the blanks with **the** where necessary.

1 I visited _____ Eiffel Tower when I was in _____ France for a tour last month.

2 _____ Republic of Singapore lies south of _____ Peninsular Malaysia.

3 Dyak people live along _____ Skrang River in _____ Sarawak.

4 _____ Prince Street is parallel to _____ Wellington Street.

5 _____ Vice-Chancellor of _____ University of New South Wales is here.

PRACTICE `C` The word **the** is missing in 10 places. Mark with ⋏ wherever it should be.

Canary Islands, also called Canaries, are part of Spain. They have a mild climate, beautiful scenery and were once called Fortunate Islands. Today holiday makers love to view Maspalomas Dunes, which resemble Sahara Desert. They also visit Canary Islands Museum and learn about history of Canary Islands. There are exhibitions featuring Guanches, who were pre-Spanish inhabitants of islands.

YOUR SCORE
10

PRACTICE `D` Rewrite the sentences. Put in **a**, **an** or **the** where necessary.

1 The manager of Westin Hotel is uncle of mine.

_____

2 River Ganges is in India.

_____

3 Prime Minister of Australia will visit Republic of China next year.

_____

4 National Theatre is opposite fire station on Stamford Road.

_____

5 Golden Gate Bridge in San Francisco is popular tourist attraction.

_____

YOUR SCORE
10

PRACTICE `E` Fill in the blanks with **the** or **–** (no article).

(1) _____ 20th century saw its last total eclipse of the sun in August, 1999. The eclipse was watched by millions of people in (2) _____ Europe and the Middle East. It began at 9.31 GMT when the shadow of the moon covered the sun completely. This was witnessed by spectators near Nova Scotia. The eclipse moved at a speed of 2,400 km per hour across (3) _____ Atlantic Ocean and at 1010 GMT, it reached (4) _____ Scilly Isles of Britain. In less than a minute, it was witnessed on the mainland. More than one million people were waiting in (5) _____ county of Cornwall to witness the historic event.

After Britain, it was (6) _____ France, (7) _____ Germany and then (8) _____ Hungary that experienced the darkness. The eclipse ended at about 1230 GMT off (9) _____ India with the setting of the sun in (10) _____ Bay of Bengal.

YOUR SCORE
10

12

PRACTICE $\boxed{F}$ Circle the letters of the sentences that are correct. There may be more than one answer for each question.

1   A   The Andaman Islands are in Bay of Bengal.
     B   Andaman Islands are in Bay of Bengal.
     C   The Andaman Islands are in the Bay of Bengal.

2   A   Bay of Bengal lies between India and Myanmar.
     B   The Bay of Bengal lies between the India and the Myanmar.
     C   The Bay of Bengal lies between India and Myanmar.

3   A   Mandalay is a city found in the Myanmar.
     B   Mandalay is a city found in Myanmar.
     C   The city of Mandalay is found in Myanmar.

4   A   Thailand is east of the Myanmar.
     B   The Thailand is east of the Myanmar.
     C   Thailand is east of Myanmar.

5   A   Capital of Thailand lies on Chao Phrayer river.
     B   The capital of Thailand lies on the Chao Phrayer river.
     C   The capital of Thailand lies on Chao Phrayer river.

6   A   The Plain of Jars is a famous monument in Laos.
     B   Plain of Jars is a famous monument in the Laos.
     C   Plain of Jars is a famous monument in Las.

7   A   Mekong River flows through Vietnam.
     B   The Mekong River flows through the Vietnam.
     C   The Mekong River flows through Vietnam.

8   A   Hanoi was once the capital of the Vietnam.
     B   The Hanoi was once the capital of Vietnam.
     C   Hanoi was once the capital of Vietnam.

9   A   Tourists visit the Royal Palace in Cambodia.
     B   Tourists visit Royal Palace in Cambodia.
     C   Tourists visit the Royal Palace in the Cambodia.

YOUR SCORE
10

UNIT 1.4 ARTICLES

with countable and uncountable nouns

Look at the **A** and **B** sentences below. Find out why **B** is correct and **A** is wrong in the **Grammar Points** section.

			GRAMMAR POINTS
1A	There is **a sand** in my shoe. / There are **sands** in my shoe.	✗	
1B	There is **sand** in my shoe.	✓	1
2A	I would like **bottle of soda**.	✗	
2B	I would like **a bottle of soda**.	✓	2
3A	**Milk** in this jug is sour.	✗	
3B	**The milk** in this jug is sour.	✓	3

GRAMMAR POINTS

1

Some nouns can be counted and they are called countable nouns. Some nouns cannot be counted and they are called uncountable nouns.

We use **a** or **an** only before countable nouns.

a/an + countable noun ✓   **a/an** + uncountable noun ✗

EXAMPLES: We use **flour** to make pancakes.
Mum added **salt** to the fish curry.
There is **water** on the table.

> **REMEMBER!**
> - An uncountable noun does not have a plural form.
>
> EXAMPLES:
>
> mud ✓   muds ✗
> rice ✓   rices ✗

2

We use **a** or **an** with uncountable nouns in this way:

a/an + countable noun + **of** + uncountable noun

EXAMPLES: I used **a cup of flour** to make pancakes.
Mum added **a teaspoon of salt** to the fish curry.
There is **a jug of water** on the table.

3

We use **the** with uncountable nouns when it is clear to the listener or reader which things we are referring to. We do not use **the** with uncountable nouns when we are talking in general.

EXAMPLES: **The water** in this jug tastes funny.
(We are referring to the water in the jug specifically.)

Plants need **water** to grow. (general)

> **REMEMBER!**
> - The word **some** can be used with both countable and uncountable nouns in these ways:
>
> some + plural countable noun
>
> EXAMPLES: I want **some apples**.
> He needs **some pencils**.
>
> some + uncountable noun
>
> EXAMPLES: I want **some flour**.
> He needs **some paper**.

PRACTICE **A** Complete the table with the words in the box. Add **a** or **an** where necessary.

| aluminium | bread | cloth | cookie | diskette | envelope |
| hamburger | music | raincoat | smoke | umbrella | wool |

countable noun
a cookie
_____
_____
_____
_____
_____

uncountable noun
bread
_____
_____
_____
_____
_____

YOUR SCORE
10

PRACTICE **B** Complete the conversation. Put in **a**, **an**, **the** or **–** (no article).

Sue : Oh! I've scalded my hand. Do you have (1) _____ honey?

Anita : Yes, there's (2) _____ tub of (3) _____ honey in (4) _____ fridge.

Sue : Where's (5) _____ honey? I don't see it anywhere.

Anita : It's on (6) _____ second shelf, in (7) _____ orange tub.

Sue : Now, I just need (8) _____ spoonful of (9) _____ honey.

Anita : Won't it be sticky?

Sue : Yes, but it'll bring relief. I always apply (10) _____ honey whenever I have a small burn. It takes the pain away.

YOUR SCORE
10

PRACTICE **C** Tick the correct boxes to complete the sentences.

1 There is

	paint
	a paint
	the paint

on the floor. Please wipe it.

2 Janice likes

	furniture
	a furniture
	the furniture

in that shop. She says that

	furniture
	a furniture
	the furniture

is well-made.

3 He has

	–
	a
	the

work to do. He'll play

	–
	a
	the

badminton with you later.

15

4 I like

soup
a soup
the soup

but only if

soup
a soup
the soup

is hot.

5 My mother makes

jam.
a jar of jam.
the jar of jam.

She keeps

jam
a jam
the jam

in jars.

She often gives our neighbour

jar of jam.
a jar of jam.
the jar of jam.

YOUR SCORE
10

PRACTICE _D_ Fill in the blanks with **a**, **an**, **the** or **–** (no article).

1 Is there _____–_____ juice in the bottle?

2 I'd like _____ cup of coffee with _____ sugar, please.

3 My teacher gave me _____ homework today. I must finish _____ homework by Wednesday.

4 We make _____ paper from wood. _____ paper is made in factories.

5 There is _____ oil along this road. That palm oil tanker spilt _____ oil.

6 Alison put _____ ounce of _____ butter into the bowl.

YOUR SCORE
10

PRACTICE _E_ There are 10 unnecessary uses of **the** in the paragraph below. Cross them out.

As a child, I loved going with my mother to the Indian grocery store in our neighbourhood. There were so many fascinating things in Mr Pandian's shop. There was the flour, the green peas, the red kidney beans, and the chickpeas in open gunny sacks. There was the white sugar in a metal container with the glass in front for easy viewing. On the floor were also large tins of the oil. Containers of the margarine and the ghee filled the lowest shelves.

I do believe Mr Pandian was fond of me for he never said anything whenever I picked up a handful of the rice, held it up in mid-air and let it drizzle back into the sack.

YOUR SCORE
10

Fill in the blanks with **a ... of ...** .

syrup

1 Jim wanted _a spoonful_

of syrup

_____ in his drink.

2 Could I have _____

_____

_____ , please?

porridge

3 Mother cooked _____

_____

_____ for me.

water

4 The cleaner mopped the

floor with _____

_____ .

MILK POWDER

5 Aunt Mary bought _____

_____

_____ for her baby.

SALT

6 Could you get me _____

_____

from the grocery shop?

PRACTICE *G*   Rewrite the passage and correct the mistakes.

Kaolin is type of clay. It is also known as a china clay. It is essential item in manufacture of a porcelain. We use a porcelain to make the cups, plates and decorative objects such as figurines.

The kaolin is also used when making a paper. A paper is coated with kaolin to make it shiny and more opaque.

_____

_____

_____

_____

_____

_____

YOUR SCORE

10

UNIT 2 **POSSESSIVES**

apostrophe (**'**), apostrophe '**s**' (**'s**), **of**

Look at the **A** and **B** sentences below. Find out why **B** is correct and **A** is wrong in the **Grammar Points** section.

CHECKPOINT

			GRAMMAR POINTS
1A	The **bird** wing is broken.	✗	
1B	The **bird's** wing is broken.	✓	1
2A	Those **women** shoes are expensive.	✗	
2B	Those **women's** shoes are expensive.	✓	2
3A	Look at the **page's top**.	✗	
3B	Look at the **top of the page**.	✓	3

GRAMMAR POINTS

1   We usually add **'s** to a person or an animal to show ownership or relationship.

EXAMPLES: the **girl's** rings   (ownership)
her **father's** boss   (relationship)
the **dog's** kennel   (ownership)
the **elephant's** trainer   (relationship)

2   We usually add **'** to plural nouns ending in 's', and **'s** to plural nouns not ending in 's' to show ownership or relationship.

EXAMPLES: the **ladies'** hats   (plural – ladies)
the **girls'** cousin   (plural – girls)
the **children's** shoes   (plural – children)
the **men's** leader   (plural – men)

3   We usually use **of** to show relation or association with a plant, place or object.

EXAMPLES: the branches **of the tree**
the roof **of the house**

REMEMBER!

■ Sometimes, it is possible to use **'s** with plants, places and objects.
  EXAMPLE: the **company's** logo

■ Sometimes, it is possible to use **of** with people.
  EXAMPLE: the father **of the bride**

---

1 Many students' parents came for our Sports Day.

2 My friend father's a policeman.

3 The leaves of that tree are turning yellow.

4 My aunt's friend is arriving tonight.

5 The fir tree fruits' are conical.

6 The legs of the table are broken.

7 The babies bottles are in this bag.

8 My cat's whiskers are long.

9 That is the cub of the white tiger.

10 My dogs' name is Rover.

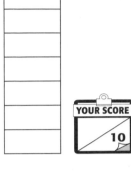

YOUR SCORE
10

PRACTICE *B*   Rewrite the sentences correctly.

1 The birds cages are large.
   The birds' cages are large.

2 Amy painting won the first prize.

3 My cousins' wife visited me at the hospital.

4 This sheep tail is very short.

5 These lady's watches are expensive.

6 The workmens' tools are in the shed.

YOUR SCORE
10

US$1,000

US$2,000

US$2,500

PRACTICE C Complete the sentences. Use the words in the brackets to guide you. You have to use **'** , **'s** or **of** in your answers.

1 _____*Mrs Chong's son*_____ won the first prize in the poster competition. (the son / Mrs Chong)

2 The players were unhappy with _____ . (the decision / the umpire)

3 _____ are spacious. (the rooms / this house)

4 Steve helped to check if _____ are faulty. (the brakes / my bicycle)

5 Manchester United is _____ . (the favourite team / my brothers)

6 Ivan left the cinema before _____ . (the end / the movie)

7 _____ will be staying with her for a week. (mother-in-law / Sheila)

8 _____ are worn out. (the soles / my sandals)

9 The chairman listened intently to _____ . (the report / the manager)

10 _____ is intriguing. (the title / your essay)

11 I have always listened to _____ . (the advice / my parents)

YOUR SCORE / 10

PRACTICE D Underline the 10 mistakes in the passage and write the correct answers in the spaces provided. You have to use **'** , **'s** or **of** in your answers.

1   Emmas eyes shone with mischief.
She pointed to the river's edge and
motioned Sam, Betty and Ming to join
her. Scotty, her highland terrier, followed
5   closely on Bettys heels.

The group crouched behind the huge
raintree's trunk and watched Nick,
Sam brother, and his friends. They were
swimming in the river. The girls decided
10 to play a trick. The boys shirts and shoes
lay in a heap on the grass. Emma noticed
some mens overalls nearby. The men
were busy fishing. She quickly switched
the shirts with the overalls. The girls
15 laughter caught Nicks attention. He
looked but saw no one. Then he heard the
dogs excited barks. He rushed out of the
water but the girls had gone.

_____
_____
_____
_____
_____
_____
_____
_____
_____
_____
_____
_____
_____
_____
_____
_____
_____
_____

YOUR SCORE / 10

20

Circle the letters of the correct sentences. There may be more than one answer for each question.

1 A We watched the finals of the women singles at Wimbledon yesterday.
  B We watched the finals of the womens singles at Wimbledon yesterday.
  C We watched the finals of the women's singles at Wimbledon yesterday.
  D We watched the finals of the womens' singles at Wimbledon yesterday.

2 A My antique sewing machine's cover is made of blackwood.
  B The cover of my antique sewing machine is made of blackwood.
  C My antique sewing machines cover is made of blackwood.
  D The cover of my antique sewing machine's is made of blackwood.

3 A At the harvest festival in my village, the cattle's horns are painted in bright colours.
  B At the harvest festival in my village, the cattles' horns are painted in bright colours.
  C At the harvest festival in my village, the cows horns are painted in bright colours.
  D At the harvest festival in my village, the cows' horns are painted in bright colours.

4 A The naval officers uniforms were dark blue with gold trimmings.
  B The naval officers' uniforms were dark blue with gold trimmings.
  C The naval officer's uniform was dark blue with gold trimmings.
  D The naval officer uniform was dark blue with gold trimmings.

5 A The boys older sister works as a nurse in a local hospital.
  B The boys' older sister works as a nurse in a local hospital.
  C The boy's older sister works as a nurse in a local hospital.
  D The boy older sister works as a nurse in a local hospital.

6 A The passengers' bags were sent through a security check.
  B The passenger's bags were sent through a security check.
  C The passenger bags were sent through a security check.
  D The passengers bags were sent through a security check.

YOUR SCORE

10

UNIT 3.1 PERSONAL PRONOUNS AS SUBJECTS AND OBJECTS

Look at the **A** and **B** sentences below. Find out why **B** is correct and **A** is wrong in the **Grammar Points** section.

			GRAMMAR POINTS
1A	I know this girl. **This girl** is clever.	✗	
1B	I know this girl. **She** is clever.	✓	1
2A	We are eating cherries. **It is** sweet.	✗	
2B	We are eating cherries. **They are** sweet.	✓	2
3A	He is tired. Give **he** a drink.	✗	
3B	He is tired. Give **him** a drink.	✓	3
4A	**I and Gary** played badminton.	✗	
4B	**Gary and I** played badminton.	✓	4

GRAMMAR POINTS

1 Pronouns are words that take the place of nouns. We use a pronoun in place of a noun so that we do not have to repeat the noun.

EXAMPLE: This is **Mr Samuel**. **He** is my teacher.
Ruby and I are good friends. **We** often go to school together.

2 The pronoun must agree with the noun in number. Singular pronouns replace singular nouns and plural pronouns replace plural nouns.

EXAMPLES: <u>Bob</u> likes ice-cream. **He** especially likes chocolate ice-cream.
(singular subject)
<u>Mary and I</u> like ice-cream. **We** especially like vanilla ice-cream.
(plural subject)

3 Pronouns used as the subject of a sentence must be in the subjective form. Pronouns used as the object of a sentence must be in the objective form.

EXAMPLE: **They** are good at carpentry. I asked **them** to repair my cupboard.

4 We use pronoun/noun + **and** + **I** in subject position and pronoun/noun + **and** + **me** in object position.

EXAMPLES: **You and I** like tennis. ✓   Mrs Todd wants to see **you and me**. ✓
I and you like tennis. ✗   Mrs Todd wants to see **me and you**. ✗

REMEMBER!

		Pronouns as subjects	Pronouns as objects
(a)	First person singular (the speaker)	I **I** remember the puppy.	me The puppy remembers **me**.
(b)	First person plural (the speakers)	we **We** teased the dolphin.	us The dolphin teased **us**.
(c)	Second person singular (the person spoken to)	you **You** greeted Mr Brown.	you Mr Brown greeted **you**.
(d)	Second person plural (the persons spoken to)	you **You** beat the new team.	you The new team beat **you**.
(e)	Third person singular (the person or thing spoken about)	he, she, it **He/She/It** likes me.	him, her, it I like **him/her/it**.
(f)	Third person plural (the persons or things spoken about)	they **They** love you.	them You love **them**.

PRACTICE A   Fill in the blanks with the correct words in the brackets.

Dear Roy,

Thank you for your interesting letter. Everyone enjoyed reading (1) _____ (him / it). The pictures are beautiful. (2) _____ (They / You) are a good photographer, Roy. (3) _____ (I / me) showed the pictures to Miss Tan, the school photographer. (4) _____ (He / She) liked (5) _____ (it / them) too so I gave (6) _____ (her / she) one.

Liz and (7) _____ (I / me) want to learn to take good pictures and Miss Tan is going to teach (8) _____ (we / us). (9) _____ (Us / We) are very excited about this.

Please send (10) _____ (I / me) more photographs.

Best wishes,
Karen

YOUR SCORE
/10

PRACTICE B   Rearrange the words to form correct sentences.

1   are — him — they — watching.

_____

2   him — saw — there — we.

_____

3   and — are — I — late — you.

_____

4   and — Dad — her — me — swimming — took.

_____

5   and — he — help — I — them — will.

YOUR SCORE
/10

_____

PRACTICE **C** Fill in the blanks with suitable pronouns to replace the underlined words.

Dad once owned a Morris Oxford. The Morris Oxford **1** | *It* | was very dear to

Dad **2** | | . Mum, however, disliked the car. Mum **3** | | said the car

4 | | was too old. Mum asked Dad to sell the car but Dad **5** | | told

Mum **6** | | the car was priceless. Then, months later, Mum did something wonderful.

It was the day before Dad's birthday. She spoke to my sister and me quietly. She asked

Jenny and me **7** | | to take Dad out for the day. Jenny and I **8** | | did as

she said. A surprise awaited Dad, Jenny and me **9** | | when

Dad, Jenny and I **10** | | returned home. Mum was at the gate with two men.

She was giving the men **11** | | some money. In the driveway was Dad's

Morris Oxford. It was gleaming white and shining like never before.

PRACTICE **D** Rewrite the sentences correctly.

1 Please give George and I your address.

_____

2 Kay ordered roast lamb. They were delicious.

_____

3 Doris and me want to join the Adventure Club.

_____

4 I asked they to finish the work. They refused.

_____

5 She helped me once so now I will help she.

_____

Fill in the blanks with suitable pronouns in the box. Each word may be used more than once.

he	her	him	I	it	me
she	them	they	us	we	you

Mrs Young : Officer, arrest that man! (1) _____ stole my purse. (2) _____ had put (3) _____ on the counter just now while I was looking for my spectacles. When I looked up, it was gone!

Officer : Madam, did you see (4) _____ taking it?

Mrs Young : My daughter Christy and (5) _____ were standing in the queue. That man was behind (6) _____ . Who else could have taken it?

Accused man : Please, Madam. The officer asked (7) _____ a question. Did you see (8) _____ stealing your purse?

Mrs Young : The cashier and the attendants were all here. (9) _____ would have seen you.

Cashier : (10) _____ didn't see him touching your purse, Madam.

Officer : Madam, could you please look into your handbag? You might have put it back inside.

Mrs Young : Well, all right … Why, this is amazing! My purse is here!

YOUR SCORE
10

PRACTICE *F* Underline the correct pronouns to complete the passage.

The little boy hid in the shadows until the riders and their horses passed by. **1** (He / She) wondered who **2** (they / we) were. The white robes they wore made **3** (them / us) look like ghost riders. A cold feeling of fear caused **4** (him / them) to shiver.

He stumbled on in the darkness. A small flicker of light caught his eye. **5** (He / It) seemed to be some distance away. He drew nearer and suddenly stopped when he heard voices. Several men, covered completely in white, were talking to someone who was tied up. The boy recognised the men. **6** (He / They) had passed him earlier on horseback. **7** (He / We) tried to catch what they were saying.

"… and **8** (he / we) are going to give **9** (him / you) one more chance to answer **10** (her / us). You'll die if you don't talk."

The boy realised that he had to act quickly if he wanted to save the prisoner.

YOUR SCORE
10

UNIT 3.2 POSSESSIVE ADJECTIVES AND POSSESSIVE PRONOUNS

Look at the **A** and **B** sentences below. Find out why **B** is correct and **A** is wrong in the **Grammar Points** section.

GRAMMAR POINTS

1A	Our club is larger than **hers club**.	✗	
1B	Our club is larger than **hers**.	✓	1
2A	Her painting is like **your one**.	✗	
2B	Her painting is like **yours**.	✓	2
3A	The blue kite is **my kite**.	✗	
3B	The blue kite is **mine**.	✓	3
4A	The cat is cleaning **it's** fur.	✗	
4B	The cat is cleaning **its** fur.	✓	4

GRAMMAR POINTS

1 We use possessive adjectives and possessive pronouns to show ownership or relationship. A possessive adjective goes together with a noun. A possessive pronoun takes the place of a possessive adjective and its noun.

EXAMPLES: their shoes — theirs

(possessive adjective) (noun) (possessive pronoun)

Possessive Adjectives		Possessive Pronouns
(a)	**my** computer	mine
(b)	**our** school	ours
(c)	**your** file	yours
(d)	**his** bicycle	his
(e)	**her** calculator	hers
(f)	**its** kennel	–
(g)	**their** house	theirs

> **REMEMBER!**
> ■ The possessive pronoun for **I** is **mine**, not **mines**.
>
> ■ The personal pronoun **it** does not have a possessive pronoun form.

2 We do not use **one** after a possessive adjective.

EXAMPLE: The guitar is **hers**.   ✓

The guitar is **her one**.   ✗

26

3 We use a possessive pronoun so that we do not repeat a noun.

    EXAMPLE: Your dress looks like **mine**.   ✓

                   Your dress looks like **my dress**.   ✗

4 We must not confuse **its** with **it's**.

  (a) **Its** is a possessive adjective.
      EXAMPLE: The rabbit is sleeping in **its** hutch.

  (b) **It's** is the short form for **It is**.
      EXAMPLE: I like orange juice. **It is** my favourite drink.
                     I like orange juice. **It's** my favourite drink.

PRACTICE *A*   Tick the correct sentences.

1 The dog is playing with a collar. The collar is its.

2 Your daughter is playing with mine.

3 I like the green blouse. It's pretty.

4 His computer looks different from my one.

5 The horse loves it's owner.

6 Our hockey team is stronger than theirs.

7 Jaffa is my cat and Purcell is hers.

8 The yellow cardigan is he's.

9 The pencils are yours and the pens are mines.

10 The old motorcycle is his.

YOUR SCORE

/ 10

PRACTICE *B*   Rearrange the words to form correct sentences.

1 are — hers — pictures — the.

_____

2 its — it's — tail — wagging.

_____

3 are — his — jeans — like — your.

_____

4 knows — mechanic — ours — their.

_____

5 flying — higher — is —mine — kite — than — your.

_____

YOUR SCORE

/ 10

Fill in the blanks with suitable possessive adjectives or possessive pronouns.

Karen : Kate, did you take my gold sandals from (1) _____ cupboard? I need them now and I can't find them.

Kate : No, I didn't take (2) _____ sandals, sis. You know that my feet are smaller than (3) _____ . Besides, all your shoes are low-heeled and (4) _____ are high-heeled. You know I don't wear low-heeled shoes.

Karen : This is strange. My cosmetics bag is open and (5) _____ things seem to be missing. Kate, have you been stealing my make-up?

Kate : I didn't steal your things. I would ask (6) _____ permission if I wanted to borrow something.

Mum : What's all the fuss about?

Karen : Mum, did anyone come into my room?

Mum : Only (7) _____ dog Pinto. No, no. Carmen, (8) _____ husband Ted and (9) _____ little girls came by. They wanted to see your newly-decorated room.

Karen : Were the little ones here by themselves?

Mum : Only for a while. Carmen wanted to show Ted our new pool. She told him she wants one just like (10) _____ .

YOUR SCORE
10

Complete the sentences with the correct forms of the words in the boxes.

1 Marie, I like _____*your*_____ costume but I don't like Lena's.
   Why is _____ so plain?

   you
   she

2 Mr Olin left _____ notes at home. I had to lend him
   _____ .

   he
   I

3 Sir, you've taken _____ Mum's bag by mistake.
   That small bag on _____ trolley is _____ .

   I
   you
   she

4 Officer, this is _____ dog. He has been _____
   for years. Now the couple in the next street are claiming Rover is
   _____ . They lost _____ dog a month
   ago and unfortunately, it looks just like Rover.

   we
   we
   they
   they

   YOUR SCORE
   10

28

Cross out the incorrect words to complete the dialogue.

Meriam :   Dan, you'd better hurry. You're already late for **1** | his | your | appointment with

Mr Sheares. You know how **2** | her | his | temper shows when he's kept waiting!

Dan :   You don't have to remind me. Miriam, have you seen **3** | his | my | briefcase?

Meriam :   Isn't the one on the chair **4** | ours | yours | ?

Dan :   No, that isn't **5** | his | mine | . My briefcase is in black leather with my initials on it.

Meriam :   I mistook it for Dora's. Your initials are the same as **6** | hers | ours | . I put it in

7 | her | his | locker. I'll get it for you.

Dan :   Thanks. Could you please phone my wife? Tell her that I won't be able to keep

8 | his | our | dinner date with the neighbours. Ask her to please return the chess set to

them. It is **9** | mine | theirs | . I borrowed it last week. **10** | Her | Their | children asked

me for it this morning.

Meriam :   I'll tell her. Now, you should be going, Dan. You're late.

YOUR SCORE **10**

PRACTICE *F*   Fill in the blanks with suitable words in the box.

her	hers	his	its	mine	my
our	ours	their	theirs	your	yours

We were going to sit for our final exams. We had already taken (1) _____ places in the exam hall. Near me John shifted uncomfortably in (2) _____ chair. It was wobbly and he wanted to move to the empty seat next to (3) _____ . However, the seats assigned to us would remain (4) _____ throughout the entire examination. No one was allowed to move to another seat.

I glanced at the candidates on (5) _____ right. (6) _____ faces were pale. I was sure my face was like (7) _____ too. There was complete silence in the hall. I looked around while waiting for the exam to begin. The grey curtains gave the hall a depressing look. (8) _____ atmosphere of gloom was made worse by the solemn faces all around.

Suddenly, my best friend Delia burst into the hall. She was in tears. The invigilators did their best to calm her. She told them she was late because (9) _____ mother's car had broken down. They asked her to sit down and she looked at me with relief on her face. My feelings were the same as (10) _____ . I was very happy that she had made it to the exam hall just in time.

YOUR SCORE **10**

UNIT 3.3 DEMONSTRATIVE ADJECTIVES AND DEMONSTRATIVE PRONOUNS

this, that, these, those

Look at the **A** and **B** sentences below. Find out why **B** is correct and **A** is wrong in the **Grammar Points** section.

				GRAMMAR POINTS
1A	**This** are good drawings.	✗		
1B	**These** are good drawings.	✓		1
2A	**These** hills are three kilometres away from us.	✗		
2B	**Those** hills are three kilometres away from us.	✓		2
3A	**These** bouquet of roses is pretty.	✗		
3B	**This** bouquet of roses is pretty.	✓		3

GRAMMAR POINTS

1 We use **this** and **that** with singular nouns. We use **these** and **those** with plural nouns.
  EXAMPLES: **This/That** boy is tall.   **These/Those** boys are tall.

2 We use **this** and **these** to point to people and things that are near us.
  We use **that** and **those** to point to people and things that are far from us.
  EXAMPLES:

3 A collective noun and the expression **a pair of** take singular verbs. We use **this** or **that** with them.

EXAMPLES: This/That **herd of buffaloes** is quite tame.
This/That **pair of spectacles** is mine.

> **REMEMBER!**
> ■ A collective noun is the name of a group of people or things.
> EXAMPLES:
> a **band** of musicians
> a **flock** of birds
> a **bunch** of bananas

> **REMEMBER!**
> ■ **This**, **that**, **these** and **those** point to specific people or things.
> EXAMPLES: Boys can be mischievous.   (not pointing to specific boys)
> Those boys can be mischievous.   (pointing to specific boys)
>
> ■ **This**, **that**, **these** and **those** are demonstrative adjectives when they are followed by nouns and demonstrative pronouns when they are not followed by nouns.
> EXAMPLES: Demonstrative adjectives   Demonstrative pronouns
> **This typewriter** is old.   **This** is an old typewriter.
> **That animal** is dangerous.   **That** is a dangerous animal.

PRACTICE *A* Circle the letters of the sentences that are correct.

1 A Look at these houses across the field.
   B Look at that houses across the field.
   C Look at those houses across the field.

2 A These are my friend's shoes.
   B These is my friend's shoes.
   C This is my friend's shoes.

3 A Bob wants to play with that children.
   B Bob wants to play with this children.
   C Bob wants to play with those children.

4 A Please ask those group of girls to come here.
   B Please ask that group of girls to come here.
   C Please ask this group of girls to come here.

5 A These are an expensive pair of jeans.
   B This is an expensive pair of jeans.
   C These is an expensive pair of jeans.

6 A Could you pass me that pile of books?
   B Could you pass me those pile of books?
   C Could you pass me these pile of books?

7 A This are not my files. Those on the table are mine.
   B These are not my files. Those on the table are mine.
   C That are not my files. Those on the table are mine.

8 A That were my grandfather's gold cufflinks.
   B These was my grandfather's gold cufflinks.
   C Those were my grandfather's gold cufflinks.

9 A Did you make this vase that I'm holding?.
   B Did you make that vase that I'm holding?
   C Did you make these vase that I'm holding?

10 A We just bought those potted plants here by the gate.
   B We just bought these potted plants here by the gate.
   C We just bought this potted plants here by the gate.

YOUR SCORE
10

31

PRACTICE *B*   Tick the correct boxes to complete the sentences.

1   ☐ These / ☐ Those books on the table by the window over there are new arrivals. ☐ This / ☐ That book here is a bestseller.

2   Is ☐ this / ☐ that your umbrella over there by the door? No, mine is ☐ that / ☐ this red one here.

3   ☐ These / ☐ This is Mark's coat, not yours. Yours is ☐ that / ☐ this one on the sofa there.

4   Please pass me ☐ that / ☐ this blue file inside the cabinet. I have to put ☐ these / ☐ those invoices here inside it.

5   Would you hand in ☐ that / ☐ this assignment for me? I'll finish the last sentence and give it to you.

6   I have all ☐ these / ☐ those essays in my file here to hand in to Mr Royce.

YOUR SCORE 10

PRACTICE *C*   Some of the underlined words have been wrongly used. Write the correct words in the spaces provided.

1   Mum, do you have any biscuit cutters like <u>these</u> here?
Teresa lent me this pair but I need a few more of them.

2   Are <u>that</u> the sunglasses that you bought? They look good
on you.

3   <u>Those</u> large parcel which the postman is carrying looks
interesting. I hope it is for me.

4   The children are looking forward to <u>this</u> trip so let's make
it really enjoyable for them.

5   <u>Those</u> are Ben's golf clubs. He left them there by the
garage door.

6   <u>This</u> are chicken sandwiches. Those in that box have a
tuna filling.

7   Which seat would you prefer, this one by the aisle or <u>that</u>
one by the window?

8   We just replaced <u>those</u> tiles here in the porch but they
have become loose again.

9   The apples on this tree are ripe. <u>Those</u> on that tree are
green.

10   Do you always buy from <u>these</u> grocery shop or that one
across the road?

YOUR SCORE 10

32

Mr Charles : Good morning, Miss. What would you like?

Miss Cruz : Could you give me five of
(1) _____ red apples here?
(2) _____ bananas look green. Are they ripe?

Mr Charles : (3) _____ are a green-skinned variety. They are ripe enough to eat.

Mrs Wright : Is (4) _____ a sweet honeydew?

Mr Charles : Yes, Madam. (5) _____ is a very sweet honeydew melon. You can see that it is golden yellow.

Mrs Wright : I would also like some of
(6) _____ celery.

Mr Charles : Alright. Let me weigh it and tell you the cost.

Mr Nathan : I want some of (7) _____ lettuce and a kilo of spinach. Are (8) _____ Australian carrots over here?

Mr Charles : Yes, Sir. Would you like some?

Mr Nathan : I'll take 200 grams, please. What are (9) _____ fruit behind you?

Mr Charles : (10) _____ are tangerines. They are flown in from the US.

YOUR SCORE

10

UNIT 3.4 REFLEXIVE PRONOUNS AS OBJECTS

Look at the **A** and **B** sentences below. Find out why **B** is correct and **A** is wrong in the **Grammar Points** section.

			GRAMMAR POINTS
1A	I bought **me** a calculator.	✗	
1B	I bought **myself** a calculator.	✓	1
2A	The boys fell and **hurt badly themselves**.	✗	
2B	The boys fell and **hurt themselves badly**.	✓	2

GRAMMAR POINTS

1   We use a reflexive pronoun as the object in a sentence to show that the subject and the object refer to the same person or thing.

> EXAMPLE: **Sandra** saw **herself** in the mirror.
>
> (subject)   (object)
>
> (**Sandra** and **herself** refer to the same person)

Subject pronouns (Singular)	Reflexive pronouns	Subject pronouns (Plural)	Reflexive pronouns
I	myself	we	ourselves
you	yourself	you	yourselves
he/she/it	himself/herself/itself	they	themselves

2   A reflexive pronoun used as an object comes immediately after the verb.

> EXAMPLE: I **pinched myself** hard to keep awake.
>
>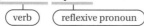
>
> (verb)   (reflexive pronoun)

REMEMBER!

- Reflexive pronouns are used in certain phrases with special meaning.

to enjoy yourself = to have fun
EXAMPLE: We **enjoyed ourselves** at the party last night.

to help yourself to something = to take something for yourself
EXAMPLE: She **helped herself** to the cake on the table.

to behave yourself = to be good
EXAMPLE: Mrs Harris asked the boys to **behave themselves** while she was out.

to make yourself at home = to behave as if in your own home when visiting another person's house
EXAMPLE: He **made himself at home** and began looking for food in the fridge.

to kick yourself = to be very annoyed because you have done something very stupid
EXAMPLE: I wanted to **kick myself** when I realised that I had forgotten my best friend's birthday.

PRACTICE *A*   Underline the correct words to complete the sentences.

1 Please do help (myself / yourself) to some of the ripe fruit in our orchard.

2 He cut (herself / himself) while he was carving the roast chicken.

3 Don't blame (himself / yourself) for the accident. The motorcyclist swerved into your path.

4 Lisa enjoyed (herself / himself) when she was working in the garden.

5 Mum and I are going shopping so please let (herself / yourselves) into the house after your game.
    Here are the house keys.

6 They considered (ourselves / themselves) fortunate to have found jobs so quickly.

7 The stray tabby cat defended (itself / myself) fiercely against our dog Caesar.

8 The boy suddenly found (himself / herself) in a deserted lane with huge trees.

9 We washed (ourselves / themselves) thoroughly after our swim in the muddy river.

10 Why don't the two of you keep (yourself / yourselves) warm with these blankets?

YOUR SCORE

10

PRACTICE *B*   Mark with ⋀ where the words in the boxes should go in the sentences.

1 Please make comfortable.

2 Mr Morris bought a caravan.

3 The elderly woman drove to the hospital.

4 I made a cup of tea.

5 We served at the cafe.

6 They arranged in a circle.

7 Help to some of the cakes on the tray.

8 The tiger cub forced through the narrow opening in the cave.

9 She made ill by forgetting to eat.

10 The boys told that they must get up early the next morning.

| yourselves |
| himself |
| herself |
| myself |
| ourselves |
| themselves |
| yourself |
| itself |
| herself |
| themselves |

YOUR SCORE

10

PRACTICE **C**   Tick the sentences that are correct.

1 I tried to scare them but I scared me.

2 Children, behave yourself.

3 They are teaching themselves to swim.

4 I told myself to reply to all the e-mail.

5 The little boys can bathe themselves.

6 The bird flew against the wall and hurt its self.

7 We locked yesterday ourselves in the house.

8 After we've finished work we'll enjoy.

9 The dog is scratching itself.

10 I like myself in that dress.

YOUR SCORE

10

PRACTICE **D**   Rearrange the words to form correct sentences.

1 about — always — he — himself — talks.

_____

2 at — enjoy — seaside — the — yourselves.

_____

3 challenge —early — finish — task — the — to — yourself.

_____

4 cleaning — is — itself — kitten — the.

_____

5 fed — girl — herself — little — the.

_____

YOUR SCORE

10

PRACTICE **E**   Rewrite the sentences correctly.

1 The kids dressed yesterday themselves for the party.

_____

2 Surprisingly, he himself behaved at the wedding.

_____

3 We ourselves made at home and enjoyed our stay.

_____

4 She herself told not to give up hope.

_____

5 The horse itself injured it when it stumbled and fell.

_____

YOUR SCORE

10

PRACTICE `F` Some of the underlined words have been wrongly used. Write the correct words in the spaces provided.

1 The students enjoyed <u>ourselves</u> very much during the excursion today.

2 Alan kept <u>herself</u> busy on the computer with his maths quiz.

3 Lyn knitted <u>himself</u> a scarf which she was going to wear with her winter outfit.

4 Come in, Charles and Sue. Make <u>yourselves</u> at home.

5 I was so hungry that I cooked <u>myself</u> some noodles for lunch.

6 The stray cat sat on the wall and scratched <u>itself</u> behind the ear.

7 Kathy, why don't you make <u>myself</u> a cup of tea and join us on the balcony?

8 Mr Singam said that he would drive <u>himself</u> to the golf club.

9 We promised <u>themselves</u> that we would go on a holiday this year.

10 They helped <u>themselves</u> to the buffet by the poolside.

YOUR SCORE

10

PRACTICE `G` Fill in the blanks with suitable words in the box. Each word may be used more than once.

herself	himself	itself	myself
ourselves	themselves	yourself	yourselves

Bill and his family arrived at the beach at about 9 a.m. and found it quite deserted. Edna, Bill's wife, said, "Let's all make (1) _____ useful." She chose a shady spot under the trees and busied (2) _____ with laying out the food on a mat. Bill's sister Betty set up the barbecue grill and began cooking the burgers and sausages.

Little Tom wandered off and decided to build (3) _____ a sandcastle in the wet sand. Sixteen-year-old Sally lay down on a large beach towel to get a tan. She rubbed (4) _____ with suntan lotion because she did not want to get sunburnt. Nearby, Rover the family dog tried to dig out a crab which had lodged (5) _____ under a rock.

Soon, the aroma of grilled meat made Bill hungry. Edna said to him, "Help (6) _____ to a hamburger." Their sons David and Ben said they would eat later and went off to amuse (7) _____ with a game of football. Betty took some sausages to Sally and said, "Why don't you have some?" Sally replied, "Thanks, Aunt Betty, but I'm not hungry now. I'll cook (8) _____ some later."

It was almost noon when Edna called out, "Come over, everyone. Serve (9) _____ while the food is still hot." Everyone gathered round, made (10) _____ burgers and then sat down on the mat to enjoy their lunch.

YOUR SCORE

10

UNIT 3.5 REFLEXIVE PRONOUNS FOR EMPHASIS

Look at the **A** and **B** sentences below. Find out why **B** is correct and **A** is wrong in the **Grammar Points** section.

			GRAMMAR POINTS
1A	I did all the sums **my own self**.	✗	
1B	I did all the sums **myself**. / I **myself** did all the sums.	✓	1
2A	The young man cooked **himself** all the dishes.	✗	
2B	The young man cooked all the dishes **himself**. / The young man **himself** cooked all the dishes.	✓	2

GRAMMAR POINTS

1 We can also use a reflexive pronoun to show that the speaker is giving emphasis to a particular noun or pronoun.

EXAMPLES: The schoolboy assembled the computer **himself**.
The movie star **herself** shook hands with us.

Reflexive pronouns for emphasis

(a) I did it **myself**. / I **myself** did it.
(b) We did it **ourselves**. / We **ourselves** did it.
(c) You did it **yourself**. / You **yourself** did it. (singular subject)
(d) You did it **yourselves**. / You **yourselves** did it. (plural subject)
(e) He did it **himself**. / He **himself** did it.
(f) She did it **herself**. / She **herself** did it.
(g) They did it **themselves**. / They **themselves** did it.

> **REMEMBER!**
> ■ The reflexive pronoun **itself** is not usually used for emphasis.

2 We usually place the reflexive pronoun at the end of the sentence or just after the subject when we use it for emphasis. In this case, the reflexive pronoun is **not** the object of the sentence and we **do not** place it immediately after the verb.

EXAMPLES: He **sweeps himself**. [✗]
He **does** the sweeping **himself**. [✓]
He **sweeps** the floor **himself**. [✓]

(Take note that 'He sweeps himself' means that he uses the broom on his own body.)

PRACTICE *A*　Circle the letters of the sentences that are correct.

1　A　The girls and I organised ourselves the concert.
　　B　The girls and I organised the concert ourselves.
　　C　The girls and I organised the concert themselves.

2　A　Mrs Pravin mops herself.
　　B　Mrs Pravin herself mops.
　　C　Mrs Pravin does the mopping herself.

3　A　The little boy brushed his teeth himself.
　　B　The little boy brushed himself his teeth.
　　C　The little boy brushed teeth own self.

4　A　Boys, catch the fish for supper yourself.
　　B　Boys, catch the fish for supper yourselves.
　　C　Boys, catch the fish for supper your own selves.

5　A　I wrote the story with my own self.
　　B　I wrote myself the story.
　　C　I wrote the story myself.

6　A　Repair the motorbike yourself. I'm not going to help you.
　　B　Repair the motorbike with yourself. I'm not going to help you.
　　C　Repair the motorbike by ourselves. I'm not going to help you.

7　A　My grandfather made that furniture themselves.
　　B　My grandfather made that furniture itself.
　　C　My grandfather made that furniture himself.

8　A　The village men constructed the community hall their own selves.
　　B　The village men constructed the community hall themselves.
　　C　The village men constructed the community hall with themselves.

9　A　Val made all the arrangements for the outing herself.
　　B　Val made all the arrangements for the outing themselves.
　　C　Val made herself all the arrangements for the outing.

10　A　Tom set up the business by his own self.
　　B　Tom set up himself this business.
　　C　Tom set up the business himself.

YOUR SCORE
10

PRACTICE *B*　Fill in the blanks with the words in the box. You may use them more than once.

> herself　　himself　　myself　　ourselves
> themselves　　yourself　　yourselves

1　He did the typing _____ .

2　Did you bake this cake _____ ?

3　My little sister completed the jigsaw puzzle _____ .

4　Did Margaret and Anita decorate the hall _____ ?

5　Our new employee John wrote the important report _____ .

6　We washed and polished Dad's car _____ .

7　Miss Locke changed the car tyres _____ .

8　I trimmed the hedge _____ .

9　Brian and Charles, prepare _____ for a surprise!

10　Sheena and I wallpapered the study _____ .

YOUR SCORE
10

39

PRACTICE C Cross out the incorrect words to complete the sentences.

1 Grace sewed her satin and lace wedding gown ☐ herself ☐ himself ☐ .

2 Dad tiled the whole bathroom ☐ himself ☐ itself ☐ .

3 "Enjoy your lunch," my teenage sister told the family. "I cooked everything ☐ herself ☐ myself ☐ ."

4 Our dog killed the two poisonous snakes ☐ itself ☐ ourselves ☐ .

5 Six-year-old Joey ironed his shirt ☐ herself ☐ himself ☐ .

6 Mrs Lee and Mrs Choo organised the whole conference ☐ herself ☐ themselves ☐ .

7 My neighbour's two young sons mowed the entire lawn ☐ ourselves ☐ themselves ☐ .

8 "Work out the answer ☐ themselves ☐ yourselves ☐ ," said the lecturer. "I want to see how many of you can do it."

9 The committee was amazed that the girls had done the beautiful mural ☐ herself ☐ themselves ☐ .

10 We tidied the park ☐ themselves ☐ ourselves ☐ as our city was short of gardeners.

PRACTICE D Fill in the blanks with suitable reflexive pronouns.

1 My mother did all the baking _____ without the help of her sisters.

2 Little Jimmy wanted to choose his clothes _____ .

3 Derek, don't copy your friend's work. Do the calculation _____ .

4 The general manager did not send his assistant to attend our function. He came _____ .

5 The chimpanzee drew the picture _____ .

6 There is no one to help us wash and iron. We have to do everything _____ .

7 "Look, Mum! I built the train _____ !" said Bobby.

8 The notice said that campers must clean the site _____ .

9 They are proud because they renovated the whole house _____ .

10 Aunt Bella repaired the leaking roof _____ .

Underline the correct words in the brackets.

My parents want us to do everything **1** (ourselves / themselves). My father looks after the garden **2** (herself / himself). My mother likes to do the cooking **3** (herself / her own self). My sisters clean their room **4** (itself / themselves). My little brother puts away his toys **5** (himself / themselves).

At first I hated cleaning my little room **6** (itself / myself). I cried and made **7** (me / myself) sick. My parents said I must behave **8** (myself / ourselves). If I work hard I would keep **9** (I / myself) happy. Now we do all the work **10** (themselves / ourselves).

YOUR SCORE
10

PRACTICE *F* Rewrite each sentence and mark with ∧ the two positions where you can use the word in brackets.

1 I made the candy.   (myself)

 I ∧ *made the candy* ∧ .
_____

2 Jennifer wrote the story.   (herself)

_____

3 They built the wall.   (themselves)

_____

4 Steve laid the tiles for the patio.   (himself)

_____

5 We washed all the curtains.   (ourselves)

_____

6 The children grew these vegetables.   (themselves)

YOUR SCORE
10

_____

UNIT 4.1 ADJECTIVES

before nouns and after verbs

Look at the **A** and **B** sentences below. Find out why **B** is correct and **A** is wrong in the **Grammar Points** section.

			GRAMMAR POINTS
1A	The **boy frightened** ran out of the house.	✗	
1B	The **frightened boy** ran out of the house.	✓	1
2A	I lucky. I won the first prize.	✗	
2B	I **was** lucky. I won the first prize.	✓	2

GRAMMAR POINTS

1 We usually place an adjective immediately before the noun that it describes.

> adjective + noun

EXAMPLES:
The **old** farmer caught the **cunning** fox.
The **cunning** farmer caught the **old** fox.

(Notice the difference in the meaning of these sentences.)

2 We also use an adjective after some verbs to describe the subject of the sentence.
(These verbs include **is**, **are**, **appear**, **seem**, **look**, **feel**, **sound** and **become**.)

> Subject + verb + complement (+ adverbial)
> adjective

EXAMPLES:

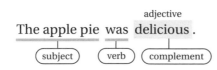

REMEMBER!

- An adjective describes a noun or pronoun (such as a person, an animal, a plant, a place or a thing) and tells us about one of its qualities.

  EXAMPLES: an **active** child
  a **playful** kitten
  a **thorny** bush
  a **noisy** market
  an **expensive** pen

- Sometimes, nouns are also used as adjectives before other nouns.

  EXAMPLES: a **Science** teacher
  a **seafood** restaurant
  a **diamond** ring

PRACTICE *A* Underline the adjectives in the sentences.

1 I prepared a special breakfast for Mum on her birthday.

2 The heavy box is already in the car.

3 Sue has an unusual hobby.

4 We saw a long queue in front of the cinema.

5 This room is bright and spacious.

6 The kind man gave the old lady his seat on the bus.

7 I feel hot. I'd like a cold drink.

PRACTICE *B* Rewrite the sentences and use the adjectives in the box.

1 It was a holiday.
It was a wonderful holiday.

| wonderful |

2 The horse drank some water.

_____

| thirsty |

3 The detective walked into the room.

_____

| smoky |

4 That man saved the baby from the fire.

_____

| fearless |

5 This road sign is new.

_____

| triangular |

6 The puppies chewed our slippers.

_____

| naughty |

PRACTICE *C* Cross out the word which is in the wrong position in each sentence.

1 Thrifty James is a thrifty man.

2 I dislike her because bossy she is bossy.

3 I enjoy walking in the quiet park when it is quiet.

4 You busy are always too busy to see me.

5 Tina is cheerful and therefore I enjoy cheerful her company.

6 Please put your dirty clothes into the dirty washing machine.

7 The children impatient were impatient to leave for the picnic.

8 Tony is going to play the jealous role of a jealous character.

9 That inquisitive squirrel is always watching us from its inquisitive tree.

10 The successful police were successful in tracking the robbers to their hideout.

43

PRACTICE *D*   Tick the correct sentences.

1.
- A The weather fine is today.
- B The weather is fine today.
- C Today is fine the weather.

2.
- A This accurate clock gives time.
- B This clock gives accurate time.
- C This clock accurate gives time.

3.
- A She slipped smooth on the floor.
- B She smooth slipped on the floor.
- C She slipped on the smooth floor.

4.
- A My sister speaks fluent French.
- B My fluent sister speaks French.
- C My sister fluent speaks French.

5.
- A She did not drink the medicine bitter.
- B She bitter did not drink the medicine.
- C She did not drink the bitter medicine.

6.
- A The careful nurses worked through the night.
- B The nurses worked through the night careful.
- C The nurses worked through the careful night.

7.
- A The paper was put into a safe important.
- B The paper important was put into a safe.
- C The important paper was put into a safe.

8.
- A The news reached wonderful them yesterday.
- B The wonderful news reached them yesterday.
- C The news wonderful reached them yesterday.

9.
- A Those office chairs are comfortable.
- B Those chairs are comfortable office.
- C Those comfortable are office chairs.

10.
- A We took home the long route.
- B We took long the route home.
- C We took the long route home.

YOUR SCORE
10

44

PRACTICE *E* Fill in the blanks with the adjectives in the box.

angry	bright	excellent	innocent	late
muddy	shady	strong	thick	tired

1 My bus is _____ today.

2 The _____ waves carried the jellyfish away.

3 The scouts walked through the _____ forest.

4 The _____ footballers went home immediately after the game.

5 Tonight the moon is _____ .

6 This essay is _____ .

7 The _____ customers demanded a refund.

8 Wipe your shoes. They are _____ .

9 It's hot so let's sit under that _____ tree.

10 John Paine insisted he was _____ of the crime.

YOUR SCORE / 10

PRACTICE *F* Rewrite the sentences so that the adjectives come after the verb 'to be'.

1 Sue has a small apartment.
   Sue's apartment is small.

2 This is an incomplete report.

   _____

3 He has an expensive watch.

   _____

4 That was an awful story.

   _____

5 My tutor gave sound advice.

   _____

6 That chef makes delicious apple pies.

   _____

YOUR SCORE / 10

UNIT 4.2 ADJECTIVES

word order, use of comma and **and**

Look at the **A** and **B** sentences below. Find out why **B** is correct and **A** is wrong in the **Grammar Points** section.

CHECKPOINT

GRAMMAR POINTS

1A	Joanna bought a **Mexican green** hat.	✗	
1B	Joanna bought a **green Mexican** hat.	✓	1
2A	The clown pulled out a **red yellow** scarf.	✗	
2B	The clown pulled out a **red and yellow** scarf.	✓	2
3A	There is a **big, silver,** Japanese car in the driveway.	✗	
3B	There is a **big silver** Japanese car in the driveway.	✓	3

GRAMMAR POINTS

1 Size, colour and nationality are three groups of adjectives we make use of commonly. When we use more than one type of adjective before a noun, we follow this order:

1 SIZE	2 COLOUR	3 NATIONALITY	
tall	–	French	lady
–	blue	Thai	silk
huge	purple	–	umbrella

EXAMPLES: I met a **tall French** lady yesterday.
Jan bought a piece of **blue Thai** silk from Bangkok.

2 When we use two adjectives from the colour group, we place **and** between them. We can use the adjectives in any order.

EXAMPLES: The **pink** and **lilac** dress is hers.
Her dress is **lilac** and **pink**.

> **REMEMBER!**
> ■ The word **colour** is not used after a colour adjective.
> **EXAMPLE:**
> a blue and white colour building ✗
> a blue and white building ✓

3 When we use adjectives from **different** groups together, we do not use a comma or **and**.

EXAMPLES:

The dancer wore a large, yellow, Korean costume. ✗

The dancer wore a large and yellow Korean costume. ✗

The dancer wore a large yellow Korean costume. ✓

PRACTICE **A** Circle N (noun), A-C (adjective of colour), A-N (adjective of nationality) or A-S (adjective of size) to indicate what the underlined words are.

1	That little <u>red</u> stone is a ruby.	N	(A-C)	A-N	A-S
2	This hotel has a small Vietnamese <u>restaurant</u>.	N	A-C	A-N	A-S
3	The <u>Canadian</u> team left for the airport immediately after the closing ceremony.	N	A-C	A-N	A-S
4	My uncle owns a <u>vast</u> orchard in Italy.	N	A-C	A-N	A-S
5	We bought a red and black <u>Turkish</u> carpet for our new home.	N	A-C	A-N	A-S
6	Mark needs a <u>spacious</u> study because he has many books and files.	N	A-C	A-N	A-S
7	We want <u>blue</u> tiles for our kitchen floor.	N	A-C	A-N	A-S
8	Those with British <u>passports</u> can go to that Immigration counter.	N	A-C	A-N	A-S
9	My dream house is a huge <u>white</u> Spanish villa.	N	A-C	A-N	A-S
10	I think that <u>slim</u> girl is Jean's sister.	N	A-C	A-N	A-S
11	The first prize in the bakery competition is a large Japanese <u>refrigerator</u>.	N	A-C	A-N	A-S

YOUR SCORE
10

PRACTICE **B** Mark with ⎰ where you would put the words in the boxes.

1 We need a cupboard for all these toys.

2 Ruth has to leave for the embassy now.

3 These tiny flowers are from my garden.

4 Our Nepalese guide waved frantically to get Mr Lee's attention.

5 I found a photo of myself when I was two years old.

6 Tina's Mum bought her a red and black shawl when she was abroad.

7 I love those miniature bowls in the shop window.

8 The workers damaged Grandma's orange sofa while they were moving it onto the lorry.

9 Those engineers over there are the ones who designed this bridge.

10 That yellow building is the city's main shopping centre.

big
American
yellow
small
black and white
Peruvian
blue and green
huge
Indian
enormous

YOUR SCORE
10

47

Tick the correct sentences.

1 Bill loves that black red sportscar.

2 Nicole likes to collect little Japanese dolls.

3 Wendy painted big purple dots on the drawing paper.

4 She wore a ring studded with tiny, blue sapphires.

5 I have a pair of brown Italian shoes.

6 They entered a white big room with paintings on the wall.

7 Mrs Brown bought a small box of Belgian chocolates for me.

8 He has an expensive gold and silver watch.

9 The black, Chinese plums are sweet.

10 I don't want to go to that French little cafe.

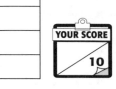

YOUR SCORE

10

PRACTICE *D*   Rearrange the words to form correct sentences.

1 an — and — bought — hat — Jo — orange — red.
Jo bought an orange and red hat.

2 and — carnations — pink — those — Vicky — wants — white.

_____

3 at — beetle — tiny — look — green — this.

_____

4 a — collection — have — huge — I — of — storybooks.

_____

5 a — came — German — man — my — school — tall — to.

_____

6 big — blue — balloons — friend — loves — my.

YOUR SCORE

10

_____

48

PRACTICE *E*   Rewrite the sentences using the words in the boxes in the correct order.
Use **and** where necessary.

1 Our guest brought us a teapot. | black   Chinese   small |
   Our guest brought us a small black Chinese teapot.

2 There was a snake at the zoo. | green   yellow |
   _____

3 My neighbour has a clock. | big   Swiss   white |
   _____

4 The taxis here are very efficient. | blue   red |
   _____

5 That building changed the skyline. | grey   tall |
   _____

6 We saw some apples as big as melons at the trade fair. | gigantic   red |

   YOUR SCORE
   10

   _____

PRACTICE *F*   Fill in the blanks with the words in the box.

cheap	expensive	fine	good	tune
bracelet	present	triangular	unusual	musical

Anna   :   I'm looking for a suitable (1) _____ for a (2) _____ friend. I

   don't want anything (3) _____ because I have just 10 dollars to spend.

Salesgirl :   How about a pretty (4) _____ ? We also have some (5) _____

   photo frames decorated with shells.

Anna   :   How much are the photo frames?

Salesgirl :   They're (6) _____ – just five dollars each.

Anna   :   What else do you have?

Salesgirl :   Does your friend like music? We have some (7) _____ boxes ... Here's a

   (8) _____ box. Listen ... It plays a lovely (9) _____ , doesn't it?

Anna   :   Yes, it does. How much is it?

Salesgirl :   Nine dollars.

   YOUR SCORE
   10

Anna   :   Yes, that's (10) _____ . I'll take it.

49

UNIT 4.3 ADJECTIVES OF COMPARISON

Look at the **A** and **B** sentences below. Find out why **B** is correct and **A** is wrong in the **Grammar Points** section.

CHECKPOINT

				GRAMMAR POINTS
1A	Dora is **more helpful** of the nurses.	✗		
1B	Dora is **the most helpful** of the nurses.	✓	1	
2A	Your cat is **more fat** than mine.	✗		
2B	Your cat is **fatter** than mine.	✓	2a	
3A	She is the **honestest** person I know.	✗		
3B	She is **the most honest** person I know.	✓	2b	
4A	Your project is **more neater** than ours.	✗		
4B	Your project is **neater** than ours.	✓	2c	

GRAMMAR POINTS

1 When we compare two nouns, we use comparative adjectives. When we compare more than two nouns, we use superlative adjectives.

EXAMPLE: **short**: Eric is **shorter** than Mark. (comparative adjective)
Steve is **the shortest** among/of the three boys. (superlative adjective)

2 (a) With one-syllable adjectives and some two-syllable adjectives, we usually use 'er' and 'est' endings for their comparative and superlative forms.
EXAMPLE: **clean**: Jean's room is **cleaner** than mine.
Anne's room is **the cleanest** in our house.

(b) With some two-syllable adjectives, adjectives of three or more syllables, and adjectives ending in 'ful', we use **more** and **most** for their comparative and superlative forms.
EXAMPLE: **attractive**: Apartment 1A is **more attractive** than Apartment 1C.
Apartment 1D is **the most attractive** of all.

(c) Since the 'er' ending and **more** are both forms of comparative adjectives, we cannot use them together.
Since the 'est' ending and **most** are both forms of superlative adjectives, we cannot use them together.

REMEMBER!			
	Positive form	**Comparative form**	**Superlative form**
one-syllable adjectives	fast	fast + 'er' = faster	fast + 'est' = fastest
some two-syllable adjectives	careful	more + careful	most + careful
adjectives of three or more syllables	expensive	more + expensive	most + expensive

PRACTICE A Tick the correct answers.

1 The antique desk is | heavier | | heaviest | than the modern one.

2 This patchwork quilt is the | lovelier | | loveliest | of them all.

3 The | prettier | | prettiest | twin sings well.

4 This restaurant has the | tastier | | tastiest | chicken pie in this area.

5 I am the | shorter | | shortest | in the family.

6 Abe's father is a | faster | | fastest | driver than my father.

7 I am | slower | | slowest | than you on the computer.

8 Alan looks | smarter | | smartest | than his brother.

9 The | more experienced | | most experienced | surgeon in that hospital operated on my grandmother.

10 My brother's room is a mess. It is | messier | | messiest | than mine.

YOUR SCORE
10

PRACTICE B Fill in the blanks with the correct forms of the words in the brackets.

1 Marie is _____ *cleverer* _____ (clever) than Rita in spelling.

2 Jason is _____ (big) than his father.

3 Cathy is _____ (enthusiastic) member of the nature club.

4 This apple is _____ (juicy) than that one.

5 Rina is _____ (practical) among her sisters.

6 Adam is _____ (tall) than Gary.

7 My father is _____ (patient) than my uncle.

8 This tiger is _____ (old) than that one.

9 Your stereo is _____ (loud) in the neighbourhood.

10 This is _____ (sweet) chocolate I have ever tasted.

11 The cheesecake is _____ (delicious) than the sponge cake.

YOUR SCORE
10

PRACTICE **C**   Look at the people in the picture and complete the sentences with the correct forms of the words in the box. Each word may only be used once.

| cheerful | curly | fashionable | large | long |
| old | plain | short | tall | thin | tired |

1   James looks _____ *more tired than* _____ Henry.

2   Rachel is _____ among all the people at the bus stop.

3   Henry looks _____ Mike.

4   Mike is _____ Rachel.

5   Evelyn is _____ Henry.

6   Evelyn's skirt is _____ Sue's.

7   Mike's tie is _____ Henry's.

8   Evelyn's hair is _____ Sue's.

9   Henry's briefcase is _____ among the three men.

10   Sue is _____ Evelyn.

11   Mike looks _____ James.

YOUR SCORE

10

PRACTICE **D**   Rearrange the words to form correct sentences.

1   expensive — is — more — motorbike — my — than — yours.
My motorbike is more expensive than yours.
_____

2   among — athletes — fittest — is — Raoul — the — the.

_____

3   handwriting — is — Mariah's — my — than — smaller.

_____

4 is — Mario — me — more — patient — than.

_____

5 among — artist — creative — Helen — is — most — the — them.

_____

6 aquarium — beautiful — fish — in — is — most — that — the — the.

_____

PRACTICE **E** Some of the underlined words have been wrongly used. Write the correct words in the spaces provided.

Agent : You'll find this apartment (1) <u>attractive</u> than Apartment 1D. Just a minute, please, while I unlock the door … Oh dear, this lock is (2) <u>more difficult</u> to open than the one for 1D. Okay, here we are … Please come in.

Mr Hill : Hm! It does have (3) <u>moderner</u> furniture than 1D.

Mrs Hill : Yes, and the arrangement is (4) <u>tastefuller</u>.

Agent : Please sit down. You'll find the seats are very (5) <u>comfortable</u>.

Mr Hill : Yes, they are.

Mrs Hill : They're the (6) <u>comfortablest</u> seats I've ever sat on!

Agent : I'm glad you like them. Let me show you around.

Mrs Hill : Let's start with the balcony…
It's such a (7) <u>big</u> balcony! Oh, and what a (8) <u>lovely</u> view of the valley!

Agent : Among all the apartments on this floor, this apartment gives you the (9) <u>lovelier</u> view of the valley.

Mrs Hill : It seems cooler here too. John, we could have some potted plants on the balcony and it would still be (10) <u>spacious</u>.

UNIT 4.4 ADJECTIVES

> irregular adjectives, 'ed' and 'ing' endings

Look at the **A** and **B** sentences below. Find out why **B** is correct and **A** is wrong in the **Grammar Points** section.

GRAMMAR POINTS

CHECKPOINT

1A	His drawing is **more good** than mine.	✗	
1B	His drawing is **better** than mine.	✓	1
2A	We heard the **shock** news about the plane crash today.	✗	
2B	We heard the **shocking** news about the plane crash today.	✓	2a
3A	The **frighten** cat hid under the bed.	✗	
3B	The **frightened** cat hid under the bed.	✓	2b

GRAMMAR POINTS

1 Some adjectives have their own comparative and superlative forms. We cannot add 'er', 'est', **more** or **most** to them.

Irregular Adjective	Comparative	Superlative
good	better	best
bad	worse	worst
little	less	least
many/much	more	most

2 We form some adjectives from verbs by adding 'ing' or 'ed' endings to them. Adjectives ending in 'ing' have different meanings from those ending in 'ed'.

(a) We use an adjective ending in 'ing' to describe a thing or situation.

verb + 'ing' ending = adjective

EXAMPLE: **excite:** You must read *The Adventures of Tom Sawyer*. It is an **exciting** book.

(b) We use an adjective ending in 'ed' to describe how a person or an animal feels.

verb + 'ed' ending = adjective

EXAMPLE: **excite:** Helen gave her brother a new bicycle. The **excited** boy showed the bicycle to all his friends.

1 The ☐ moving / ☐ moved news of how the young boy saved his friend was in the newspaper.

2 The storm last night was ☐ frightening. / ☐ frightened.

3 You have ☐ least / ☐ less work than Jessie.

4 The ☐ terrified / ☐ terrifying girl hid from the burglar.

5 To my surprise, Mum found the roller-coaster ride ☐ excited. / ☐ exciting.

6 This is a ☐ boring / ☐ bored book. Don't bother to read it.

7 He is ☐ the better / ☐ the best badminton player in my school.

8 This clinic has ☐ much / ☐ more doctors than the one in Hicks Road.

9 She was ☐ pleased / ☐ pleasing with my gift.

10 We enjoyed the ☐ thrilling / ☐ thrilled detective film.

YOUR SCORE 10

PRACTICE $\boxed{B}$ Fill in the blanks with the correct form of the adjectives in the brackets. Use **than** or **the** where necessary.

(a) That man's temper is **1** _____ (bad) his wife's but their son George has

   2 _____ (bad) temper in the house.

(b) Ken gets $50 a month as pocket money. Richard gets **3** _____ (much) him.

   He gets $70 a month.

(c) It is not **4** _____ (good) to borrow money. It is even

   5 _____ (bad) to borrow money and then not return it.

(d) This month, Helen made **6** _____ (much) sales among the sales executives

   in our company. That was surprising because the previous month she had done

   7 _____ (little) work among them.

(e) William has **8** _____ (little) gardening experience than Peter but his flower-

   beds are **9** _____ (good) Peter's. In fact, Mr Jones

   the landscape architect thinks William is **10** _____ (good)

   all his other gardeners.

YOUR SCORE 10

Fill in the blanks with the correct words from the boxes.

1 (a) The many crossroads in this town are very _____ .

   (b) She is _____ about how to get to her hotel.

| confused |
| confusing |

2 (a) Julie's journey was long and _____ .

   (b) The doctor advised the _____ patient to rest.

| tired |
| tiring |

3 (a) We completed the project successfully and that was _____ .

   (b) The _____ customer paid a compliment to the customer service executive.

| satisfied |
| satisfying |

4 (a) Sarah makes _____ jam tarts than Susie.

   (b) Susie's mother makes the _____ jam tarts of all.

| best |
| better |

5 (a) The winter this year is _____ than it was last year.

   (b) We had the _____ winter ever four years ago.

| worse |
| worst |

YOUR SCORE
10

PRACTICE D Some of the underlined adjectives have been wrongly used. Write the correct words in the spaces provided.

1 My neighbours are such <u>annoying</u> people. They often quarrel at the top of their voices.

2 There was a <u>terrified</u> sound of glass breaking when his car crashed into a shop window.

3 The <u>humiliating</u> girl ran into her bedroom and cried.

4 We were able to see the spaceship go into orbit via satellite. It was an <u>amazing</u> sight.

5 The <u>exhausting</u> waiters hurriedly cleared up the banquet hall after the wedding reception.

6 It was almost midnight and Mrs Hall was still not home yet. A <u>worried</u> Mr Hall phoned her parents to check if she was with them.

7 The <u>touched</u> scene where the soldier said 'goodbye' to his family made most of the audience cry.

8 The <u>daring</u> boy made his way carefully down the cliff to rescue the little girl.

9 The <u>pleased</u> atmosphere in the restaurant made us stay there longer than we intended.

10 The <u>stunned</u> pedestrian stood open-mouthed as the van stopped inches away from him.

YOUR SCORE
10

Tick the sentences that use adjectives correctly. There may be more than one answer for each question.

1 embarrass

- [ ] **A** I found that remark embarrassing.
- [ ] **B** Joe apologised to the embarassing group for his remark.
- [ ] **C** The embarrassed group didn't like Joe's remark.

2 astonish

- [ ] **A** Ray's photos of the volcano were astonishing.
- [ ] **B** The astonishing photos of the volcano were hung in the art gallery.
- [ ] **C** The astonished viewers looked at the photos of the volcano in silence.

3 inspire

- [ ] **A** The songwriter gave his inspiring fans tips on how to write memorable songs.
- [ ] **B** The inspired songwriter composed a new song in two hours.
- [ ] **C** The producer's words to the songwriter were inspiring.

4 disappoint

- [ ] **A** The disappointing holiday saddened the whole family.
- [ ] **B** The disappointing family felt depressed when they returned home.
- [ ] **C** The family were disappointing with the holiday.

5 surprise

- [ ] **A** Ken is a surprising man who always has wonderful ideas.
- [ ] **B** Ken explained how he gets his ideas to a surprised group of scientists.
- [ ] **C** Ken's surprised ideas are often featured in magazines.

YOUR SCORE /10

PRACTICE *F* Complete the sentences with the correct form of the words in the brackets. Use the 'ed' or 'ing' ending.

1 I go fishing every Sunday. It is a _____ (relax) hobby.

2 I will complete my story next week. I will send the _____ (complete) story to the newspaper.

3 I have been working from 8 a.m. to 7 p.m. It has been a _____ (tire) day.

4 I like Susan because she is an _____ (interest) girl.

5 Ronnie is photocopying some exercises. The _____ (photocopy) papers are for the students.

6 Mr Lim rented two houses last week. The _____ (rent) houses are on Maxwell Road.

7 I often press flowers and use the _____ (press) flowers to decorate cards.

8 The storm damaged many houses. The _____ (damage) houses belong to some fishermen.

9 Mr Bean is an _____ (amuse) character. I like his movies.

YOUR SCORE /10

10 I want iced lemon tea. It is such a _____ (refresh) drink.

UNIT 4.5 ADJECTIVES OF QUANTITY

a few, a little, many, much, some

Look at the **A** and **B** sentences below. Find out why **B** is correct and **A** is wrong in the **Grammar Points** section.

				GRAMMAR POINTS
1A	He has **many** respect for her.	✗		
1B	He has **much** respect for her.	✓		1
2A	I bought **a little** stamps.	✗		
2B	I bought **a few** stamps.	✓		2
3A	There **are** some butter in that dish.	✗		
3B	There **is** some butter in that dish.	✓		3

GRAMMAR POINTS

1 **many, much**
We use **many** with plural countable nouns. We use **much** with uncountable nouns.
EXAMPLES: There are **many** tables in this room.
There was **much** cooperation in the group.

2 **a few, a little**
We use **a few** with plural countable nouns. We use **a little** with uncountable nouns.
EXAMPLES: **A little** sugar is enough.
A few children want mint sweets.

3 **some**
We use **some** with both countable and uncountable nouns in these ways:

(a)   some + plural countable noun — with plural verb
EXAMPLE: There **are** some buns on the table.

(b)   some + uncountable noun — with singular verb
EXAMPLE: There **is** some bread on the table.

> **REMEMBER!**
> - **A few, a little, many, much** and **some** are examples of adjectives of quantity. They are used to indicate indefinite quantities.
> - **Many** means 'a large number of'.
> - **Much** means 'a large amount of'.
> - **A little** means 'a small amount of'.
> - **A few** means 'a small number of'.
> - **Some** means 'an unknown number of' or 'an unknown amount of'.

PRACTICE *A* Cross out the incorrect adjectives to complete the sentences.

1 That plant needs just | a few | a little | water.

2 There are | much | some | telephone messages on your desk.

3 | Many | Much | motorists had to take another route to work because the highway was under repair.

4 | A few | Some | money is missing from the safe!

5 He showered his children with | many | much | love.

6 Even | a few | a little | aid for the orphans is welcome.

7 | A little | Some | diseases in this world have no cure.

8 | Many | Much | effort was put into making the exhibition a success.

9 Let's spend | many | some | time working out this puzzle.

10 | A little | Many | students need to attend a course on speed-reading.

PRACTICE *B* Tick the correct words in the boxes.

1 | Many | | Much | | people do not exercise regularly.

2 You can add | a few | | some | | sugar to the juice.

3 I don't have | many | | much | | hours to complete this job.

4 This scrambled egg needs | a little | | a few | | pepper.

5 | Many | | Much | | of the machinery was damaged in the floods.

6 Heat | much | | some | | oil in a frying pan.

7 There was | a few | | much | | development in the city.

8 We gave the youths | many | | some | | training in leadership.

9 There were | a few | | a little | | mistakes in your essay.

10 Give me | a little | | many | | time to get used to my new job.

PRACTICE **C** Underline the correct words to complete the sentences.

1 He added (a little / a few) soya sauce to the soup.

2 (Many / much) members agreed with our suggestion.

3 Only (a little / a few) tourists are at the museum today.

4 Please give me (a few / some) ketchup.

5 They are making too (many / much) noise.

6 Vanessa wants (a little / many) salt in her food.

7 There (is / are) some birds on that tree.

8 A little advice (is / are) welcome.

9 There was much (laughter / conversations) in the room.

10 A few (dishes / food) were excellent.

YOUR SCORE
10

PRACTICE **D** Fill in the blanks with the correct words in the boxes.

1 Your composition has many _____ in it.

| errors |
| information |

2 There is some _____ in the red container over there.

| cheese |
| slices of cheese |

3 Hurry up! We don't have much _____ left. The taxi will be here soon.

| minutes |
| time |

4 My car suffered only a little _____ in the accident.

| damage |
| dents |

5 Please get me a few _____ from the fridge.

| oranges |
| orange juice |

6 There are some _____ on the top shelf.

| copper |
| copper sheets |

7 All he needs is a little _____.

| kindness |
| kind acts |

8 That store sells many _____.

| perfume |
| types of perfume |

9 He hurriedly packed a few _____ into his suitcase and rushed to the airport.

| clothes |
| clothing |

10 He doesn't get much _____ from his office colleagues.

| cooperation |
| suggestions |

YOUR SCORE
10

PRACTICE *E* Tick the correct sentences.

1 You need many oil to cook the vegetables.
2 A few plates are still dirty.
3 There are some milk in the jug.
4 She received many information from him.
5 I need a little jam on my bread.
6 There are much blue whales in the ocean.
7 She spends much time with her children.
8 Many people are without jobs nowadays.
9 There are some plums in the fridge.
10 A little students are here for the meeting.

YOUR SCORE
10

PRACTICE *F* Rewrite the sentences correctly.

1 There are much deep valleys in this country.
   There are many deep valleys in this country.

2 They borrowed a few equipment from us.

3 A few money is enough to make her happy.

4 Please give me a few advice on how to study.

5 In November many rain falls in the east coast.

6 There are much mushroom farms on those highlands.

YOUR SCORE
10

PRACTICE *G* Rewrite the sentences that are not correct.

1 Some chairs in the hall is broken.

2 There is many traffic on the road.

3 A few boys want to study Spanish.

4 A little baking powder are what you need for the batter.

5 Many soldiers passed the difficult test.

YOUR SCORE
10

UNIT 5.1 ADVERBS OF MANNER

Look at the **A** and **B** sentences below. Find out why **B** is correct and **A** is wrong in the **Grammar Points** section.

			GRAMMAR POINTS
1A	He spoke **angry**.	✗	
1B	He spoke **angrily**.	✓	1
2A	She worked **hardly** to finish her painting.	✗	
2B	She worked **hard** to finish her painting.	✓	2
3A	Sara **drank slowly** the hot tea.	✗	
3B	Sara **drank** the hot tea **slowly**.	✓	3

GRAMMAR POINTS

1 We do not use adjectives to describe verbs. We use adverbs. Many adverbs are formed by adding the 'ly' ending to adjectives. These are usually adverbs of manner.

Adjectives	Adverbs (+ 'ly')	Adverbs ('y̶' 'i' + 'ly')
angry	–	angrily
happy	–	happily
kind	kindly	–
quiet	quietly	

EXAMPLE: Mrs Gordon gazed **happily** at her baby.

verb   adverb

REMEMBER!
- An adverb of manner tells us how something is done.
  EXAMPLE:
  How did he work?
  He worked **slowly**.

REMEMBER!
- Adverbs are words which tell us more about verbs, adjectives or other adverbs. Adverbs are usually placed next to the words they describe.

(a) **adverbs with verbs**
  EXAMPLE: verb ⌒ adverb
  The child smiled sweetly at me.

(b) **adverbs with adjectives**
  EXAMPLE:
  The leather handbag is
  adverb ⌒ adjective
  very   expensive .

(c) **adverbs with other adverbs**
  EXAMPLE: adverb ⌒ adverb
  I waited rather anxiously
  for the exam results.

2 Some adverbs do not take the 'ly' ending. They have the same form as adjectives.
EXAMPLES:

far	fast	hard	high	last
late	long	low	near	straight

Hank is a **fast** swimmer.
adjective   noun

Hank swims **fast**.
verb   adverb

We had a **late** supper.
adjective   noun

The show started **late**.
verb   adverb

3 When the sentence has an object, we cannot place an adverb between the verb and its object.

EXAMPLES: He crossed the road.
<u>subject</u> <u>verb</u> <u>object</u>

He crossed **carefully** the road. ☒

Carefully he crossed the road. ✓

He crossed the road **carefully**. ✓

He **carefully** crossed the road. ✓

PRACTICE *A* Tick the correct sentences.

1 **A** We finished easily the race.
   B We finished the race easily.

2 **A** The girl sang happily.
   B The girl happily sang.

3 **A** Frankie cycled home fastly.
   B Frankie cycled home fast.

4 **A** The crowd cheered noisy during the match.
   B The crowd cheered noisily during the match.

5 **A** He spoke gently to the child.
   B He spoke to gently the child.

6 **A** Mark showed us proudly his trophies.
   B Mark proudly showed us his trophies.

7 **A** Grace worked hard all year.
   B Grace worked hardly all year.

8 **A** Sandra speaks fluently Japanese.
   B Sandra speaks Japanese fluently.

9 **A** The motorcyclist rode on the wet road recklessly.
   B The motorcyclist rode on recklessly the wet road.

10 **A** Henry sat quiet at the dental clinic.
   B Henry sat quietly at the dental clinic.

YOUR SCORE

10

63

Underline the correct words to complete the sentences.

1 Ted is driving too fast. In fact he's driving (danger / dangerously).

2 The singers were (joyful / joyfully) when they sang the new anthem.

3 The speaker looked (stern / sternly) at the rowdy audience.

4 She appeared (tired / tiredly) after the long climb up the hill.

5 Adam felt (confident / confidently) when he walked into the interview.

6 "I don't want to come with you," she said (stubborn / stubbornly).

7 Farah wears (elegant / elegantly) suits to the office.

8 The men worked (hard / hardly) under the hot sun to repair the road.

9 "This movie is so sad," she said (tearful / tearfully) to me.

10 Our group performed (good / well) in the drama competition.

PRACTICE C Circle the marks ($\wedge$) to show the possible places where you could put the adverbs in the brackets.

1 $\wedge$ The young executive dresses $\wedge$. (beautifully)

2 The firemen dashed into the burning hotel $\wedge$ to rescue $\wedge$ the trapped children. (bravely)

3 $\wedge$ The little $\wedge$ girls smiled at us as we entered the house. (cheerfully)

4 The tourist guide spoke $\wedge$ and therefore many of us could not hear her $\wedge$. (softly)

5 $\wedge$ They danced to welcome $\wedge$ the Prime Minister to their village. (gracefully)

6 Mum $\wedge$ hugged us when $\wedge$ we returned home from our school camp. (lovingly)

7 She gazed at $\wedge$ the painting $\wedge$. (admiringly)

8 The hungry children grabbed $\wedge$ the cakes $\wedge$. (eagerly)

9 Mark sat $\wedge$ in $\wedge$ the doctor's waiting room. (listlessly)

10 The archaeologists $\wedge$ guarded the entrance $\wedge$ to the ruins of an ancient city. (zealously)

Some of the underlined words have been wrongly used. Write the correct words in the boxes provided.

1   The people stared <u>curious</u> at us as we entered their village.

2   I was so engrossed in my book that I tripped and hit my head <u>hardly</u> against the pillar.

3   The animal moved <u>straightly</u> towards us as we stood frozen with fear.

4   The staff speak <u>highly</u> of their new manager.

5   The actress smiled <u>charming</u> as she walked into the reception hall.

6   We walked <u>hurriedly</u> into the forest to get to the campsite.

7   The refugees looked <u>hopeful</u> at us as we began to distribute the food.

8   The old lady screamed so <u>loudly</u> that everyone rushed towards her.

9   The car stopped <u>abruptly</u> at the junction and would not start again.

10 We slept <u>comfortably</u> on the wooden floor under woollen blankets.

YOUR SCORE

10

PRACTICE $\boxed{E}$ Fill in the blanks with the correct adverb forms of the words in the brackets.

We went on the expedition (1) _____ (confident). Our research indicated that the soil conditions were stable. However, tremors started (2) _____ (unexpected) when we were halfway up the mountain. We held on to our ropes and anchors (3) _____ (tight). Our guide instructed us to climb (4) _____ (fast) and (5) _____ (steady) upwards.

We crawled (6) _____ (painful) along a narrow ledge and found an opening in the rock. Squeezing our way in, we trudged (7) _____ (deep) into the cave. We were just in time. Boulders, rocks and earth crashed (8) _____ (thunderous) down the slope as the tremors began again. The place shook (9) _____ (violent) and we clung to each other (10) _____ (fearful). Thankfully, the cave saved us from being crushed by the falling rocks.

YOUR SCORE

10

UNIT 5.2 ADVERBS OF TIME AND PLACE

Look at the **A** and **B** sentences below. Find out why **B** is correct and **A** is wrong in the **Grammar Points** section.

 CHECKPOINT

GRAMMAR POINTS

1A	We **yesterday** saw Mr Neat at the shopping mall.	✗	
1B	We saw Mr Neat at the shopping mall **yesterday**.	✓	1
2A	**There** I put the books.	✗	
2B	I put the books **there**.	✓	2

 GRAMMAR POINTS

1 We often put **adverbs of time** at the end of sentences.

    EXAMPLES: Father left for Tokyo **today**.
               We will reach the hotel **soon**.

Some **adverbs of time** can also be put at the beginning of sentences for emphasis.

    EXAMPLE: **Today** Father left for Tokyo.

Other **adverbs of time** can be put in the middle of sentences just before the main verb.

    EXAMPLE: We will **soon** reach the hotel.

2 We usually put **adverbs of place** after the main verb and the object (if there is one).

    EXAMPLES: He will go **out** at 7 p.m.

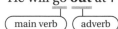
main verb   adverb

    The men have carried the table **upstairs**.

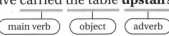
main verb   object   adverb

REMEMBER!

- An **adverb of time** tells us when something takes place.
  EXAMPLE: **When** will your aunt arrive?
                My aunt will arrive **tomorrow**.

- The following are some adverbs of time:

again	just	now	recently

- An **adverb of place** tells us where someone or something is.
  EXAMPLE: **Where** is my bag?
                Your bag is **here**.

- The following are some adverbs of place:

anywhere	away	downstairs	here
inside	near	somewhere	there

PRACTICE | *A* | Tick the correct sentences.

1 The messenger late came.

2 Mrs Danton stepped outside to collect the newspaper.

3 My cousins visited me yesterday.

4 Sam ran to upstairs shut the windows.

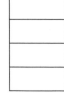

5 My neighbours are away in Switzerland.

6 You now must leave or you'll miss the bus.

7 Mary visited me recently.

8 I placed there the dictionaries.

9 He couldn't find his spectacles anywhere.

10 Richard yesterday played at the concert.

PRACTICE *B*   Rearrange the words to form correct sentences.

1 be — I — in — Morocco — tomorrow — will.

_____

2 badminton — finals — in — Mary — played — the — today.

_____

3 children — during — indoors — rain — stayed — the — the.

_____

4 ago — an — here — hour — repairmen — the — were.

_____

5 and — father — for — his — left — Mike — Singapore — yesterday.

_____

PRACTICE *C*   Mark with ⎰ the possible places in the sentences where you could put the adverbs.

1 **again** — 2 places

   The alarm went off.

2 **already** — 2 places

   I have finished my report.

3 **nearby** — 1 place

   The strange man was standing.

4 **here** — 1 place

   Please write your name.

5 **later** — 1 place

   I'll deliver the parcel.

6 **downstairs** — 1 place

   Steve ran and turned off the tap.

7 **tomorrow** — 2 places

   I have to go to the dentist's.

PRACTICE *D* Cross out the adverbs that are in the wrong position.

1 He has just arrived ~~just~~ at the station.

2 The lioness sleeps beside her cubs beside to protect them against any danger.

3 The rescue helicopter flew over the canyon over to search for the hikers.

4 Cora was recently offered recently a scholarship to study in the UK.

5 The doctor said that Henry's injury yet has not healed yet.

6 I will be meeting tomorrow Robin at the airport tomorrow.

7 Mrs Hall anywhere can't find her dog anywhere.

8 Nowadays Grandma nowadays doesn't travel a lot.

9 Everywhere Ben looked everywhere for his missing wallet.

10 They parked nearby the car nearby and walked to the restaurant.

11 We already have already spoken to the manager about the anti-smoking campaign.

YOUR SCORE
10

PRACTICE *E* Complete the sentences by putting the words in the boxes in the correct order.

1 I am going | today | to the bank | to cash my cheque | .

_____

2 | came | here | last night | Nina | to return my book.

_____

3 | at home | called me | just | she | to discuss the committee meeting.

_____

4 We drove | yesterday | downtown | to look in the shops there | .

_____

5 The game is about to begin so | are going | inside | now | the spectators | .

_____

YOUR SCORE
10

68

PRACTICE **F** Rewrite the sentences and correct them.

1 We later will go to the Italian cafe.
   We will go to the Italian cafe later. / Later we will go to the Italian cafe.

2 We reached soon the village.

3 Uncle Bob lives now in an apartment.

4 I searched the room but was not there my diary.

5 Kevin has booked already the tickets for the show.

6 A hot-air balloon overhead flew.

YOUR SCORE
10

PRACTICE **G** Fill in the blanks with the words in the box. Each word may only be used once.

| downstairs | everywhere | immediately | late | nowhere | |
| out | soon | suddenly | there | upstairs | yesterday |

(1) _____Yesterday_____ , the whole house was in an uproar. Two-year-old Tess was missing.
We looked (2) _____ for her. Jessica searched (3) _____ ,
starting with the kitchen and moving into the hall and dining area. Mum tried her luck
(4) _____ in the bedrooms. She went (5) _____ onto the
balcony and leaned over to look into the garden. Tess was (6) _____ to be found.
It was getting (7) _____ and still there was no sign of Tess. Justin peeped into her
toy cupboard. He did not see her (8) _____ either. (9) _____
everyone started to panic. (10) _____ , Jessica remembered the old unused fridge
in the storeroom. (11) _____ she ran there and found the fridge door slightly ajar.
She opened the door fully and found Tess hiding inside. Everyone was relieved. Mum decided to get
rid of the fridge right away.

YOUR SCORE
10

UNIT 5.3 ADVERBS OF COMPARISON

Look at the **A** and **B** sentences below. Find out why **B** is correct and **A** is wrong in the **Grammar Points** section.

			GRAMMAR POINTS
1A	Nita speaks English **more fluently** among her classmates.	✗	
1B	Nita speaks English the **most fluently** among her classmates.	✓	1
2A	Ray works the **most hardest** in the factory.	✗	
2B	Ray works the **hardest** in the factory.	✓	2
3A	Sam played the drums **more better** than Henry.	✗	
3B	Sam played the drums **better** than Henry.	✓	3

GRAMMAR POINTS

1 When we compare the actions of two people, we use comparative adverbs. When we compare the actions of more that two people, we use superlative adverbs.

EXAMPLES: Emma runs **faster** than Joe.   (comparative adverb)
Emma runs the **fastest** in class.   (superlative adverb)

Linda dances **more gracefully** than me.   (comparative adverb)
Linda dances the **most gracefully** among us.   (superlative adverb)

REMEMBER!

	One-syllable adverbs	Two-syllable adverbs
Comparative form	adverb + 'er' ending	more + adverb
	EXAMPLES: soon – sooner late – later	EXAMPLES: carefully – more carefully slowly – more slowly
Superlative form	adverb + 'est' ending	most + adverb
	EXAMPLES: soon – soonest late – latest	EXAMPLES: carefully – most carefully slowly – most slowly

Take note that the comparative and superlative forms of the adverb **early** are **earlier** and **earliest**.

70

2 We do not use two different comparative or superlative forms of adverbs together. Adverbs ending in 'er' or 'est' cannot be used with **more** or **most** in the same sentence.

EXAMPLE: They studied **more harder** than us.   ✗

They studied **harder** than us.   ✓

3 Some adverbs have irregular comparative and superlative forms.

Positive Adverbs	well	badly	much	little
Comparative Adverbs	better	worse	more	less
Superlative Adverbs	best	worst	most	least

EXAMPLES: David sang **well** at the concert.
Soraya sang **better** than him at the concert.
Ted sang the **best** among them.

PRACTICE *A* Cross out the incorrect adverbs to complete the sentences.

1 Among the family members, Mother waited the | more eagerly | most eagerly | for news about her first grandchild.

2 We worked fast and finished | soonest | sooner | than the other group.

3 He spoke | more courteously | most courteously | than the other waiter.

4 Among all my friends, David has travelled the | more widely | most widely |.

5 Sam did | more badly | worse | than his sister Nisha in the tennis tournament finals.

6 Lisa sang | more sweetly | most sweetly | than her sister.

7 My grandmother walks | more briskly | most briskly | than my father.

8 Adam eats the | more | most | among his brothers.

9 Ben drives the | more cautiously | most cautiously | in my neighbourhood.

10 Among the gymnasts in the championship, Susie scored the | least | less |.

11 Little Ben cries | more easily | most easily | than his brother.

YOUR SCORE

10

Fill in the blanks with the correct adverb forms of the words in the brackets.

Among those who taught us, we loved our form teacher Miss Wong (1) _____
(dear). She scolded us (2) _____ (thorough) from time to time but we
knew that she wanted us to do (3) _____ (good) in our studies. Miss Wong
stayed back (4) _____ (often) than her colleague Miss Gomez to give us extra
coaching in Science and English. We had to work (5) _____ (hard) among all
the classes. Her efforts paid off. Of all the classes in the school, we did
(6) _____ (good). We will never forget how she coped (7) _____
(patient) with those students who were slow. She dealt (8) _____ (gentle)
with problem students as well. They changed (9) _____ (remarkable)
after she had counselled them. Two weeks ago, my class planned a wonderful farewell for her.
At the party, Miss Wong said with a smile that she would miss cheeky Joe
(10) _____ (terrible) among all her students.

YOUR SCORE
10

PRACTICE **C** Fill in the blanks with the suitable adverbs in the box.

| better | calmer | earliest | least nervous | more composed |
| more dearly | more emotional | more gracefully | radiantly | prettiest |

There was no one else in the church when Tom arrived. He was the (1) _____
there. Soon, the bridal party came. Katy looked the (2) _____ among the girls. In her
lace wedding gown, she walked (3) _____ than her maids of honour who appeared
very nervous. Katy seemed the (4) _____ among them. Her face glowed
(5) _____ when she saw Tom.

Her father, John Kelly, looked (6) _____ than her mother, Mary. He understood
Katy (7) _____ than his wife did. He loved Katy (8) _____ than he
did, Kevin or Bob. She was the youngest and the most precious of his children. As the ceremony came
to an end, John appeared (9) _____ than his wife. She looked
(10) _____ than he. She was happy Katy was going to have a
new life with Tom.

YOUR SCORE
10

PRACTICE $\boxed{D}$ Underline the mistakes in the sentences and write the correct answers in the spaces provided.

1 Sandra debated the <u>more eloquently</u> among all the members of her team.

_____ *most eloquently*
_____

2 Little Toby made the less noise among all the children in the kindergarten.

_____
_____

3 She did badly than me in her driving test and failed.

_____

4 I spent the most on food and transport this month than I did last month.

_____
_____

5 Mr Liew worked harder among the partners to build up the business.

_____
_____

6 Of all the secretaries, she did her work the most efficient.

_____

YOUR SCORE
10

PRACTICE $\boxed{E}$ Rearrange the words to form correct sentences.

1 faster — father — his — jogs — than — Voss.
   Voss jogs faster than his father.

2 among — classmates — clearly — his — Johan — most — speaks — the.

_____

3 dresses — her — more — sister — smartly — Susan — than.

_____

4 among — most — Richard — runs — swiftly — the — us.

_____

5 earlier — goes — me — Mimi — school — than — to.

_____

6 Celine — exercises — her — husband — more — regularly — than.

_____

YOUR SCORE
10

UNIT 6.1 SUBJECT–VERB AGREEMENT

positive statements

Look at the **A** and **B** sentences below. Find out why **B** is correct and **A** is wrong in the **Grammar Points** section.

CHECKPOINT

			GRAMMAR POINTS
1A	Nigel in that shop.	✗	
1B	Nigel **is** in that shop.	✓	1
2A	My cousins **visits** me on Fridays.	✗	
2B	My cousins **visit** me on Fridays.	✓	2
3A	The furniture **are** on sale.	✗	
3B	The furniture **is** on sale.	✓	3
4A	His diary and pen **is** in that drawer.	✗	
4B	His diary and pen **are** in that drawer.	✓	4

GRAMMAR POINTS

1 Every sentence must have a subject and a verb. The subject can be a noun or a pronoun.

EXAMPLES: Adam **cooks** every Sunday.

(noun subject) (verb)

They **play** tennis every weekend.

(pronoun subject) (verb)

2 We use singular verbs for singular subjects and plural verbs for plural subjects.

EXAMPLES:

My neighbour **takes** the bus to school.

(singular subject) (singular verb)

My neighbours **take** the bus to school.

(plural subject) (plural verb)

The ladder **is** against the wall.

(singular subject) (singular verb)

The ladders **are** against the wall.

(plural subject) (plural verb)

REMEMBER!

■ The verb usually states what a subject is or does.

EXAMPLES:

Julia swims twice a week.   (what she does)

(subject) (verb)

Julia is my best friend.   (what she is)

(subject) (verb)

■ The two basic types of verbs are main verbs and auxiliary verbs. The majority of verbs are main verbs. Auxiliary verbs are a small group of verbs including 'to be', 'to do', 'to have', **can**, **may**, etc. An auxiliary verb is also known as a 'helping verb'. It is used in combination with a main verb; it cannot stand on its own in a sentence.

EXAMPLE: I **will wash** the dishes after dinner.

(auxiliary verb) (main verb)

■ The verbs 'to be', 'to do' and 'to have' can be used as main verbs as well as auxiliary verbs.

EXAMPLES:

My uncle **is** a computer engineer.
                ('to be' as main verb)

My uncle **is visiting** us this weekend.
                ('to be' as auxiliary verb)

Take note that the singular pronouns **I** and **you** are the only exceptions as they do not make use of singular verb forms.

EXAMPLES: I **take** the bus to school.
                singular subject

You **take** the bus to school.
                singular subject

I **am** in the first class.
                singular subject

You **are** in the first class.
                singular subject

3 Uncountable nouns take singular verb forms.
EXAMPLES: The rice **is** in the pot.
                The news **is** shocking.

4 Two or more subjects joined by **and** always take a plural verb.
EXAMPLE: Bob **goes** fishing once a month.
                subject   verb

Bob and Helen **go** fishing once a month.
                subjects   verb

PRACTICE *A*   Tick the correct sentences.

1 Michael call for his mother.

2 The paint is still wet.

3 My mother cooks chicken every Sunday.

4 The monkey jump from branch to branch.

5 The charity ask for a contribution.

6 He always helps his classmates.

7 Mr and Mrs Chang are here.

8 Anna is my best friend.

9 I cleans the room every morning.

10 These boxes belongs to the Art Club.

YOUR SCORE
10

PRACTICE *B*   Fill in the blanks with the correct form of the verbs in the boxes.

1 Michael _____ every morning.

2 It _____ heavily every day.

3 The fish curry _____ hot.

4 Kitty _____ biscuits.

5 Pat and her brother _____ badminton champions.

6 We _____ new shoes.

7 The club members _____ the sanctuary every month.

8 Allen _____ in a soap factory.

9 These farmers _____ fruit and vegetables.

10 The children _____ table tennis on Saturdays.

| exercise |
| rain |
| be |
| like |
| be |
| need |
| visit |
| work |
| grow |
| play |

YOUR SCORE
10

PRACTICE *C* Cross out the incorrect verb forms to complete the sentences.

1 The manager and his staff | is | are | attending an important meeting.

2 Both Alex and Shanta | participate | participates | in outdoor sports.

3 The antelopes | is | are | climbing the hill slopes.

4 Simon | has | have | a pilot's licence and will be joining a commercial airline soon.

5 The latest information on cancer treatment | was | were | on the nine o'clock news today.

6 The Minister | intend | intends | to set up more youth centres.

7 Peter and his wife | do | does | the housework and laundry on Saturdays.

8 The national hockey team and their coach | return | returns | home tomorrow from Delhi.

9 Hurricanes | cause | causes | great damage in the coastal areas of our country.

10 Many women today | work | works | outside the home.

YOUR SCORE
10

PRACTICE *D* Some of the underlined verbs have been wrongly used. Write the correct words in the spaces provided.

1 My parents hope to buy a cottage by the sea. _____

2 Phil's car require a lot of repair and maintenance. _____

3 His trousers are torn and need to be mended. _____

4 The dairy cattle roams in the pasture for long hours in the summer. _____

5 Technology make life easier for people throughout the world. _____

6 The grapes are ripe and are ready to be picked. _____

7 Wheat and rye are nutritious cereals. _____

8 The primary schoolchildren wait here for their bus every morning. _____

9 Sheep-rearing are a major occupation in New Zealand. _____

10 The election results was a surprise to everyone. _____

YOUR SCORE
10

Circle the letters of the correct sentences. There may be more than one answer for each question.

1   **A**   Brian am at the bank now.
    B   Brian is at the bank now.
    C   Brian at the bank now.

2   **A**   My friends and I cycle to the park every Sunday.
    B   My friends and I cycles to the park every Sunday.
    C   My friends and I are cycled to the park every Sunday.

3   **A**   Oil spills in the oceans endangers fish and marine life.
    B   Oil spills in the oceans endanger fish and marine life.
    C   Oil spills in the oceans endangered fish and marine life.

4   **A**   The food at the wedding is insufficient.
    B   The food at the wedding are insufficient.
    C   The food at the wedding was insufficient.

5   **A**   The machinery in this factory are out of date.
    B   The machinery in this factory is out of date.
    C   The machinery in this factory was out of date.

6   **A**   The plantation workers want fairer wages.
    B   The plantation workers wants fairer wages.
    C   The plantation worker wants fairer wages.

YOUR SCORE
10

PRACTICE F Rewrite the paragraph and use the verbs in the box to complete it.

call	carries	causes	cuts	falls	wear

Strong winds and rain down rocks and reduce them to gravel. When rain on the bare earth, it the gravel into streams and rivers. As a river meanders, the gravel the sides of the riverbank. This the river to widen. We this process 'Erosion'.

Strong winds and rain wear down rocks and reduce them to gravel.

_____

_____

_____

_____

_____

_____

YOUR SCORE
10

UNIT 6.2 SUBJECT–VERB AGREEMENT

negative statements

Look at the **A** and **B** sentences below. Find out why **B** is correct and **A** is wrong in the **Grammar Points** section.

			GRAMMAR POINTS
1A	She **don't** know Richard.	✗	
1B	She **doesn't** know Richard.	✓	1
2A	Those workers **isn't** technicians.	✗	
2B	Those workers **aren't** technicians.	✓	2
3A	I **amn't** sleepy.	✗	
3B	**I'm not** sleepy.	✓	3
4A	Carrie and he **isn't** cousins.	✗	
4B	Carrie and he **aren't** cousins.	✓	4

GRAMMAR POINTS

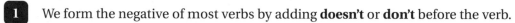

1   We form the negative of most verbs by adding **doesn't** or **don't** before the verb.

(a)   For a singular subject, we add **doesn't** and change the verb to its base form:
    EXAMPLES: Pat **likes** dancing.   →   Pat **doesn't like** dancing.
                 She **needs** paper clips.   →   She **doesn't need** paper clips.

(b)   For a plural subject, and the singular pronouns **I** and **you**, we add **don't**:
    EXAMPLES: My sisters **like** dancing.   →   My sisters **don't like** dancing.
                 We **need** paper clips.   →   We **don't need** paper clips.

2   We form the negative of the verb 'to be' by changing it to **isn't** or **aren't**.

(a)   For a singular subject, we change the verb to **isn't**:
    EXAMPLES: Sandra **is** in school today.   →   Sandra **isn't** in school today.
                 It **is** in Joe's briefcase.   →   It **isn't** in Joe's briefcase.

(b)   For a plural subject and the singular pronoun **you**, we change the verb to **aren't**:
    EXAMPLES: The twins **are** in school today.   →   The twins **aren't** in school today.
                 You **are** the second contestant.   →   You **aren't** the second contestant.

3   For the singular pronoun **I**, we form the negative of the verb 'to be' like this:
    EXAMPLES: I **am** tired.   →   I **am not** tired. / **I'm not** tired.
                 I **am** at the airport now. →   I **am not** at the airport now. / **I'm not** at the airport now.

     Ain't should not be used as a contracted form of **am not**.

4   Two or more subjects joined by **and** always take **don't** or **aren't** in negative statements:
    EXAMPLES: She and I **are** good friends.   →   She and I **aren't** good friends.
                 Anna, Eve and Kim **study** together.   →   Anna, Eve and Kim **don't study** together.

PRACTICE *A* Use the correct verbs in the boxes to complete the sentences.

1 Anita and Steven _____ in. They were at the cinema. | wasn't / weren't |

2 We _____ in town. We live in the suburbs. | doesn't live / don't live |

3 She _____ TV every day. | doesn't watch / doesn't watches |

4 My mother and my aunt _____ members of the Art Society. | aren't / isn't |

5 Those ships from Rio _____ passengers. | doesn't carry / don't carry |

6 He _____ pleased with his English test marks. | wasn't / weren't |

7 Lewis _____ a timid child. | aren't / isn't |

8 He _____ Tamil. | doesn't speak / don't speak |

9 Cyprus and Sicily _____ in Asia. | aren't / isn't |

10 Spiders _____ six legs. They have eight legs. | don't has / don't have |

YOUR SCORE /10

PRACTICE *B* Write negative statements in answer to the questions.

1 Is Greta the president of the science club?

Greta isn't the president of the science club.

2 Are they working on the project now?

_____

3 Do you know that the concert is on tonight?

_____

4 Does Bill like the way she sings?

_____

5 Do the players need more refreshments?

_____

6 Are the secretaries interested in the lunchtime fashion show?

_____

YOUR SCORE /10

PRACTICE C Fill in the blanks with the negative forms of the words in the brackets.

1 We _____*aren't going*_____ to the performance. (go)

2 You _____ present in school yesterday. (be)

3 The customers are unhappy. They _____ the bad food in the restaurant. (like)

4 Steve _____ keen on golf. He prefers tennis. (be)

5 The child has a terrible toothache but she _____ to go to the dentist. (want)

6 Judith and her mother _____ in France now. They will be there next week. (be)

7 Maria _____ happy with the new duties she has been given. (be)

8 I _____ the address of that veterinary clinic but Janet has it. (have)

9 Jill _____ told of the changes in the exam timetable and so she missed the Geography paper. (be)

10 The chairman _____ the meeting now. He will do it this afternoon. (conduct)

11 Mrs Roberts _____ to work because she gets a lift from her neighbour. (drive)

PRACTICE D Complete the dialogue with negative statements.

A: You play tennis very well.
B: I (not) play as well as my brother.

1 *I don't play as well as my brother.* _____

A: Is your brother a member of this club?
B: He (not).

2 _____

A: Does he take part in tournaments?
B: He (not) like to take part in tournaments.

3 _____

A: Are you interested in playing for this club?
B: I (not) good in competitions.

4 _____
I get nervous. Those two players over there are never nervous and they're very good.

A: They (not) better than you.

5 _____

B: They're confident but I (not).

6 _____

PRACTICE *E* Fill in the blanks with the negative forms of the words in the brackets.

Vijay and Arun are brothers. Vijay prefers to stay at home. He (1) _____ (be) an outgoing person and he (2) _____ (have) many friends. He (3) _____ (play) football and he (4) _____ (have) an interest in swimming. He spends hours on the computer. Sometimes he plays chess with his father. He finds the chess challenging.

His brother Arun is sociable and enjoys going out with his friends. He (5) _____ (like) to stay at home alone. He also swims and plays football. Arun (6) _____ (believe) in sitting in front of the computer for too long. He and his friends (7) _____ (be) interested in chess. They (8) _____ (understand) how a teenager like Vijay prefers to stay at home.

The boys' parents agree that the two of them (9) _____ (be) the same. They (10) _____ (worry) about the differences in their personalities. They accept them for who they are.

YOUR SCORE

10

PRACTICE *F* Some of the underlined verbs have been wrongly used. Write the correct words in the spaces provided.

1 Michael <u>aren't</u> happy with the food at the students' hostel.

2 The mayor and his team <u>isn't</u> visiting the flood victims tonight.

3 Betty and I <u>don't know</u> why the accident happened.

4 Economics <u>isn't</u> an easy subject to understand. It consists of complicated theories and their application.

5 The children <u>don't like</u> the type of car their father wants to buy.

6 The basketball players <u>doesn't have</u> any practice tomorrow as their coach is ill.

7 She <u>doesn't realise</u> how important it is to follow the instructions exactly.

8 Eddy and Patrick <u>aren't</u> attending the function tonight.

9 He <u>doesn't remembered</u> where he put the important letter.

10 She dropped the tin of baking powder. The lid came off and there <u>were</u> baking powder all over the floor.

YOUR SCORE

10

81

UNIT 6.3 SUBJECT–VERB AGREEMENT

positive questions

Look at the **A** and **B** sentences below. Find out why **B** is correct and **A** is wrong in the **Grammar Points** section.

			GRAMMAR POINTS
1A	**He is** hungry?	✗	
1B	**Is he** hungry?	✓	1
2A	**Is** Ken and Tim in the library?	✗	
2B	**Are** Ken and Tim in the library?	✓	2
3A	Does she **knows** the time?	✗	
3B	Does she **know** the time?	✓	3

GRAMMAR POINTS

1 Statements are sentences which give us information. Questions are sentences which ask the listener to give information. We normally do not make use of the statement form when asking for information. We use the question form.

EXAMPLES:

Statements	**Questions**
That is your car.	Is that your car?
They are coming.	Are they coming?

2 We form questions with the verb 'to be' by placing the verb before the subject. Compare this to the statement form where the subject comes before the verb 'to be'.

EXAMPLES:

Statements	**Questions**
Subject + verb 'to be'	Verb 'to be' + subject
Sammy **is** in your class.	**Is** *Sammy* in your class?
The tools **are** in the box.	**Are** *the tools* in the box?

Singular subjects take the verb **is**, except for the singular pronouns **I** and **you** which take **am** and **are** respectively. Plural subjects take the verb **are**.

3 We can form questions with most verbs by changing the verb to its base form, and adding the verb 'to do' before the subject.

(a) For a singular subject, we add the verb **does** before the subject.

EXAMPLES:

Statements	**Questions**
Subject + verb	Does + subject + base form of verb
Julie **sings** classical songs.	**Does** *Julie* **sing** classical songs?
He **enjoys** swimming.	**Does** *he* **enjoy** swimming?

(b) For a plural subject, and the singular pronouns **I** and **you**, we add the verb **do** before the subject.

    EXAMPLES: **Statements**

                  Subject + verb

                  The ladies **sing** classical songs.

                  They **enjoy** swimming.

                  Questions

                  Do + subject + base form of verb

                  Do *the ladies* **sing** classical songs?

                  Do *they* **enjoy** swimming?

PRACTICE *A* Tick the correct boxes to complete the questions.

1 ☐ Do / ☐ Does she ☐ enjoy / ☐ enjoys needlework?

2 ☐ Is / ☐ Are you comfortable?

3 ☐ Do / ☐ Does he ☐ has / ☐ have your address?

4 ☐ Is / ☐ Are that pen yours?

5 ☐ Do / ☐ Does we ☐ has / ☐ have to go now?

6 ☐ Do / ☐ Does they ☐ has / ☐ have their notebooks with them?

YOUR SCORE 10

PRACTICE *B* Complete the questions with the correct words in the boxes.

1 Do _____ need a lift? | Eric / Eric and Paul

2 Are _____ afraid of being alone? | he / you

3 Does _____ perform every night? | that band / those bands

4 Is _____ in the boot of the car? | it / they

5 Do _____ have to go now? | I / she

6 Is _____ at home? | your brother / your brothers

7 Are _____ ready to vote? | the committee / the committee members

8 Do _____ belong to that gentleman? | this suitcase / these suitcases

9 Are _____ on the right road? | she / we

10 Does _____ begin at 6 p.m.? | the parade / the parades

YOUR SCORE 10

PRACTICE *C* Rearrange the words to form questions.

1 does — like — Richard — tea?
Does Richard like tea?

2 cousins — do — have — pets — your?

_____

3 cut — does — grass — himself — Joe — the?

_____

4 a — chess — club — is — Jerry — member — of — the?

_____

5 and — fruit — cake — do — Harry — like — Vanessa?

_____

6 are — children — in — park — the — the?

_____

PRACTICE *D* Complete the conversation using the words in the box. Each word may be used more than once.

is	am	are	do	does

Police : (1) _____ you realise you did not stop at the traffic lights?

Driver : I can't believe I did that.

Police : (2) _____ you have your driving licence with you?

Driver : (3) _____ you want it right now?

Police : (4) _____ it with you or not?

Driver : (5) _____ I in trouble, officer?

Police : Let me see. (6) _____ your brake lights work? I notice that they didn't work just now.

Driver : Nobody told me that. (7) _____ you sure?

Police : (8) _____ you arguing with me? That's an offence too.

Driver : This is not my car. Actually, …

Police : (9) _____ this a stolen car, then?

Driver : This is my wife's car.

Police : (10) _____ she know you borrowed it? If she doesn't, she might have reported it stolen.

Driver : Good grief! It's just not my day. Please give me a ticket, officer.

84

PRACTICE *E*   Change the following statements into questions.

1 She likes dairy products.
   Does she like dairy products? _____

2 This is their first visit to Paris.

   _____

3 There are many good restaurants in this area.

   _____

4 Ken and Eva own a bakery.

   _____

5 Anita has a college degree.

   _____

6 Those factories observe laws on the environment.

   _____

YOUR SCORE
10

PRACTICE *F*   Fill in the blanks with the correct forms of the verb 'to be' or 'to do'.

Lawyer   : Mrs Marshall, (1) _____ you _____ (know) the defendant Mr Rubin?

Mrs Marshall : Yes. He lives next door to me.

Lawyer   : (2) _____ (be) he a well-mannered person?

Mrs Marshall : Yes. He is very polite.

Lawyer   : (3) _____ he _____ (treat) his household well?

Mrs Marshall : Yes, he does. There are times, though, when he and his brother quarrel.

Lawyer   : You said that on the evening of June 8 you saw Mr Rubin chasing his brother with a bat.

                    (4) _____ you _____ (watch) your neighbours all the time?

Mrs Marshall : I don't watch them all the time. I happened to be in the garden when I saw them.

Lawyer   : (5) _____ (be) you sure that Mr Rubin wasn't playing a game with his family?

                    (6) _____ you _____ (think) one of the children could have done it?

Mrs Marshall : No. They're too young.

Lawyer   : (7) _____ (be) the son John taller than his uncle?

Mrs Marshall : Yes, he is but he's a very gentle boy. He didn't hit his uncle. Mr Rubin must have done it.

Lawyer   : In other words, you didn't see Mr Rubin hit his brother. (8) _____ (be) I right?

Mrs Marshall : I didn't see him do it.

Lawyer   : (9) _____ you _____ (realise) what you just said? You jumped to

                    conclusions, Mrs Marshall. (10) _____ (be) you certain that you saw

                    Mr Rubin hit his brother?

YOUR SCORE
10

Mrs Marshall : No, I'm not sure that he did it.

85

UNIT 7.1 PRESENT TENSE

simple and continuous

Look at the **A** and **B** sentences below. Find out why **B** is correct and **A** is wrong in the **Grammar Points** section.

GRAMMAR POINTS

				GRAMMAR POINTS
1A	Nora's father **is being** a police inspector.	✗		
1B	Nora's father **is** a police inspector.	✓		1a
2A	A spider **is having** eight legs.	✗		
2B	A spider **has** eight legs.	✓		1b
3A	Lisa **fries** noodles now.	✗		
3B	Lisa **is frying** noodles now.	✓		2
4A	I **am wanting** a glass of cold water.	✗		
4B	I **want** a glass of cold water.	✓		3

GRAMMAR POINTS

Simple Present Tense

1   We use the simple present tense in these ways:

   (a)   to show habits and regular actions or to refer to current situations

      EXAMPLES: I **wake** up at six o'clock every morning. (habit)
                   Anna **works** in a factory. (current situation)

   (b)   to state general truths or facts

      EXAMPLE: Fish **breathe** through their gills.

REMEMBER!

■ The following are some words that are often used with verbs in the simple present tense to show habits or regular actions:

> always   every day   every week
> often   sometimes   usually

■ Verbs in the simple present tense are formed in these ways:

For singular nouns and the pronouns **he/she/it**:	For plural nouns and the pronouns **I/you/we/they**:
(a) base form of verb + 's'	base form of verb = present tense
EXAMPLE: bake + s = bakes	**EXAMPLES:**

For plural nouns and the pronouns **I/you/we/they**:

Base form	bake	wash	fly
Present Tense	bake	wash	fly

(a) base form of verb + 's'
    EXAMPLE: bake + s = bakes

(b) base form of verb + 'es'
    EXAMPLE: wash + es = washes

(c) base form of verb ending in '~~y~~' 'i' + 'es'
    EXAMPLE: fl~~y~~i + es = flies

Present Continuous Tense

2 We use the present continuous tense to show that an action is going on at the time of speaking or writing or is planned for the future.

EXAMPLES:
He **plays** basketball every weekend. (regular action)
He **is playing** basketball now.
He **is playing** tennis tomorrow.

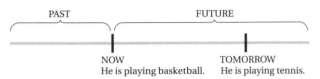

PAST   FUTURE

NOW
He is playing basketball.

TOMORROW
He is playing tennis.

3 Certain verbs do not take the continuous tense.
EXAMPLES: Hannah **is liking** chocolates.   ✗
Hannah **likes** chocolates.   ✓

> **REMEMBER!**
> ■ The present continuous tense is formed in this way:
>
> > present tense form of the verb 'to be' + base form of verb + 'ing'
>
> **EXAMPLES:**
> They fly.   → They are flying.
> He studies. → He is studying.
>
> ■ The following verbs do not usually take the continuous tense:
>
> | believe | belong | contain |
> |---------|--------|---------|
> | hear | know | like |
> | own | see | smell |

PRACTICE *A*   Underline the correct verbs in the brackets to complete the sentences.

1 The hotel guest (is waiting / wait) for a taxi.

2 Mother is busy now. She (is baking / bakes) cookies for us.

3 Tasha and Bob (are flying / fly) to Australia on Monday.

4 Our neighbour Mrs Lim often (is visiting / visits) us.

5 Aida (is going / goes) to school by bus every morning.

6 The kittens (are chasing / chase) a ball of wool now.

7 The club (is celebrating / celebrate) Cultural Day tomorrow.

8 The trees in my garden (are producing / produce) a lot of fruit every year.

9 We (are listening / listen) to the news on television every night.

10 Roy seldom (is coming / comes) late to the office.

YOUR SCORE

10

PRACTICE *B*   Fill in the blanks with the correct tense of the verbs in the brackets.

Dear Sally,

I (1) _____*am writing*_____ (write) to you from Santa Cruz. Santa Cruz (2) _____ (be) a seaside town in California. Its beaches (3) _____ (be) really beautiful.

Every morning I (4) _____ (wake) up early to see the glorious sunrise. I (5) _____ (jog) along the beach before breakfast. Now I (6) _____ (sit) on the beach. Nina (7) _____ (sit) next to me. We (8) _____ (watch) a group of tourists. Some of them (9) _____ (learn) to parasail. It looks adventurous and fun to us! The others (10) _____ (swim). Nina and I plan to swim later. Both of us (11) _____ (think) this place is wonderful.

I wish you could be here with us.

Love,

Susan

PRACTICE C Cross out the incorrect verb forms to complete the passage.

Photosynthesis in green plants (1) | uses | use | the energy from sunlight to convert carbon dioxide, water and minerals into organic food. Photosynthesis (2) | occur | occurs | in the leaves of plants. The roots (3) | takes | take | in water from the soil and this (4) | goes | go | up the stem to the leaves. Tiny holes in the leaf (5) | absorb | absorbs | carbon dioxide from the air. The leaf (6) | obtain | obtains | light energy from the sun's rays. The chloroplasts (7) | trap | traps | the light energy and use it to manufacture food. The leaf (8) | make | makes | carbohydrates. These (9) | provide | provides | nutrition for healthy plant growth. In the process of photosynthesis, oxygen (10) | escapes | escape | through the tiny holes in the leaf's surface into the atmosphere.

PRACTICE D Underline the correct verbs in the brackets to complete the dialogue.

Manager : Ann, I **1** (need / am needing) the documents on the Eden Housing Project.

Ann : Just give me a minute, Sir. I **2** (type / am typing) them out now.

Manager : My meeting **3** (are / is) scheduled for 4 p.m. today.

Ann : I'll have them ready. Mary and I **4** (organise / are organising) the file now for you to take to your meeting. Mr Long **5** (finish / is finishing) the statistics and the sketches for your presentation.

Manager : I **6** (require / requires) all my notes as well. I **7** (has / have) a big job ahead of me. All the important people **8** (are coming / come) today. I **9** (am thinking / think) we **10** (has / have) a wonderful project. I hope the clients like it too.

PRACTICE *E* Some of the underlined verbs have been wrongly used. Write the correct verbs in the spaces provided.

1 Usually Ken <u>is working</u> on his computer in the evenings.

2 Alice and Adam <u>intend</u> to renovate their house.

3 In the morning Adam <u>is driving</u> a taxi and at night he teaches karate.

4 At the moment, Sam is busy. He <u>is repairing</u> the brakes of his motorcycle.

5 The cookbook <u>contains</u> a number of unusual recipes.

6 Mum, I <u>go</u> the the pharmacy now to get your medicine.

7 My cousins <u>are leaving</u> for Taiwan next week to visit their sister.

8 My neighbour always <u>talk</u> about politics.

9 They <u>reach</u> home after work before six every evening.

10 We <u>are hurry</u> to the station now. We don't want to miss the train.

YOUR SCORE
10

PRACTICE *F* Fill in the blanks with the correct present tense forms of the words in the box. Each word may only be used once.

attend	cover	fly	hope	lead
record	see	take	tell	put

Peter (1) _____ an adventurous life. His job as a photojournalist with an influential magazine (2) _____ him to different parts of the world. He (3) _____ on camera important world events and sometimes this (4) _____ his life in danger. His desire to publish pictures of what he (5) _____ and experiences brings him joy and sadness. His photographs (6) _____ the story of times of great happiness as well as suffering and how people react to such situations.

At the moment, he (7) _____ a cultural festival in South Korea. In two days' time he (8) _____ to Rumania to take some candid shots of the orphanages there. Next week, Peter (9) _____ the Middle East on an assignment and he (10) _____ to capture on film the beauty of the desert and its wildlife.

YOUR SCORE
10

UNIT 7.2 SIMPLE PAST TENSE

regular and irregular verbs

Look at the **A** and **B** sentences below. Find out why **B** is correct and **A** is wrong in the **Grammar Points** section.

				GRAMMAR POINTS
1A	I **live** in Glasgow last year.	✗		
1B	I **lived** in Glasgow last year.	✓		1
2A	We **awaked** at six o'clock this morning.	✗		
2B	We **awoke** at six o'clock this morning.	✓		2
3A	The car **hits** the tree just now.	✗		
3B	The car **hit** the tree just now.	✓		3

 GRAMMAR POINTS

1 We use the simple past tense to show that an action happened in the past.

EXAMPLES: I **visited** Cairo in 1995.
Adi **studied** in London two years ago.

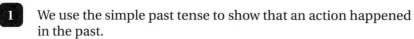

PAST		FUTURE
1995	two years ago	
	PRESENT	

REMEMBER!
- The following are some words that may be used with verbs in the past tense:

  > earlier
  > just now
  > last night
  > three days ago

2 We add 'ed' to regular verbs to form the simple past tense. Irregular verbs take different forms.
EXAMPLE: Tanya **painted** a beautiful scene yesterday.   (regular verb – paint)
Little Nicky **slept** all morning.   (irregular verb – sleep)

REMEMBER!
- The following are some ways of forming the past tense of regular verbs:

  (a) base form of verb + 'ed'
      EXAMPLES: clean + ed = cleaned
                    pick + ed = picked

  (b) base form of verb ending in 'y̶' 'i' + 'ed'
      EXAMPLES: carr~~y~~ i + ed = carried
                    hurr~~y~~i + ed = hurried

  (c) base form of verb ending in a consonant + the same consonant + 'ed'
      EXAMPLES: drag + g + ed = dragged
                    stop + p + ed = stopped

- Irregular verbs take different forms.

EXAMPLES:

Base form	awake	bring	catch	dream	eat
Past Tense	awoke	brought	caught	dreamt	ate

The verb 'to be':

Pronouns	I	He/She/It	We/You/They
Present Tense	am	is	are
Past Tense	was	was	were

3 Some irregular verbs do not change to form the simple past tense. They keep the base form.
EXAMPLE: They **put** the chairs out to dry.

REMEMBER!

Base form	beat	cut	hit	hurt	let	set
Past Tense	beat	cut	hit	hurt	let	set

PRACTICE *A* Fill in the blanks with the present tense or past tense form of the verbs in the brackets.

1 Our cat, Punch, _____*cleans*_____ (clean) himself every day after meals.

2 Linda _____ (cut) the flowers and arranged them in a vase.

3 The dish _____ (slip) from Sue's hands and broke.

4 Amphibians _____ (live) on land and in water.

5 Anand _____ (dry) the towels in the sun yesterday.

6 We _____ (hear) about the accident two weeks ago.

7 I always _____ (listen) to music while I do my work.

8 John _____ (put) all his tools in a box this morning.

9 The students _____ (assemble) in the field yesterday afternoon.

10 Dad _____ (go) to Hong Kong every year.

11 They _____ (be) in the stadium last night.

PRACTICE *B* Complete the passage using the past tense form of the verbs in the brackets.

Last Friday, Alfred and I (1) _____*joined*_____ (join) the students on a trip to Fraser's Hill. We (2) _____ (leave) early in the morning. On arrival there we quickly (3) _____ (unpack) and (4) _____ (pitch) our tents. Later we (5) _____ (trek) into the forest to gather wood. We (6) _____ (pile) logs on top of one another and (7) _____ (build) a fire. Nigel and Peter (8) _____ (spend) the afternoon fishing. They (9) _____ (be) lucky! They (10) _____ (catch) four large fish. Mr Roberts, our teacher-in-charge, (11) _____ (grill) the fish over the fire. What a feast we had!

YOUR SCORE
10

Fill in the blanks with the correct forms of the verbs in the box.

catch	grab	jump	know	manage
run	see	throw	tie	woke

Something (1) _____ me up. I found it hard to breathe. I (2) _____ out of bed and (3) _____ downstairs. I (4) _____ smoke billowing out of the kitchen and (5) _____ something was wrong. I shouted to my parents, "Mum, Dad, come quickly! The kitchen is on fire!" Mum and Dad rushed down the stairs. Mum (6) _____ me a large wet towel which I (7) _____ and (8) _____ round my body. I (9) _____ the fire extinguisher from the storeroom and sprayed foam over the burning stove. We (10) _____ to put out the fire after some time. We were lucky the fire had not spread to the rest of the house.

YOUR SCORE

/ 10

PRACTICE $\boxed{D}$ Cross out the incorrect verb forms to complete the sentences.

1 My elderly aunt sometimes $\boxed{\text{forgets} \quad \text{forgot}}$ to switch off her television set late at night.

2 After Mum finished cooking, we $\boxed{\text{scrub} \quad \text{scrubbed}}$ the greasy kitchen floor until it gleamed.

3 Nisha's diamond ring $\boxed{\text{glitters} \quad \text{glittered}}$ each time it reflected the light.

4 I $\boxed{\text{had} \quad \text{have}}$ a bad headache this morning so I went to the clinic for some medication.

5 Nelly $\boxed{\text{is bringing} \quad \text{brings}}$ over a batch of jam tarts that she baked herself.

6 The neighbour's cat $\boxed{\text{sprang} \quad \text{springs}}$ up a tree when it saw my dog heading its way.

7 Mr Miles $\boxed{\text{is speaking} \quad \text{spoke}}$ to a customer right now. Could you wait a while?

8 My brother $\boxed{\text{let} \quad \text{lets}}$ me drive his new car around the neighbourhood this afternoon.

9 The old ferry $\boxed{\text{sank} \quad \text{sinks}}$ when it hit the cargo ship.

10 The women $\boxed{\text{are weeping} \quad \text{wept}}$ with pity when they saw the starving children.

YOUR SCORE

/ 10

PRACTICE *E*   Rewrite the passage using the simple past tense.

Every morning, Dad stands out on the verandah, ready to begin his exercise. He **stretches** his arms sideways, **pulls** his shoulders straight and **breathes** in deeply. He **raises** himself up on his toes and **lowers** his body slowly. Then he **moves** his arms to a vertical position and **squats** down as he **exhales**. Dad **continues** this routine for 15 minutes before he **comes** in for a cup of hot coffee.

Yesterday morning, Dad stood out on the verandah, ready to begin his exercise.

_____

_____

_____

_____

_____

_____

_____

_____

_____

_____

YOUR SCORE
10

PRACTICE *F*   Fill in the blanks with the present, present continuous or past tense form of the verbs in the brackets.

Ravi   :   I (1) _____ (tidy) the kitchen last night and I (2) _____ (refuse) to do it again. It's your turn today.

Sheila :   You (3) _____ (be) so unfair! I (4) _____ (spend) most of last week cleaning the house. I (5) _____ (not bother) you because you (6) _____ (have) exams.

Ravi   :   I (7) _____ (beg) you now, Sheila. Please do it for me just this once. I don't have the time. I (8) _____ (type) out my Chemistry project. I have to hand it in tomorrow morning.

Sheila :   You always (9) _____ (try) to wriggle your way out of doing housework and somehow you (10) _____ (succeed). I'll let you off this time.

YOUR SCORE
10

UNIT 7.3 **PAST CONTINUOUS TENSE**

Look at the **A** and **B** sentences below. Find out why **B** is correct and **A** is wrong in the **Grammar Points** section.

			GRAMMAR POINTS
1A	At about eight o'clock last night, the police **are** driving around my area.	✗	
1B	At about eight o'clock last night, the police **were** driving around my area.	✓	1
2A	While Mother **was cleaning** the house, Father **read** the papers.	✗	
2B	While Mother **was cleaning** the house, Father **was reading** the papers.	✓	2
3A	I was sleeping when you **were** coming home.	✗	
3B	I was sleeping when you **came** home.	✓	3
4A	We **were knowing** about his plan last night.	✗	
4B	We **knew** about his plan last night.	✓	4

GRAMMAR POINTS

1 We use the past continuous tense to show that an action was going on or being carried out in the past.

EXAMPLE: At 10.30 a.m. yesterday, Roy **was making** a kite.
Now he **is flying** the kite.

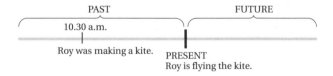

2 To show that two actions were going on at the same time in the past, we use the past tense for both actions or the past continuous tense.

EXAMPLES:

While I **was cooking** lunch, my sister **was ironing**.

While I **cooked** lunch, my sister **ironed**.

REMEMBER!

■ The past continuous tense is formed in this way:

For singular nouns and the pronouns **I/ he/she/it**:
was + base form of verb + 'ing'

EXAMPLE: Jason **was reading** this book.

For plural nouns and the pronouns **you/we/they**:
were + base form of verb + 'ing'

EXAMPLE: The kids **were sleeping** in their room.

3 To show that something happened while a longer action was going on, we do the following:
  (a) first or longer action — use the past continuous tense
  (b) second action — use the simple past tense

EXAMPLE: I **was doing** my homework last night when Lin **phoned** me.

(longer action)   (second action)

doing homework
7 p.m.   8 p.m.
phoned
PAST   PRESENT   FUTURE

4 Certain verbs do not usually take the past continuous tense.
  EXAMPLE:

  We **were understanding** your problem after the meeting.   ✗

  We **understood** your problem after the meeting.   ✓

PRACTICE *A*   Underline the correct verb forms to complete the story.

It was about 1.30 p.m. I **1** (wait / <u>was waiting</u>) in a queue at the bank to cash my cheque. Two well-dressed men **2** (walked / walking) into the bank. They **3** (went / go) up to the counter while I **4** (counting / was counting) my money. Suddenly, the men **5** (shouted / was shouting), "Give us the money!" One of them **6** (pointed / pointing) a gun at the cashier while the other **7** (tie / tied) up the security guards.

All this while, the customers **8** (was trembling / were trembling) with fear. While the men **9** (were waiting / was waiting) for the cashier to put the money into bags, the manager secretly pressed the alarm buzzer to alert the police. The men **10** (were leaving / left) the bank when they **11** (came / coming) face-to-face with the police squad outside.

YOUR SCORE
10

PRACTICE *B*   Fill in the blanks with the simple past tense or past continuous tense form of the verbs in the brackets.

1 At 9.30 last night, my brother _____ (work) on his computer.

2 From 4 p.m. to 6 p.m. yesterday, Mrs Hanes _____ (sew) curtains.

3 I _____ (forget) to lock the front door this morning.

4 The woman _____ (sleep) when the robbers _____ (break) into her house.

5 While I _____ (bake) a cake, Tommy was doing his sums.

6 They _____ (paint) the house all day yesterday.

7 While Beatrice cut the vegetables, Joyce _____ (fry) noodles.

8 She _____ (get) into the car when a cyclist _____ (knock) into her.

YOUR SCORE
10

95

PRACTICE C Fill in the blanks with the simple past tense or past continuous tense form of the verbs in the brackets.

At about 6.30 yesterday evening, Tom (1) _____ (get) ready all the ingredients needed to cook his speciality – chicken in sweet and sour sauce. He (2) _____ (mutter) to himself while he (3) _____ (search) in the pantry for the various things he needed. His little sister Inez (4) _____ (stroll) into the kitchen and sat quietly as Tom (5) _____ (rummage) in the fridge for tomatoes. Inez (6) _____ (offer) to help and Tom greatfully accepted.

While Tom (7) _____ (stir) the sauce in the pan, Inez (8) _____ (chop) up the onions and vegetables. Soon, the dish (9) _____ (simmer) on the stove. Half an hour later, Tom (10) _____ (lay) the table for dinner and Inez went off to call the rest of the family.

YOUR SCORE
10

PRACTICE D Some of the underlined verbs have been wrongly used. Write the correct answers in the spaces provided.

1 Aaron was minding the baby while Ida <u>was preparing</u> lunch.

_____

_____

2 Sarah was chatting on the phone when her manager <u>was coming</u> into the office.

_____

_____

3 From 4 p.m. to 7.30 p.m. yesterday, Julia and Jess <u>were playing</u> badminton at the sports complex.

_____

_____

4 I <u>shopped</u> at the supermarket last Sunday when I met Angela.

_____

_____

5 They were driving along the highway when a truck <u>cut</u> across their path.

_____

_____

6 We <u>waited</u> at the airport for Dad's flight to arrive when we saw the movie star.

_____

_____

7 While the children were watching a horror movie, they <u>heard</u> strange noises outside.

_____

_____

8 Rita mixed the batter for the cake while Mum <u>get</u> the baking tins ready.

_____

_____

9 The three boys <u>roamed</u> around the mall during school hours when the principal caught them.

_____

_____

10 The men <u>appeared</u> nervous when we asked them what they wanted.

_____

YOUR SCORE
10

PRACTICE *E*   Circle the letters of the sentences which are correct. There may be more than one answer for each question.

1 **A** He said, "Don't disturb me now because I watch a movie on television."

   B He said, "Don't disturb me now because I am watching a movie on television."

   C He said that he didn't want to be disturbed because he watched a movie on television.

   D He said that he didn't want to be disturbed because he was watching a movie on television.

2 **A** I was getting ready to go out when Gina called me.

   B I was getting ready to go out when Gina call me.

   C When I was getting ready to go out, Gina called me.

   D When I getting ready to go out, Gina called me.

3 **A** Bill cooked the noodles while I make the sauce.

   B Bill cooked the noodles while I made the sauce.

   C Bill cook the noodles while I made the sauce.

   D Bill was cooking the noodles while I was making the sauce.

4 **A** While I was typed the invitations, Ling was pasting the stamps on the envelopes.

   B While I type the invitations, Ling paste the stamps on the envelopes.

   C While I typed the invitations, Ling pasted the stamps on the envelopes.

   D While I was typing the invitations, Ling was pasting the stamps on the envelopes.

5 **A** At 5.30 yesterday evening, Mary was writing a letter and I was writing a report.

   B While Mary was writing a letter at 5.30 yesterday evening, I was writing a report.

   C While Mary writing a letter at 5.30 yesterday evening, I was writing a report.

   D While Mary wrote a letter yesterday evening at 5.30, I write a report.

YOUR SCORE

10

UNIT 7.4 **PRESENT PERFECT TENSE**

Look at the **A** and **B** sentences below. Find out why **B** is correct and **A** is wrong in the **Grammar Points** section.

CHECKPOINT

			GRAMMAR POINTS
1A	I **have done** the work yesterday.	✗	
1B	I **did** the work yesterday.	✓	1
2A	I **knew** Sam since 1995.	✗	
2B	I **have known** Sam since 1995.	✓	2
3A	She **has chose** blue curtains for her room.	✗	
3B	She **has chosen** blue curtains for her room.	✓	3

 GRAMMAR POINTS

1 We use the present perfect tense to talk about an action in the past without stating the exact time of the action.

EXAMPLES:

Past Tense	Present Perfect Tense
We **visited** the Science Museum **yesterday**.	We **have visited** the Science Museum before.
The bird in the cage **flew** away **last week**.	The bird in the cage **has flown** away.

When the time of action is mentioned, we use the simple past tense.

2 We use the present perfect tense to talk about an action that started in the past and is still going on.

EXAMPLE: I **have taught** in this school for three years.

> **REMEMBER!**
> - The following are some words that may be used with the present perfect tense:
>
>   > already
>   > before
>   > for (a week, a month, several days)
>   > since (last year, last month, 1980)

3 We form the present perfect tense in this way:

has/have + past participle of verb

EXAMPLES:
have + completed: The engineers **have completed** the project.
has + taken   :   Lily **has taken** her son to the clinic.

> **REMEMBER!**
> - The following are some examples of the past participle of verbs:
>
>   Regular Verbs
>
> | Base form of verb | ask | boil | dance | live | play | wash |
> |---|---|---|---|---|---|---|
> | Past Tense | asked | boiled | danced | lived | played | washed |
> | Past Participle | asked | boiled | danced | lived | played | washed |

Irregular Verbs

Base form of verb	bring	leave	make	pay
Past Tense	brought	left	made	paid
Past Participle	brought	left	made	paid

Base form of verb	choose	do	fly	write
Past Tense	chose	did	flew	wrote
Past Participle	chosen	done	flown	written

Base form of verb	cut	hit	put	read
Past Tense	cut	hit	put	read
Past Participle	cut	hit	put	read

Base form of the verb 'to be'	be
Past Tense	was/were
Past Participle	been

PRACTICE *A* Tick the correct sentences.

1 Dad polished his shoes yesterday.

2 Aida has cut the vegetables just now.

3 Mr Lee teach English for the past ten years.

4 The ripe fruit has fallen from the tree.

5 Rover our dog has dug a hole under the fence.

6 The spectators have thrown rubbish all over the field last night.

7 Alfred has flown a plane before.

8 Someone has broke the best blue platter.

9 I have studied French since 1998.

10 The police have catch the motorcyclist for speeding.

YOUR SCORE

10

PRACTICE *B* Underline the correct words in the brackets to complete the passage.

Tomorrow is Chinese New Year's Day. We **1** (have been busy / were busy) for the past two weeks
and now everything is ready. Emily **2** (has hung / hanged) up the new curtains. Maggie **3** (has washed
/ washed) the floor on Tuesday and **4** (has polished / polished) all the silverware yesterday.
We **5** (have decorated / decorated) the house with balloons two days ago. Little Cindy
6 (has drawn / drew) a beautiful poster for the New Year this morning. We **7** (have invited / invited)
Mrs Lim to welcome the New Year with us. May **8** (has baked / was baked) a delicious fruit cake.
I **9** (bought / have bought) a small gift for Mrs Lim and my little sister **10** (tied / has tied) a big bow
on it. I **11** (have even made / even made) my list of new year resolutions.

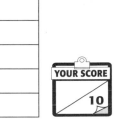

YOUR SCORE

10

PRACTICE **C** Cross out the incorrect verb forms to complete the passage.

Since our parents moved to the city, we children (1) | faced | have faced | some problems. Mum

(2) | has enrolled | enrolled | us in a co-ed school, something we are not used to. My sister Betty and I

(3) | have been | were | in an all-girls' school since we started going to school. For the past few weeks

we (4) | experienced | have experienced | some difficulty in adjusting.

We really miss our old schoolmates. We (5) | did | do | a lot of things together and had such

good times. We (6) | had | have | some very good friends who for the past five years

(7) | have always been | were always | there for us.

Betty and I (8) | already discovered | have already discovered | that some city kids are not quite as

friendly as the children we knew in the small town school. Furthermore, we (9) | had | have | to wake

up very early to catch the school bus which comes to our house at 6.15 a.m. We

(10) | never wake up | have never woken up | this early for school! We wish we could go

back to our little town where life was so relaxed.

YOUR SCORE
10

PRACTICE **D** Rewrite the sentences in the correct tenses.

1 Adam has already completing his 'A' levels.

_____

2 Joyce has enrol in a college.

_____

3 Tina has apply for several jobs.

_____

4 I seen some interesting advertisements.

_____

5 Tim has decide to work in a bank.

_____

YOUR SCORE
10

PRACTICE *E* Fill in the blanks with the present perfect tense or simple past tense form of the words in the box.

> be   dare   dream   go   meet   realise
> ride   sail   see   scream   visit

Hello Lydia,

I (1) _____*have dreamt*_____ of this moment for many months! Here I am at last in Disneyland! I

(2) _____ busy, enjoying all the wonders of this place. So far, we

(3) _____ Sleeping Beauty's castle and gone on a quick tour of Disneyland by the sky

train. We (4) _____ Mickey Mouse, Donald Duck and Goofy. We

(5) _____ so many cartoon characters that I cannot keep count of them!

This morning, Dave and I (6) _____ for a ride in Alice in Wonderland's cup and

saucer. It is like a crazy ferris wheel. Yesterday we (7) _____ in an old-fashioned boat to

see the different countries of the world. Then I (8) _____ that the world is a small place

after all! Dave and I even (9) _____ to go on a roller-coaster called Space Mountain. I

(10) _____ until I almost lost my voice. I also (11) _____ in a stage coach

to the wild, wild West.

I'll tell you more when I come back next week. Till then, take care.

Love,
Tessa

YOUR SCORE 10

PRACTICE *F* Underline the mistakes in the sentences and write the correct words in the spaces provided.

1 Mr Young has joined our company more than ten years ago.

2 The local paper has announcing that our team won the championship.

3 The Old Boys' Association already contributed cash and books for the students affected by the floods.

4 Everyone is happy that Lyn gets a promotion and is now our branch manager.

5 The prices of crude oil products have fell and this has affected many countries.

YOUR SCORE 10

101

UNIT 7.5 SIMPLE FUTURE TENSE

Look at the **A** and **B** sentences below. Find out why **B** is correct and **A** is wrong in the **Grammar Points** section.

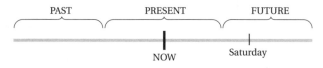

CHECKPOINT

				GRAMMAR POINTS
1A	I **go** out for dinner this evening.	✗		
1B	I **will go** out for dinner this evening.	✓	1
2A	Ralph and Anna **returns** home for the holidays next year.	✗	
2B	Ralph and Anna **will return** home for the holidays next year.	✓	2a
3A	Cory **be** in Singapore next Tuesday.	✗	
3B	Cory **will be** in Singapore next Tuesday.	✓	2b
4A	She **going to attend** a wedding tonight.	✗	
4B	She **is going to attend** a wedding tonight.	✓	3

GRAMMAR POINTS

1 We use the future tense to show future action.

EXAMPLE: We **will meet** you on Saturday.

```
   PAST          PRESENT          FUTURE
 ⌢⌣⌢⌣         ⌢⌣⌢⌣          ⌢⌣⌢⌣
————————————————|——————————|————————
              NOW        Saturday
```

2 We form the simple future tense using **will** in this way:

(a) **will** + base form of verb

EXAMPLE: Meg **will revise** her history notes this weekend.

(b) **will** + base form of the verb 'to be'

EXAMPLE: We **will be** busy with our work next week.

> **REMEMBER!**
> - The following are some words that may be used with verbs in the future tense:
>
> | | |
> |---|---|
> | tomorrow | next week |
> | this Saturday | next month |
>
> - In the past, the simple future tense was formed using **shall** for **I** and **we**, and **will** for other pronouns and nouns.
>   **EXAMPLES:**
>   I **shall attend** the Business Club meeting tomorrow.
>   We **shall have** a picnic this Sunday.
>
>   Nowadays, it is more common to use **will** for all nouns and pronouns.

3 We can also use the **going to** form for future action that is planned earlier or events that we think are likely to happen in the future. We form the simple future tense using **going to** in this way:

present tense of the verb 'to be' + **going to** + base form of verb

EXAMPLES: Peter **is going to watch** the football finals tomorrow evening.
They **are going to investigate** the break-in.

Underline the correct verbs to complete the sentences.

1 These coming holidays, Irene (visited / is going to visit) her uncle in Australia.

2 Annie (drew / will draw) the plans for her new house three months ago.

3 We (donating / are going to donate) the money we raised to a children's home.

4 The company (will build / built) the factory at the end of this year.

5 Hannah (going to buy / has bought) a new set of furniture.

6 I (join / will join) the Environment Society this weekend.

7 Everyone (taken / has taken) a lunch packet from the box.

8 Both of us (are going to attend / attend) the meeting tonight.

9 Wild geese (migrate / migrating) south for the winter.

10 My daughter (is learning / learning) how to write.

PRACTICE *B* Fill in the blanks with the correct forms of the verbs in the brackets.

1 The film _____*will start*_____ (start) at 5.30 this evening.

2 The party _____ (end) at 11 o'clock last night.

3 We _____ (clean) the house thoroughly for the coming Chinese New Year.

4 I _____ (take) Kate to the dentist yesterday afternoon.

5 Miriam _____ (meet) my sister Julia before.

6 The boat _____ (arrive) at Sydney Harbour last night.

7 I _____ (be) in the library since 3 p.m. today.

8 The farmers _____ (prepare) the fields for planting last week.

9 Mary often _____ (wash) her car during the week.

10 A herd of wild elephants _____ (attack) the village last night.

11 He _____ (be) in Australia next week.

PRACTICE *C* Cross out the incorrect verb forms to complete the dialogue.

Dr Bernard Tan : For this 'Clean up the Environment' campaign, I have decided to divide you into five teams. Paul, you (1) | will | will be | in charge of the campaign. Ranjit, Lee and Aaron (2) | will help | helped | to clear the tall grass and weeds in the field. Pat and the younger boys (3) | will carry | carry | away all the rubbish dumped under the trees. Paul, please tell the others what to do.

Paul : Right. Everyone (4) | is going | are going | to do different things. Vicki, Jean and Jess, you (5) | will sweep | sweeping | up the road and remove all the stones, loose soil and dead leaves. You (6) | use | will use | the black garbage bags to dispose of the rubbish. Christy and gang (7) | cleaning | will clean | the blocked drains. Clear the drains so water (8) | will be | will | able to flow freely. You (9) | will put | put | all garbage disposal bags neatly on one side of the road. The disposal company (10) | will collect | collecting | them later.

YOUR SCORE

/10

PRACTICE *D* Fill in the blanks with the present perfect tense or future tense form of the verbs in the brackets.

Trisha : Listen, everyone. Our graduation (1) _____ (be) in a month's time. We (2) _____ (get) so many things to do before that.

Jon : We (3) _____ (make) it a night all of us (4) _____ (remember) for a very long time.

Ling : We (5) _____ (hire) a good band and order a variety of food. Good food and good music are important.

Trisha : That's true but we (6) _____ (look) at our budget first before planning anything grand.

Jon : I (7) _____ (come) up with a wonderful idea already. To cut costs, we (8) _____ (have) our own college band to perform at our graduation.

Trisha : That sounds practical. I (9) _____ (ask) Farah's mother for some ideas about the food tomorrow. She (10) _____ (manage) a restaurant.

YOUR SCORE

/10

104

PRACTICE *E* Some of the underlined verbs in the sentences have been wrongly used. Write the correct verbs in the spaces provided.

1 He is going to participate in the grand prix next month.

2 My brother will be 21 years old next month and the family is planning a celebration.

3 They will followed all the old customs at Mala's wedding next week.

4 Sally will being our new supervisor next month.

5 Dad will angry when he finds out you dented his car.

6 Rose and I were admiring the furniture on sale when we saw Mrs Smith.

7 Nick will not break the promise he made to come tonight.

8 Lucy is coming over now. I talk to her about the problem later.

9 David is going to repair my roller blades tomorrow.

10 Property prices are going to fallen when the economy goes into a recession.

YOUR SCORE
10

PRACTICE *F* Complete the answers in the future tense. Use the words in the brackets.

1 Will Jenny come next Saturday for my birthday party? (come — next — Saturday)

Yes, she *will come next Saturday.*

2 What are you going to do on Sunday morning? (at — exercise — gym — the)

I _____

3 Who can take Grandpa to the dental clinic next week? (take — dental clinic — Grandpa — the)

I _____

4 Ed, are you going to the post office today? (a — parcel — post — today)

Yes, Sandra, _____

5 Dan, what is your departure date for New York? (leave — New York — 24th May)

I _____

6 Is it easy to get a taxi from here? I need to go to the train station tonight. (give — lift — train station — the — to)

Don't worry, Sam. I _____

_____

YOUR SCORE
10

UNIT 7.6 FUTURE CONTINUOUS TENSE

Look at the **A** and **B** sentences below. Find out why **B** is correct and **A** is wrong in the **Grammar Points** section.

				GRAMMAR POINTS
1A	The soldiers **will returning** home on Sunday.	✗		
1B	The soldiers **will be returning** home on Sunday.	✓	1	
2A	The helicopter **landing** at 6 a.m. this morning.	✗		
2B	The helicopter **will be landing** at 6 a.m. this morning.	✓	2	
3A	Press this button and you **will be hearing** music.	✗		
3B	Press this button and you **will hear** music.	✓	3	

GRAMMAR POINTS

1 We use the future continuous tense to show that an action will be going on in the future.
EXAMPLE: At 5 p.m. tomorrow Sue **will be playing** badminton.

YESTERDAY ~ 5 p.m.	NOW ~ 5 p.m.	TOMORROW ~ 5 p.m.
Sue was playing badminton.	Sue is playing badminton.	Sue will be playing badminton.

2 We form the future continuous tense in this way:
will be + base form of verb + 'ing'
EXAMPLE: We **will be working** for Mr Jenkins next year.

3 Some verbs cannot be used in the future continuous tense.
EXAMPLE:
I **will be remembering** your wedding always.   ✗
I **will remember** your wedding always.   ✓

REMEMBER!

■ The following are some verbs which do not usually take the continuous tense:

forget	hear	last
reach	remember	see
want	wish	

■ The future continuous tense can also be formed using **shall** for **I** and **we**, although it is more common to use **will** for all nouns and pronouns.

EXAMPLE:
I **shall be attending** their wedding ceremony this Friday.

PRACTICE *A* Tick the correct verbs to complete the sentences.

1 Amin [ ] will sitting / [ ] will be sitting for a basic French exam this year.

2 He [ ] chopped / [ ] will chopping some wood for the campfire.

3 The children [ ] will be touring / [ ] toured a textile factory at 4 p.m. today.

4 I [ ] will be moving / [ ] will moving to my new home on Saturday.

5 Jim and Ted [ ] wish / [ ] are wishing to go to Europe next year.

6 Nobody [ ] will be believing / [ ] will believe this silly story.

7 Ally [ ] will getting married / [ ] will be getting married to Michael at the end of the month.

8 I [ ] will enrolled / [ ] will be enrolling for the Business Management course next year.

9 They [ ] will be knowing / [ ] will know which road to take tomorrow when they see our road sign.

10 The entire town [ ] will cheered / [ ] will be cheering the badminton team when they come

YOUR SCORE 10

home tomorrow with the championship trophy.

PRACTICE *B* Fill in the blanks with **will** or **will be**.

1 Mr and Mrs Hayes _____ visiting Tokyo next week.

2 They _____ stop at Dubai on their way to London next month.

3 I _____ reach New York at about 3 p.m. tomorrow.

4 At 10 a.m. this Saturday we _____ cleaning the school hall.

5 I _____ see you at the cinema at 3 p.m. tomorrow.

6 We _____ meeting Mrs Adams this afternoon.

7 At 4 p.m. tomorrow I _____ on my way to the airport.

8 The hospital _____ organising a public fitness campaign very soon.

9 Tina's parents _____ go to Malaysia at the end of the week.

10 The concert next week _____ last for two hours.

YOUR SCORE 10

Rewrite these sentences in the future tense or future continuous tense form correctly.

1 We are going to breaking our journey at a little village by the sea.
   We are going to break our journey at a little village by the sea.

2 They will disappointed to hear that we are not going fishing with them.

3 She will arranging accommodation for the team in Sydney.

4 The girls decorating the stage at 5 p.m. today.

5 The pub will holding a karaoke contest on Saturday night.

6 We will be remembering to call you tomorrow regarding the schedule.

YOUR SCORE
10

PRACTICE *D* Fill in the blanks with the future tense or present perfect tense form of the verbs in the brackets.

Dear Jackie,

This is just a short note to let you know that I (1) _____*will be coming*_____ (come) to San Francisco next Thursday. I (2) _____ (stay) at the Cental Hotel. My secretary (3) _____ (already make) the reservations.

I (4) _____ (contact) you after I (5) _____ _____ (check) into the hotel. I hope you (6) _____ (be) free to join me for dinner. I (7) _____ (not see) you for more than three months.

We (8) _____ (have) a lot to talk about next week. On Friday and Saturday, I (9) _____ (be) completely involved in the conference. That leaves me with Sunday. I (10) _____ (fly) back home on Sunday night, but I'll be free in the morning. Perhaps you (11) _____ (be) able to go shopping with me.

See you soon.

Love,
Donna

YOUR SCORE
10

PRACTICE **E** Complete the sentences with the correct verbs in the box.

> are going to leave   has drawn   has struggled
> have already cleared   were going to reveal   will be
> will be interviewing   will be setting up   will be sponsoring
> will be thronging

1 Our club _____ an exhibition and sale of handicrafts this week.

2 Chris and I _____ for a tour of Greece on Friday.

3 She _____ alone for many years to keep the business going.

4 The board of directors _____ applicants for the job next Monday.

5 The girls _____ all our plans when we interrupted them.

6 The weather _____ fine tomorrow so we can go on our excursion.

7 The hired labourers _____ the land for planting.

8 The natural beauty of this place _____ many tourists here.

9 The young couple _____ home in a quiet suburb of the city.

10 Crowds of visitors _____ the city centre this weekend
for the annual computer fair.

YOUR SCORE
10

PRACTICE **F** Use the correct verbs in the box to describe what the writer will be doing next week.

> will be flying   will join   will be shopping   will be touring
> will go   will participate   will be sitting   will watch
> will have   will relax   will be staying

I am so tired of cooking and washing dirty dishes. Next Monday, at this time, I (1) ____*will be*____

____*flying*____ to Spain for my vacation. For 10 wonderful days I (2) _____ at the

Las Palmas Hotel by the sea in Barcelona. Lina and Abby (3) _____ me there. Every

morning, we (4)_____ in the warm sunshine under beach umbrellas, enjoying fresh

tropical fruit and juices. We (5) _____ sailing, fishing and water skiing. On Friday

morning, I (6) _____ historic Spanish palaces while the others (7) _____

at the open-air markets.

At night, we (8) _____ and listen to the music of Spain. We (9) _____

_____ in the dancing too! We (10) _____ such an exciting time!

Just before our holiday ends, we (11) _____ a bullfight – something

which Spain is famous for. I am really looking forward to my holiday.

YOUR SCORE
10

UNIT 8.1 ACTIVE AND PASSIVE VOICE

Look at the **A** and **B** sentences below. Find out why **B** is correct and **A** is wrong in the **Grammar Points** section.

GRAMMAR
POINTS

1A	Rose **was played** the violin.	✗	
1B	Rose **played** the violin.	✓	1
2A	The robbers **were chase** by the dogs.	✗	
	The robbers **chased** by the dogs.	✗	
2B	The robbers **were chased** by the dogs.	✓	2

GRAMMAR POINTS

1 A sentence which begins with the person or thing that does the action is in the active voice. It must have an active verb.

EXAMPLE: Mechanics repair cars.

- subject: the people who do the action (who repair)
- active verb: the action (repair)
- object: the things that receive the action (that get repaired)

2 A sentence which begins with the person or thing that receives the action is in the passive voice. It must have a passive verb.

EXAMPLE: Cars are repaired by mechanics.

- subject: the things that receive the action (that get repaired)
- passive verb: the action done (are repaired)

REMEMBER!

- In a sentence using the passive voice, the object comes after the verb and the preposition **by**.

EXAMPLE:
Cars **are repaired** by mechanics.

- object: the people who do the action (who repair)

We form passive verbs in this way:

the verb 'to be' + past participle of main verb

EXAMPLES: is + cleaned = is cleaned
were + caught = were caught

Active Verbs	Passive Verbs
repairs	is repaired
repair	are repaired
repaired	was/were repaired

REMEMBER!

- For some words, the past tense and the past participle are the same.

  EXAMPLES:

Past Tense	caught	taught	fed	heard	kept	swept
Past Participle	caught	taught	fed	heard	kept	swept

- For some words, the past tense and the past participle are different.

  EXAMPLES:

Past Tense	ate	beat	find	flew	took	write
Past Participle	eaten	beaten	found	flown	taken	written

PRACTICE _A_ Underline the correct words in the brackets to complete the paragraph.

Anna **1** (is loves / loves) animals. Many birds and squirrels are **2** (fed / feeded) by Anna every day. One morning, she **3** (found / was found) a sick bird under a tree. She **4** (carried / was carried) it carefully to her house. The bird **5** (was taken / was took) to a vet by Anna's father. After that, it **6** (was look after / was looked after) by the whole family. It was **7**(encouraged / encourage) to fly again by Anna. One day, it **8** (flew / was flown) back to the tree. Its happy chirps **9** (heard / are heard) by Anna every day. Sometimes it **10** (is join / joins) the other birds around Anna.

YOUR SCORE

10

PRACTICE _B_ Rearrange the words to form correct sentences.

1 car — driver — locked — the — the.

_____

2 by — door — Jill — opened — the — was.

_____

3 chased — dog — me — Mr Lim's.

_____

4 by — floor — is — maid — mopped — the — the.

_____

5 are — by — caused — diseases — germs — many.

_____

YOUR SCORE

10

PRACTICE *C*   Fill in the blanks with suitable words.

1   Active Voice :   Six monkeys rode two horses in the circus act.
    Passive Voice :   Two horses _____ ridden by six monkeys in the circus act.

2   Active Voice :   Many teenagers wear jeans and t-shirts.
    Passive Voice :   Jeans and t-shirts are _____ by many teenagers.

3   Active Voice :   The explosion rocked the building.
    Passive Voice :   The building was _____ by the explosion.

4   Active Voice :   Today, children in many countries read her books.
    Passive Voice :   Today, her books _____ read by children in many countries.

5   Active Voice :   All of us miss him.
    Passive Voice :   He is _____ by all of us.

6   Active Voice :   A group of mountain climbers _____ a strange animal.
    Passive Voice :   A strange animal was seen by a group of mountain climbers.

7   Active Voice :   The nervous actors _____ some of their lines.
    Passive Voice :   A lot of lines were forgotten by the nervous actors.

8   Active Voice :   Nowadays, girls as well as boys _____ judo clubs.
    Passive Voice :   Nowadays, judo clubs are attended by girls as well as boys.

9   Active Voice :   Most other animals in the jungle _____ the tiger.
    Passive Voice :   The tiger is feared by most other animals in the jungle.

10   Active Voice :   The little girl _____ pretty baskets.
    Passive Voice :   Pretty baskets are woven by that little girl.

YOUR SCORE   /10

PRACTICE *D*   Tick the correct sentences.

1   The doctor was examined the patient carefully.
2   That old pipe smoke by my uncle.
3   Three wolves were spotted by the cameraman.
4   A young man is managed the factory.
5   The puppy buried bones all over the garden.
6   The man was questioned by the police.
7   Meals by efficient waiters were served.
8   Experienced writers produce the script.
9   More food is needed by the flood victims.
10   The girls were poured the tea into little cups.

YOUR SCORE   /10

PRACTICE *E* Rewrite the sentences correctly.

1 My father was received a letter yesterday.

_____

2 A treasure hunt organised by the Rotary Club twice a year.

_____

3 Your torn sock was mend by Mum this morning.

_____

4 The little boy's nails is trimmed by his sister every month.

_____

5 The rice by the chef himself was fried.

_____

YOUR SCORE

10

PRACTICE *F* Fill in the blanks with the words in the box.

acted	am	are	borrows	enjoy
entertained	exchanged	is	joined	thrilled

I (1) _____ a reading group early this year. Every Monday each of the five

members (2) _____ a book from the library. On Saturday morning the books

(3) _____ discussed at our meeting. We (4) _____ these

discussions very much. Plots and ideas are (5) _____ . Sometimes we are

(6) _____ by a frightening incident in a book. Very often, I (7) _____

amused by funny characters and my friends' comments on them.

Last week, Lynne (8) _____ the rest of us with a comical scene from a novel.

She (9) _____ three different roles very well. Every week my interest in reading

(10) _____ increased by these meetings.

YOUR SCORE

10

UNIT 8.2 ACTIVE AND PASSIVE VOICE

tense and number

Look at the **A** and **B** sentences below. Find out why **B** is correct and **A** is wrong in the **Grammar Points** section.

			GRAMMAR POINTS
1A	Active Voice: Mr Jenkins bought 20 roses. Passive Voice: Twenty roses **are** bought by Mr Jenkins.	✗	
1B	Active Voice: Mr Jenkins bought 20 roses. Passive Voice: Twenty roses **were** bought by Mr Jenkins.	✓	1
2A	The children **was saved** by a fireman.	✗	
2B	The children **were saved** by a fireman.	✓	2

GRAMMAR POINTS

When we **change** a sentence from the **active voice** to the **passive voice**,

1   the tense of the verb has to remain the same

EXAMPLES: Sally **sweeps** the floor every day.   (active, present tense)
The floor **is swept** by Sally every day.   (passive, present tense)

Sally **swept** the floor yesterday.   (active, past tense)
The floor **was swept** by Sally yesterday. (passive, past tense)

2   the verb has to agree with the subject of the sentence

EXAMPLES:
My dog chased the postman.   (active)
The postman was chased by my dog. (passive)

singular subject   singular verb

My dog chased the neighbour's children.   (active)
The neighbour's children were chased by my dog. (passive)

plural subject   plural verb

114

PRACTICE *A*   For each sentence in the active voice, circle the letter of the correct sentence in the passive voice.

1 The boy kicked the ball.
   A The ball was kick by the boy.
   B The ball is kicked by the boy.
   C The ball was kicked by the boy.

2 My grandfather plants many vegetables in our garden.
   A Many vegetables in our garden are planted by my grandfather.
   B Many vegetables in our garden planted my grandfather.
   C Many vegetables in our garden are plant by my grandfather.

3 The headmistress called Mr Lim to her office.
   A The headmistress was called by Mr Lim to her office.
   B Mr Lim was called by the headmistress to her office.
   C Mr Lim was call by the headmistress to her office.

4 The bear attacked the hunter.
   A The hunter was attacked by the bear.
   B The hunter was by the bear attacked.
   C By the bear the hunter was attacked.

5 Fans cool these rooms.
   A These fans are cooling rooms.
   B The rooms are cool by fans.
   C These rooms are cooled by fans.

6 Cheryl invented the game.
   A The game invented by Cheryl.
   B The game was invented by Cheryl.
   C The game is invented by Cheryl.

7 Architects design buildings.
   A Buildings are designed by architects.
   B Buildings arc by architects design.
   C Buildings are design by architects.

8 A lifeguard saved him.
   A He was save by a lifeguard.
   B A lifeguard was saved by him.
   C He was saved by a lifeguard.

9 Wild animals fear fire.

    A Fire is feared by wild animals.

    B Fire feared by wild animals.

    C Fire are feared by wild animals.

10 Her voice soothed me.

    A I am soothed by her voice.

    B I was soothed by her voice.

    C I was soothe by her voice.

PRACTICE *B*   Tick the correct sentences.

1 The room were swept by the boys.

2 A lot of money was save by the student.

3 Our team was beaten by theirs.

4 We were stopped by the traffic policeman.

5 The women was helped by the guard.

6 Rats are ate by snakes.

7 We were taught by Mrs Lopez.

8 The fish was fry by Barbara.

9 The vases were made by Rosemary.

10 The letters are typed by Meg every day.

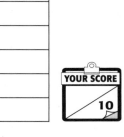

PRACTICE *C*   Rearrange the words to form correct sentences.

1 a — by — man — said — those — wise — were — words.

_____

2 boys — ground — on — spun — tops — the — the — their.

_____

3 armed — by — couple — men — robbed — the — two — was.

_____

4 by — fish — fishermen — freshest — is — sold — the — the — themselves.

_____

5 flowers — knows — many — names — of — scientific — she — the.

_____

PRACTICE *D* Underline the incorrect sentences and rewrite them correctly.

In this monastery the discipline is quite good. The rules are explain by the discipline master very clearly. Most of the time the rules are obeyed by everyone. Once in a while a rule is broke by a novice. The senior monk who catches the novice breaking the rule gives him a warning. A novice who keeps breaking rules are punished by the discipline master.

Counselling is also provided by the monastery. Some years ago two monks are sent by the monastery to attend a counselling course. They are now experienced counsellors. A counsellor helps young monks to understand and improve their own behaviour. In this way the novices were given a chance to learn self-discipline.

1 _____
   _____
2 _____
   _____
3 _____
   _____
4 _____
   _____
5 _____
   _____

YOUR SCORE
10

PRACTICE *E* Change the sentences from the active voice to the passive voice.

1 A bee stung me this morning.
   _____

2 Commuters use that pedestrian crossing every day.
   _____

3 The music centre holds three concerts every year.
   _____

4 The players chose Adam to be their captain.
   _____

5 Many Europeans enjoy Asian art.
   _____

YOUR SCORE
10

UNIT 9 SUBJECT AND PREDICATE

finite and non-finite verbs

Look at the **A** and **B** sentences below. Find out why **B** is correct and **A** is wrong in the **Grammar Points** section.

				GRAMMAR POINTS
1A	Can swim there.	✗	
1B	**We** can swim there.	✓	1
2A	Made me angry **that man**.	✗	
2B	**That man** made me angry.	✓	2
3A	She **doing** her homework now.	✗	
3B	She **is doing** her homework now.	✓	3
4A	I kept **there** my coins.	✗	
4B	I kept my coins **there**.	✓	4

GRAMMAR POINTS

1 A sentence usually has a **subject** (what the sentence is about) and a **predicate** (the part of the sentence which gives information about the subject).

EXAMPLES:

SUBJECT	PREDICATE
Mr Tan	drives well.
Linda	is a dancer.

> **REMEMBER!**
> ■ A sentence with only **one** finite verb is called a simple sentence.

2 The subject usually comes before the predicate.

EXAMPLE: That boy can run fast. ✓   Can run fast that boy. ✗

3 The predicate must have at least one finite verb. A verb that ends in 'ing' or comes with **to** before it is a non-finite verb.

EXAMPLES:

Sentences with only non-finite verbs		Sentences with finite verbs	
The bell **ringing**.	✗	The bell **is ringing**.	✓
All of us **to keep** quiet.	✗	All of us **have to keep** quiet.	✓

> **REMEMBER!**
> ■ A finite verb changes its form according to the tense and subject of the sentence but a non-finite verb remains the same.
> EXAMPLES:
>
> Present tense : She **wants** [finite] to go [non-finite] shopping today.
>
> Past tense : She **wanted** [finite] to go [non-finite] shopping yesterday.
>
> Singular subject : My sister **wants** [finite] to go [non-finite] shopping.
>
> Plural subject : My parents **want** [finite] to go [non-finite] shopping.

4 The predicate may also contain an object, a complement or an adverbial. The object or complement comes immediately after the verb.

REMEMBER!
- The object is the person or thing that the subject does something to.
- A complement often describes a quality or characteristic of the subject or object. It can also tell us the identity of the subject or object.
- An adverbial tells us more about the action, event or state mentioned in the sentence (such as: when it happened, where it happened, and how it happened).

EXAMPLES:

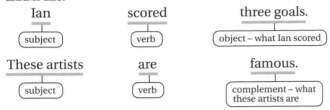

Ian	scored	three goals.
subject	verb	object – what Ian scored

These artists	are	famous.
subject	verb	complement – what these artists are

The adverbial often appears at the end of the sentence: after the verb, object or complement.

EXAMPLES:

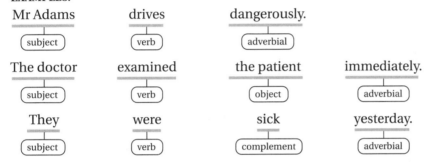

Mr Adams	drives	dangerously.	
subject	verb	adverbial	

The doctor	examined	the patient	immediately.
subject	verb	object	adverbial

They	were	sick	yesterday.
subject	verb	complement	adverbial

PRACTICE *A* Underline the predicates in the sentences.

1 My parents <u>are out.</u>

2 That calculator is too expensive.

3 We can return to our rooms.

4 Our neighbours, Mr and Mrs Hughes, like to grow flowers.

5 My friends and I are going to a party tonight.

6 Kathy's ambition is to be a pilot.

7 The little boy prepares his own breakfast every day.

8 Most trees in temperate climates shed their leaves in autumn.

9 Sports Day for our school was last Saturday.

10 The girl in blue may win the spelling competition.

11 You always make us laugh with your stories.

YOUR SCORE

10

PRACTICE *B* Circle the letters of the correct sentences. There may be more than one answer for each question.

1 A Can come tomorrow you.
　B You can come tomorrow.
　C Tomorrow you can come.

2 A At five o'clock this morning Ron went jogging.
　B At five o'clock this morning Ron jogging.
　C At five o'clock this morning Ron was jogging.

119

3
A She finished everything this morning.
B She finished this morning everything.
C This morning she finished everything.

4
A Everybody to go to the hall now.
B Everybody is to go to the hall now.
C Everybody has to go to the hall now.

5
A The children are very noisy today.
B Today the children are very noisy.
C Very noisy the children today.

PRACTICE **C** Rewrite each sentence, inserting the word or words in the brackets in **one of** the places marked ⋏ .

1 The teachers are marking ⋏ in the staff room ⋏ .   (our test papers)

_____

2 Grandpa was ⋏ a fine athlete ⋏ .   (in his youth)

_____

3 All employees ⋏ to assemble ⋏ in front of the building at once.   (are)

_____

4 The children decorated ⋏ their kindergarten ⋏ .   (beautifully)

_____

5 She will be ⋏ on this tour ⋏ .   (our guide)

_____

6 One of the scenes ⋏ in the movie ⋏ very frightening.   (is)

_____

7 The little boy greeted ⋏ his aunt ⋏ .   (with a cheeky smile)

_____

8 He ⋏ attending a meeting ⋏ in Hawaii.   (will be)

_____

9 Mrs Lee made ⋏ pineapple jam ⋏ .   (for her family)

_____

10 Good managers ⋏ to be firm and fair to ⋏ everyone.   (have)

_____

PRACTICE *D*　Rearrange the words to form correct sentences.

1　Christine — drinking — is — green tea.

_____

2　come — have — now — to — you.

_____

3　a — doctor — good — is — she — very.

_____

4　classroom — cleaned — pupils — the — the.

_____

5　her — may — she — sister — take — there.

_____

PRACTICE *E*　Underline the correct words in the brackets to complete the passage.

It **1** (is raining / raining) heavily. It **2** (rained yesterday / yesterday rained) too. The river near my house will overflow **3** (its banks soon / soon its banks). My neighbours and I **4** (need to / to) get ready **5** (are to / to) cope with a flood. Floods are **6** (a problem here / here a problem). Sometimes the water **7** (rises / rising) very high. Then we all **8** (have to / to) move to higher ground until the water level goes down. Floods damage **9** (badly our crops / our crops badly). Some of us **10** (to / want to) move away permanently.

PRACTICE *F*　Underline the incorrect sentences and rewrite them correctly.

1　A fresh wind is blowing from across the sea. The coconut palms are swaying gently. I sitting quietly on the beach. It is lovely and peaceful.

2　Two schoolboys came to our house this morning. Offered to wash our car. They were raising funds to build a new laboratory for their school. We gave them quite a lot of money for a good car wash.

3　My brother lives alone in the city. He tidies his room every day. He cleans the floor three times a week. He does twice a week his laundry.

4　Driving me crazy the noise. It is coming from a construction site in the neighbourhood. I am trying to concentrate on my science textbook and notes. I have to sit for a test tomorrow.

5　We plan hold a party next Saturday. We want to make it a really enjoyable one. We need to start early. This is because all of us have to be home by 11 p.m.

1　_____
2　_____
3　_____
4　_____
5　_____

UNIT 10 QUESTION TAGS

isn't, aren't, doesn't, don't

Look at the **A** and **B** sentences below. Find out why **B** is correct and **A** is wrong in the **Grammar Points** section.

			GRAMMAR POINTS
1A	A bear loves honey, **isn't** it?	✗	
1B	A bear loves honey, **doesn't** it?	✓	1
2A	She is a nice girl, **is not** she?	✗	
2B	She is a nice girl, **isn't** she?	✓	2
3A	Mr Lee is helpful, **isn't it**?	✗	
3B	Mr Lee is helpful, **isn't he**?	✓	3

GRAMMAR POINTS

1 We use negative question tags with positive statements. In a statement with the verb 'to be', the question tag uses the negative form of the same verb.

EXAMPLES:

This computer **is** expensive, **isn't** it?

These computers **are** expensive, **aren't** they?

In a statement with a main verb, the question tag uses the negative form of the verb 'to do'. The verb 'to do' must agree with the main verb.

EXAMPLES: Dad **walks** fast, **doesn't** he?

Ants **love** sugar, **don't** they?

2 We use short forms in question tags.

EXAMPLE:

Your brothers play chess, **don't** they? ☑

Your brothers play chess, **do not** they? ☒

3 We use pronouns, not nouns or noun phrases, in question tags. The pronoun must agree with the subject of the statement.

EXAMPLE:

The musicians are good, aren't **they**? ☑

The musicians are good, aren't **you**? ☒

REMEMBER!

- A statement can be turned into a question by adding a question tag at the end of it.
  EXAMPLE:
  This shuttlecock is yours, isn't it?

  (statement) (question tag)

- A question tag is used to:
  (a) check whether something is true
    EXAMPLE:
    You are an artist, **aren't you**?
  (b) find out if someone agrees with us
    EXAMPLE:
    The room looks colourful, **doesn't it**?

- There is no short form for **am not** so **aren't** is used to form question tags instead.
  EXAMPLE: I **am** very untidy, **aren't** I?

122

PRACTICE *A* Fill in the blanks with the correct question tags.

1 You are ready to go, _____ ?

2 We need a map and a compass, _____ ?

3 The front door is locked, _____ ?

4 That motorist drives recklessly, _____ ?

5 The cars ahead are slowing down, _____ ?

6 You need your sunglasses, _____ ?

7 Our car is making a funny noise, _____ ?

8 That policewoman wants us to stop, _____ ?

9 The waiters here give good service, _____ ?

10 I am a good driver, _____ ?

YOUR SCORE
10

PRACTICE *B* Circle the letters of the sentences with correct question tags. There may be more than one answer for each question.

1 **A** Whales are mammals, are they?

   B Whales are mammals, aren't they?

   C A whale is a mammal, isn't it?

2 **A** I am very noisy, amn't I?

   B You are very noisy, aren't you?

   C I am very noisy, aren't I?

3 **A** Aunt Rosie and Aunt Jane knit baby clothes, don't they?

   B Aunt Rosie knits baby clothes, doesn't she?

   C Aunt Rosie knits baby clothes, aren't they?

4 **A** These girls dance well, don't they?

   B These girls dance well, aren't they?

   C This girl dances well, doesn't she?

5 **A** You and I enjoy funny stories, don't we?

   B You and she enjoy funny stories, isn't it?

   C You and she enjoy funny stories, don't you?

YOUR SCORE
10

123

PRACTICE $\boxed{C}$ Rearrange the words to form correct sentences with question tags.

1 | hot | | isn't | | it | | it's | | , | | ? |
_____

2 | cats | | don't | | fish | | like | | they | | , | | ? |
_____

3 | doesn't | | he | | here | | works | | Tim | | , | | ? |
_____

4 | and | | are | | aren't | | going | | I | | we | | you | | , | | ? |
_____

5 | a | | costs | | doesn't | | it | | lot | | piano | | this | | , | | ? |
_____

YOUR SCORE 10

PRACTICE $\boxed{D}$ Underline the mistakes and write the correct answers in the boxes.

1 These mangoes are delicious, aren't <u>them</u>? | _they_ |

2 She wants this book, don't she? | |

3 They lives here, don't they? | |

4 That is the Ritz Hotel, isn't that? | |

5 Joseph and I am right, aren't we? | |

YOUR SCORE 10

6 Stella and Steve work well together, aren't they? | |

PRACTICE $\boxed{E}$ Rewrite the sentences and correct the question tags.

1 Monaco is just 1.5 square km in area, is not it?
_____

2 Canada and the United States grow wheat, doesn't they?
_____

3 Raisins and currants are dried grapes, isn't it?
_____

4 You do have my book 'Robinson Crusoe', you don't?
_____

5 Your brother likes the cartoon character in this book, isn't he?
_____

YOUR SCORE 10

124

Fill in the blanks with suitable words from both boxes. Each word may be used more than once.

Box A

he	I	it	she	they	we	you

Box B

are	aren't	doesn't	don't	is	isn't

1 _____ is brilliant, _____ she?

2 You and _____ are adventurous, _____ we?

3 Both he and _____ love travelling, don't _____ ?

4 This cough mixture makes you sleepy, _____ _____ ?

5 The streets _____ crowded today, aren't _____ ?

6 I bring you a lot of problems, _____ _____ ?

7 _____ expresses himself well, _____ he?

8 The scenery _____ awesome, _____ it?

9 Tapirs feed on leaves, _____ _____ ?

10 You _____ a nature lover, aren't _____ ?

YOUR SCORE
10

PRACTICE *G* Underline the sentences in which question tags are used correctly.

Mr Yong : This party is really enjoyable, isn't it?

Mrs Yong : Oh yes. The desserts are delicious, aren't they?

Mr Yong : You are supposed to be dieting, isn't it?

Mrs Yong : You know how to spoil my fun, don't you?

Mr Yong : Sorry, dear. Hey, our son looks smart, don't he?

Mrs Yong : He is wearing your favourite shirt, isn't he?

Mr Yong : I noticed that. It looks fine on him. But it looks even better on me, doesn't it?

Mrs Yong : Men are vain, are they?

Mr Yong : Not me. You and I argue a lot, don't we?

Mrs Yong : Our arguments make life interesting, don't they?

Mervyn : Hi, Mum. Hi, Dad. You are staying till the end of the party, aren't you?

Mr Yong : Yes, if you are. We are going home together, are not we?

Mrs Yong : We have to stay, Mervyn. Our hostess wants you to play the piano for the dance, doesn't she?

Mervyn : I am important, aren't I?

Mrs Yong : You are happy to be needed, don't you?

Mr Yong : He is as vain as I am, doesn't he?

YOUR SCORE
10

125

UNIT 11.1 **WH-QUESTIONS**

Look at the **A** and **B** sentences below. Find out why **B** is correct and **A** is wrong in the **Grammar Points** section.

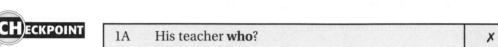

CHECKPOINT

			GRAMMAR POINTS
1A	His teacher **who**?	✗	
1B	**Who** is his teacher?	✓	1
2A	**Where those** boys?	✗	
2B	**Where are those** boys?	✓	2
3A	What did Janet **wanted**?	✗	
3B	What did Janet **want**?	✓	3a
4A	Why don't you **comes** with us?	✗	
4B	Why don't you **come** with us?	✓	3b

GRAMMAR POINTS

1 We always begin a wh-question with a wh-word. The wh-words are as follows:

Who	Whom	Whose	What	Which	Where	When	Why	How

EXAMPLE: Whose ring is this? ✓

This ring is whose? ✗

2 Every wh-question must have a finite verb to make it complete.

EXAMPLES:

Where **is** the hammer? ✓

Where the hammer? ✗

Which students **are** representing our school? ✓

Which students representing our school? ✗

3 We use the verb 'to do' with wh-words in these ways:

(a) Wh-word + the verb 'to do' + noun/pronoun + base form of main verb

EXAMPLE:

How **did** Emma **go** home? ✓

〔base form〕

> **REMEMBER!**
> ■ Wh-words are also known as interrogative words or question words. They are words used in the asking of questions and they are called wh-words as most of them begin with 'wh'.
>
> ■ During conversation, a wh-word alone can be used as a question. However, this is not acceptable in writing.
> **EXAMPLE:**
> In conversation:
> A: Someone here likes dried fruit.
> B: Who?
> In writing:
> Who likes dried fruit?

How **did** Emma **goes** home? ✗

How **did** Emma **went** home? ✗

How **did** Emma **going** home? ✗

(b) Wh-word + the negative of the verb 'to do' (**doesn't/don't/didn't**) +
noun/pronoun + base form of main verb

EXAMPLE:

Why **doesn't** Eva **finish** her work? ✓

Why **doesn't** Eva **finishes** her work? ✗

Why **doesn't** Eva **finished** her work? ✗

Why **doesn't** Eva **finishing** her work? ✗

(base form)

PRACTICE *A*   Rewrite the wh-questions correctly.

1 My umbrella is where?
Where is my umbrella?

2 Why your brother is so happy today?

3 Kim's occupation is what?

4 Is how your backache now?

5 Anne's flight is when?

6 Is suitcase which your?

YOUR SCORE
10

PRACTICE *B*   Mark with ⅄ where the missing verbs or parts of the verb should be.

1 Who ⅄ Edith Cavell ?	is
2 How fast does that fighter jet ?	fly
3 Where the headquarters of the United Nations ?	are
4 What the old name for Istanbul ?	is
5 Who helping you with the housework ?	is
6 Why Steve look so pleased ?	did
7 How many seats there in this auditorium ?	are
8 Which country that tourist come from ?	did
9 How much money did the thief ?	steal
10 When Nelson Mandela become the President of South Africa ?	did
11 Why did the Europeans to the Americas in the fifteeth century ?	go

YOUR SCORE
10

127

PRACTICE $\boxed{C}$ Underline the correct words to complete the questions.

1 What do the children (want / wants) for tea?

2 How much sugar do you (take / takes) in your coffee?

3 Whose shoes did your dog (chew / chewed)?

4 Who doesn't James (know / knows) at the party?

5 Where did Mary and Eva (find / finding) the wallet?

6 When did Maxine (leave / left) her job?

7 Which magazines do you (read / reads)?

8 How did Jenny (get / gets) my telephone number?

9 Why didn't we (ask / asked) the policeman for directions just now?

10 How many employees does that firm (have / having)?

PRACTICE $\boxed{D}$ Tick the questions that are correct.

1 A Whose answer is correct?
   B Whose answer correct?

2 A What did the salesgirl give you?
   B What did the salesgirl gave you?

3 A Your birthday is when?
   B When is your birthday?

4 A How old is your brother?
   B How old your brother is?

5 A Which journalist this article wrote?
   B Which journalist wrote this article?

6 A You have how many hamsters?
   B How many hamsters do you have?

7 A How much paint is there?
   B How much paint there is?

8 A Victor put my file where?
   B Where did Victor put my file?

9 A Why didn't you finish your breakfast?
   B Why didn't you finished your breakfast?

10 A Who wanting this calendar?
    B Who wants this calendar?

PRACTICE *E* Complete the questions with the correct words in the boxes.

1 _____ the highest mountain in the world?

| Which |
| Which is |

2 _____ to the airport?

| How did you go |
| How you went |

3 _____ in a hurry?

| Kevin why was |
| Why was Kevin |

4 _____ a Japanese garden?

| Whose house has |
| Whose house having |

5 _____ the hair stylist _____ ?

| What didn't – bring |
| What – didn't bringing |

6 Whose father _____ to dress up as a clown?

| going |
| is going |

7 _____ Anne _____ you about the meeting?

| Why – didn't tell |
| Why didn't – tell |

8 _____ your parents returning from Scotland?

| When |
| When are |

9 Which student _____ for the History paper?

| didn't sit |
| didn't sat |

10 What _____ for dinner?

| are you cooking |
| you are cooking |

YOUR SCORE
10

PRACTICE *F* Some of the following questions are wrong. Correct them.

1 Which town that is?
  Which town is that?

2 Whose initials are those?

3 Where did Joe bought that shirt?

4 Why did they refuse to come?

5 Which classes decorating the hall now?

6 How does this machine works?

YOUR SCORE
10

129

UNIT 11.2 WH-QUESTIONS

who

Look at the **A** and **B** sentences below. Find out why **B** is correct and **A** is wrong in the **Grammar Points** section.

CHECKPOINT

GRAMMAR POINTS

1A	Who **was** your visitors?	✗	
1B	Who **were** your visitors?	✓	1
2A	Who **like** cricket?	✗	
2B	Who **likes** cricket?	✓	2
3A	Who is **shout** upstairs?	✗	
3B	Who is **shouting** upstairs?	✓	3
4A	Who does not **likes** orange juice?	✗	
4B	Who does not **like** orange juice?	✓	4

GRAMMAR POINTS

1 In a **Who** question, the verb 'to be' must agree in tense and number with the noun or pronoun it points to.

singular

EXAMPLES: Who **is** your favourite **singer**?

plural

Who **are** your favourite **singers**?

2 We usually use the **singular** form of a **main verb** with a **Who** question that is in the **present** tense.

EXAMPLES: Who **wants** some cake? ✓

Who **want** some cake? ✗

Who **plays** the violin? ✓

Who **play** the violin? ✗

3 We must use the verb 'to be' together with the 'ing' form of the main verb in a **Who** question.

EXAMPLES: Who is **singing** now? ✓   Who was **watching** TV just now? ✓

Who **singing** now? ✗   Who **watching** TV just now? ✗

REMEMBER!

■ **Who** is used to ask questions about people's identity.

■ Traditionally, **who** is used as the subject of the verb in a question, and **whom** is used as the object of the verb.

EXAMPLE: subject   object
Question: Who called Peter ?
              object   subject
Question: Whom did Annie call?
              subject   object
Answer: Annie called Peter .

However, nowadays, it is more common to use **who** as both the subject and the object of the verb.

130

4 We can use the negative form of the verb 'to do' with **Who** in this way:

Who + the negative form of the verb 'to do' + base form of main verb

EXAMPLE:

Who doesn't **like** jazz? ✓
    └─ (base form)

Who doesn't **likes** jazz? ✗

Who doesn't **liked** jazz? ✗

Who doesn't **liking** jazz? ✗

PRACTICE *A*   Tick the correct verbs.

1 Who [is | are] your sister's tutor?

2 Who [is | are] Mr Tate's tenants?

3 Who [was | were] the committee members of the Chess Club last year?

4 Who [was | were] the chairman of the Chess Club last year?

5 Who [doesn't study | doesn't studies] Japanese?

6 Who [require | requires] transport to the stadium?

7 Who [was deliver | was delivering] a speech just now?

8 Who [is using | are using] the computer now?

9 Who [wish | wishes] to subscribe to this magazine?

10 Who [didn't understand | didn't understood] Miss Lee's explanation?

YOUR SCORE / 10

PRACTICE *B*   Circle the verbs you can use to fill the blanks. You may circle more than one verb for each question.

1 Who _____ the winner?

| is | are | was | were |

2 Who _____ the organisers for the photography exhibition?

| is | are | was | were |

3 Who _____ Lara is a good actress?

| think | thinks |
| doesn't think | don't think |

4 Who _____ a beautiful silk saree?

| wear | wore |
| was wearing | were wearing |

5 Who _____ the doors and windows of the office?

| lock | locks |
| don't lock | didn't lock |

YOUR SCORE / 10

PRACTICE C Complete the questions with the correct words in the boxes.

1 Who _____*doesn't like*_____ Italian food? [doesn't   don't   like   likes]

2 Who _____ the latest issue of *Students' Digest*? [has   have]

3 Who _____ leaves in the garden? [is   are   burn   burning]

4 Who _____ the women in the car with your mother? [is / are]

5 Who _____ to solve the mystery of the missing letterbox? [intend   intends]

6 Who _____ the ten mile race? [don't   attempt / didn't   attempts]

7 Who _____ the finalists in the choral-speaking competition? [was / were]

8 Who _____ the way to Emily's house? [doesn't   don't   know   knows]

9 Who _____ old coins and stamps? [collect   collecting / collects   are collecting]

10 Who _____ you to pitch the tents? [help   is helping / helping   are helping]

11 Who _____ another form? [need   needs]

PRACTICE D Rewrite the questions and correct the verbs.

1 Who is the elderly women on the bridge?
   Who are the elderly women on the bridge?

2 Who were the person you spoke to just now?
   _____

3 Who prefer tennis to badminton?
   _____

4 Who doesn't liked to travel anywhere by train?
   _____

5 Who coaching the boys now for the football tournament?
   _____

6 Who doesn't takes sugar in her coffee?
   _____

YOUR SCORE

10

132

PRACTICE *E* Tick the questions that are correct.

1 ☐ **A** Who in the attic?
   ☐ **B** Who is in the attic?

2 ☐ **A** Who does not has a comb?
   ☐ **B** Who does not have a comb?

3 ☐ **A** Who brought these flowers?
   ☐ **B** Who was brought these flowers?

4 ☐ **A** Who is painting a picture now?
   ☐ **B** Who painting a picture now?

5 ☐ **A** Who did not take the driving test?
   ☐ **B** Who did not taking the driving test?

6 ☐ **A** Who those wonderful singers?
   ☐ **B** Who are those wonderful singers?

7 ☐ **A** Who makes the best cakes in your family?
   ☐ **B** Who make the best cakes in your family?

8 ☐ **A** Who at your house this morning?
   ☐ **B** Who was at your house this morning?

9 ☐ **A** Who does not like sardines?
   ☐ **B** Who does not liking sardines?

10 ☐ **A** Who is play the piano?
   ☐ **B** Who is playing the piano?

YOUR SCORE 10

PRACTICE *F* Rearrange the words to form questions.

1 a — sandwich — wants — who?
   Who wants a sandwich?

2 are — children — those — who?
   _____

3 a — drawing — does — have — not — of — paper — sheet — who?
   _____

4 camera — is — my — using — who?
   _____

5 a — dictionary — doesn't — need — who?
   _____

6 box — slides — has — of — the — who?
   _____

YOUR SCORE 10

133

UNIT 11.3 WH-QUESTIONS

what

Look at the **A** and **B** sentences below. Find out why **B** is correct and **A** is wrong in the **Grammar Points** section.

			GRAMMAR POINTS
1A	What magazines did Mr Singer **buys**?	✗	
1B	What magazines did Mr Singer **buy**?	✓	1
2A	What that cinema **is showing** now?	✗	
2B	What **is** that cinema **showing** now?	✓	2
3A	What **have** black and white stripes?	✗	
3B	What **has** black and white stripes?	✓	3
4A	What date **it is**?	✗	
4B	What date **is it**?	✓	4

GRAMMAR POINTS

1 In a **What** question, we use the verb 'to do' in these ways:

(a) **What** + the verb 'to do' + noun/pronoun + base form of main verb

EXAMPLES: What **does** she **mean**?
What **did** you **take** from the cupboard?

(b) **What** + noun + the verb 'to do' + noun/pronoun + base form of main verb

EXAMPLES: What information **does** that lady **want**?
What games **do** you **play**?

Take note that the main verb must be in the base form and the verb 'to do' must have the right tense and must agree with the noun or pronoun in number.

2 We use the verb 'to be' with the 'ing' form of a main verb in this way:

What + the verb 'to be' + noun/pronoun + base form of main verb + 'ing'

Take note that, unlike statements, the verb 'to be' always comes before the noun or pronoun in questions.

EXAMPLES: What were they doing after dinner?

They were doing their chores.

What was she holding in her hand?

She was holding a bunch of keys in her hand.

> **REMEMBER!**
> - **What** is used to ask questions about things and actions.
> - **What** can be used as the subject or object of the verb in a question.
>
> EXAMPLES:
>
> subject
> **What** is in the box?
> **The new laser printer** (is in the box).
>
> object
> **What** does he want?
> He wants **a new computer**.

134

3 We usually use the singular form of a main verb with a **What** question that is in the present tense. We often come across this type of question in the form of riddles and during quizzes.

> EXAMPLES: What **has** horns on its head?
> What **twinkles** in the sky at night?

4 We sometimes use **What** with a noun to ask for details about the noun. When the wh-word **What** is followed by a noun, the word after the noun has to be a finite verb.

> **What** + noun + the verb 'to be' + noun/pronoun

> EXAMPLES: What nationality **are they**?   ☐ ✓
> What nationality **they are**?   ☐ ✗

PRACTICE *A*   Complete the questions with **Who** or **What**.

1 _____ books do you enjoy?

2 _____ is that parrot saying?

3 _____ is that elderly gentleman?

4 _____ colour were the thief's shoes?

5 _____ did not pass the driving test?

6 _____ wants another slice of bread?

7 _____ indoor game is that?

8 _____ music do your parents like?

9 _____ visited Anne yesterday?

10 _____ is organising the concert?

YOUR SCORE

10

PRACTICE *B*   Underline the correct verbs.

1 What birds (is / are) those?

2 What books (do / does) Larry read?

3 What (keep / keeps) the baby happy?

4 What musical instruments do James and Janet (play / plays)?

5 What (are / is) you complaining about?

6 What items (was / were) in the store cupboard?

7 What airline (is / are) that?

8 What (grow / grows) easily without much water?

9 What report (was / were) Mr Wells reading through just now?

10 What classes (do / does) you attend every evening?

YOUR SCORE

10

135

PRACTICE **C** Complete the questions with the correct words in the boxes.

1 A _____ well with this dress?

  B _____ you have in your jewellery box?

What do
What goes

2 A _____ we doing this evening?

  B _____ you suggest we do?

What are
What do

3 A _____ Kim want to tell the policeman?

  B _____ she saying to him?

What is
What does

4 A _____ good for the skin?

  B _____ Sally use?

What soap is
What soap does

5 A _____ this cake so light?

  B _____ in this cake? It's so light!

What is
What makes

 YOUR SCORE 10

PRACTICE **D** Tick the correct words to complete the questions.

1 What
| | cause | the dough to rise?
|---|---|
| | causes |

2 What forms
	these are?
	are these?

3 What
| | is | in the pot – coffee or tea?
|---|---|
| | are |

4 What type of envelope
	does Elaine want?
	does Elaine wants?

5 What
| | were you saying | just now?
|---|---|
| | you were saying |

6 What crops
	does they grow?
	do they grow?

7 What
| | has legs | but cannot walk?
|---|---|
| | have legs |

8 What perfume
	Mavis uses?
	does Mavis use?

9 What
	Anne is serving for dessert?
	is Anne serving for dessert?

10 What
	instrument measures the temperature of our bodies?
	instrument the temperature of our bodies measures?

YOUR SCORE 10

136

PRACTICE **E**   Rearrange the words to form questions.

1   Cecilia — doing — is — this — weekend — what?
    What is Cecilia doing this weekend?

2   baby — drinking — is — the — what?
    _____

3   irritates — sister — what — your?
    _____

4   do — films — like — what — you?
    _____

5   colour — is — room — what — your?
    _____

6   behind — Bill — cupboard — did — hide — that — what?
    _____
    _____

YOUR SCORE
10

PRACTICE **F**   Write questions with the words underlined as the answers.

1   Diana is painting <u>a portrait of her mother</u>.
    What is Diana painting?

2   <u>Loud music</u> gives my grandfather a headache.
    _____

3   <u>Dad and Peter</u> are going to the airport to meet Aunt Ruth.
    _____

4   Sheila recommends <u>egg and tomato</u> sandwiches.
    _____

5   <u>Mr Adams</u> informed the landlord about the rodent problem.
    _____

6   Clarence used <u>turpentine</u> to remove paint from the brushes.
    _____

YOUR SCORE
10

137

UNIT 11.4 WH-QUESTIONS

> answering **Who** and **What** questions – main verbs and the verb 'to be'

Look at the **A** and **B** sentences below. Find out why **B** is correct and **A** is wrong in the **Grammar Points** section.

				GRAMMAR POINTS
1A	Who has a camera? Ken and Kim **has** cameras.	✗		
1B	Who has a camera? Ken and Kim **have** cameras.	✓	1	
2A	What are these things? **These things** are can openers.	✗		
2B	What are these things? **They** are can openers.	✓	2a	
3A	Who is he? **Is my** football coach.	✗		
3B	Who is he? **He is my** football coach.	✓	2b	
4A	What are they making? They **making** puppets.	✗		
4B	What are they making? They **are making** puppets.	✓	3	

GRAMMAR POINTS

1 When we answer a question where **Who** or **What** is the subject of a verb, we replace **Who** or **What** with a suitable noun or pronoun and make sure the verb agrees with the subject.

EXAMPLES:　Who **needs** an umbrella?　　Who **was** talking to you just now?

　　　　　Susie **needs** an umbrella.　　Mack and Philip **were** talking to me just now.

　　　　　What **fell** just now?　　　What **is** in that box?

　　　　　A stool **fell** just now.　　Some eggs **are** in that box?

2 When **Who** or **What** is **not** the subject of a verb, we usually do the following:

(a) change the noun in the question to a suitable pronoun and move it to the beginning of the sentence

EXAMPLES:　Who is that handsome man ? He is Sue's brother.

　　　　　What nationality are those people ? They are Australian.

(b) repeat the pronoun in the question

EXAMPLES:

Who is he ? He is Sue's brother.

What nationality are they ? They are Australian.

> **REMEMBER!**
> ■ Normally, answers to wh-questions do not include **yes** or **no**.
> EXAMPLE:
> Q: Who has the hammer?
> A: Yes, Nick has the hammer. | ✗ |
> A: Nick has the hammer. | ✓ |

138

3 When **What** is not the subject in a question which has the 'ing' form of a verb, we usually answer in this way:

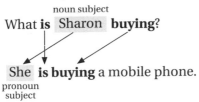

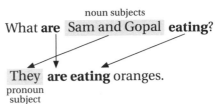

PRACTICE **A** Circle the correct words in the boxes to complete the answers.

1 Who has the keys to the storeroom?
   Janet _____ the keys to the storeroom.

   | has | have |

2 What is in the parcel?
   A calendar and a notebook _____ in the parcel.

   | is | are |

3 Who is that man walking towards us?
   _____ is the new superintendent.

   | He | She |

4 Who was helping Kim just now?
   James and Fiona _____ Kim just now.

   | was helping / were helping |

5 Who was signalling to you just now?
   Richard was signalling to _____ just now.

   | me | you |

6 What documents are those?
   _____ are the ones on the development project in India.

   | They | Those |

7 What gets rid of those stains?
   Vinegar or lime juice _____ rid of those stains.

   | get | gets |

8 Who gave the two of you permission to take these hockey sticks?
   Mr Thomas gave _____ permission to take these hockey sticks.

   | us | we |

9 What are the women making?
   _____ rattan baskets.

   | They are making / They making are |

10 What caused the landslide on Saturday?
   _____ on Saturday.

   | The landslide caused heavy rain / Heavy rain caused the landslide |

YOUR SCORE
10

Correct the answers to the questions.

1 Q: What are your core subjects?
   A: Core subjects are Science and English.

   _____

2 Q: Who brought you home?
   A: Mrs Tanner brought I home.

   _____

3 Q: What are those?
   A: They children's magazines.

   _____

4 Q: Who was practising with you?
   A: Anna and Laila was practising with me.

   _____

5 Q: What is Kenneth pointing to?
   A: He pointing to something strange in the sky.

   _____

YOUR SCORE / 10

PRACTICE C Answer the questions by using the words in the boxes.

1 What is that in your hand?
   It is a laser pointer. | a laser pointer |

2 Who works in a hospital?

   _____ | Mrs Rama |

3 Who is that tall man?

   _____ | Mr Watson |

4 What is your favourite game?

   _____ | soccer |

5 What is Jonathan drawing?

   _____ | a village scene |

6 Who is printing the cards?

   _____ | Joe |

YOUR SCORE / 10

Circle the letters of the correct answers. There may be more than one answer for each question.

1 What paint is this?
   A Acrylic paint is this.
   B It is acrylic paint.
   C This paint is acrylic paint.

2 What is the correct answer?
   A What the correct answer is ten kilos.
   B The correct answer is ten kilos.
   C Ten kilos the correct answer.

3 Who intends to study law?
   A Alan and Pat intends to study law.
   B Alan intends to study law.
   C Pat and I intend to study law.

4 Who are those musicians?
   A Those are 'The La Palma Brothers'.
   B Musicians are those 'The La Palma Brothers'.
   C They are 'The La Palma Brothers'.

5 What flew into your room just now?
   A A bat flew into my room just now.
   B Flew into my room just now a bat.
   C A bat flew into your room just now.

6 Who is investigating the boy's story?
   A The police are investigating the boy's story.
   B Our teachers is investigating the boy's story.
   C Our headmaster is investigating the boy's story.

7 What was Paul trying to catch?
   A What was Paul trying to catch a spider.
   B He was trying to catch a spider.
   C He trying to catch was a spider.

8 Who gave all of you advice on how to behave at the interview?
   A Mrs Kent gave all of us advice on how to behave at the interview.
   B Mrs Kent who gave all of us advice on how to behave at the interview.
   C Mrs Kent gave all of you advice on how to behave at the interview.

YOUR SCORE

10

UNIT 11.5 WH-QUESTIONS

> answering **Who** and **What** questions – main verbs and the verb 'to do'

Look at the **A** and **B** sentences below. Find out why **B** is correct and **A** is wrong in the **Grammar Points** section.

			GRAMMAR POINTS
1A	Who does the gardening? Richard and Lisa **does** the gardening.	✗	
1B	Who does the gardening? Richard and Lisa **do** the gardening.	✓	1
2A	What games does Janice play? She **play** tennis and netball.	✗	
2B	What games does Janice play? She **plays** tennis and netball.	✓	2
3A	Who does not like lizards? Does not like lizards **is Jan**.	✗	
3B	Who does not like lizards? **Jan does not** like lizards.	✓	3

GRAMMAR POINTS

1 When we answer a question where **Who** is the subject of the verb 'to do', we replace **Who** with a suitable noun or pronoun and make sure the verb agrees with the subject.

    EXAMPLES: Who **does** the laundry? The maid/She **does** the laundry.

                    Who **does** the ironing? My brother and I/We **do** the ironing.

2 When **Who** or **What** is **not** the subject of the verb 'to do', we usually change the noun in the question to a suitable pronoun, leave out **do**, **does** or **did** in the answer and make sure the main verb agrees with the subject.

    EXAMPLES: Who **does** Steve **like**? He **likes** Shane and Rachel . *(object)*

                    What **did** Anita **get** for her birthday? She **got** a pearl necklace . *(object)*

                    Who **do** your classmates **like**? They **like** Mr Hunt . *(object)*

                    What books **do** the boys **want**? They **want** science fiction books . *(object)*

3 When a **Who** or **What** question has the negative form of the verb 'to do', we repeat the negative **don't**, **doesn't** or **didn't** and the base form of the main verb in the answer.

    EXAMPLES: Who **doesn't want** milk? He **doesn't want** milk. / He and I **don't want** milk.

                    What **don't** the tourists **like**? They **don't like** expensive hotels.

PRACTICE **A** Tick the correct words to complete the questions and answers.

1 Who [ ] do / [ ] does the cleaning and tidying in your house?

My mother and our housekeeper [ ] do / [ ] does the cleaning and tidying.

2 [ ] What / [ ] Who does Arthur have in his bag?

[ ] He / [ ] His has some magazines in his bag.

3 What do you [ ] like / [ ] likes for tea?

[ ] I / [ ] You like cakes for tea.

4 What [ ] don't / [ ] doesn't we have for the picnic?

We [ ] don't / [ ] doesn't have mats and umbrellas.

5 [ ] What / [ ] Who doesn't like pizza?

They [ ] don't / [ ] doesn't like pizza.

YOUR SCORE / 10

PRACTICE **B** Fill in the blanks with the correct words.

1 What do you keep in that safe?

_____ _____ money and documents in it.

2 Who did Mr Bolton employ for the post of general manager?

_____ _____ Maria.

3 Who doesn't know the way to the camp?

Paul and I _____ _____ the way to the camp.

4 What does Aunt Molly like about him?

_____ _____ his thoughtfulness.

5 What do you and Brian want for dinner?

_____ both _____ lamb chops.

YOUR SCORE / 10

143

PRACTICE | C | Circle the correct words in the boxes to complete the questions and answers.

1 Who / the weekly cleaning with you?

do	does

My brothers do the weekly cleaning with / .

I	me

2 What / the salesman have?

do	does

He / some new gadgets.

has	have

3 Who doesn't / the new computer games?

play	plays

Alan and John / play the new computer games.

don't	doesn't

4 What did Pamela / to do?

refuse	refused

She / to postpone the meeting.

refuse	refused

5 Who didn't the members / for?

vote	votes

/ didn't vote for Richard.

They	We

YOUR SCORE

10

PRACTICE | D | Answer the questions by using the words in the boxes.

1 What do Yvonne and Macy have?

a tortoise

They have a tortoise.

2 Who doesn't play hockey?

Susan

_____

3 What doesn't your cat like?

sardines

_____

4 What do Mr and Mrs Chan want?

a two-storey house

_____

5 Who do you want to speak to?

Trisha

_____

6 Who did the landscaping of your garden?

my uncle

_____

YOUR SCORE

10

144

PRACTICE E Form questions about the words in the brackets based on the sentences. Use the verb 'to do'.

Bob gave the report to Mrs Laker.

1 *Who did Bob give the report to?* _____ (Mrs Laker)

2 *What did Bob give Mrs Laker?* _____ (the report)

Steve didn't understand the instructions.

3 _____ (Steve)

4 _____ (the instructions)

They don't have passports.

5 _____ (passports)

I handed over the wallet to the police.

6 _____ (the wallet)

7 _____ (the police)

YOUR SCORE
10

PRACTICE F Study the diagram and answer the questions.

Names	Indra	Carol	Michiyo
Household chores	cleans the apartment	washes the dishes	cooks all the meals
Things they have	a car	a bicycle	a bicycle
Languages spoken	English, French, Hindi	English, French, Italian	English, Japanese

1 Who does the cooking?

_____

2 What languages does Indra speak?

_____

3 Who does the cleaning and washing up?

_____

4 What don't Carol and Michiyo have?

_____

5 Who doesn't speak Italian?

_____

YOUR SCORE
10

145

UNIT 11.6 WH-QUESTIONS

where and when

Look at the **A** and **B** sentences below. Find out why **B** is correct and **A** is wrong in the **Grammar Points** section.

			GRAMMAR POINTS
1A	**Where your** bag?	✗	
1B	**Where is your** bag?	✓	1a
2A	When **you are** leaving for Rome?	✗	
2B	When **are you** leaving for Rome?	✓	1b
3A	Where Sue **will be** at 3 p.m. today?	✗	
3B	Where **will** Sue **be** at 3 p.m. today?	✓	2
4A	When did Shukor **left** for India?	✗	
4B	When did Shukor **leave** for India?	✓	3

GRAMMAR POINTS

1   We use the verb 'to be' with **Where** and **When** questions in these ways:

(a)   **Where/When** + the verb 'to be' + noun/pronoun

EXAMPLES:

Where **is** ⬚Tokyo⬚ ?   When **was** ⬚the skateboard competition⬚ ?
⬚It⬚ **is** in Japan.   ⬚It⬚ **was** on 10th January.

(b)   **Where/When** + the verb 'to be' + noun/pronoun + base form of main verb + 'ing'

EXAMPLES:

Where **are** ⬚you⬚ **taking** that box?   When **are** ⬚they⬚ **playing** volleyball?
⬚I⬚ **am taking** it to the garage.   ⬚They⬚ **are playing** volleyball on Saturday.

> ### REMEMBER!
>
> ■ **Where** is used to ask questions about places, directions and locations.
>
> EXAMPLES:
>
> **Where** is Steven?   **Where** do you keep your tennis racquet?
> He is **in his study**.   I keep it **in my locker**.
>
> ■ **When** is used to ask questions about dates and time.
>
> EXAMPLES:
>
> **When** is the float procession?   **When** will they get their exam results?
> It is **on Friday night**.   They will get their exam results **next month**.

2 We use **will** with **Where** and **When** questions in this way:

Where/When + **will** + noun/pronoun + base form of main verb

EXAMPLES:

Where **will** ⌐the singers⌐ **perform** tomorrow?　　　When **will** ⌐Jenny⌐ **finish** her work?

⌐They⌐ **will perform** at the Music Centre tomorrow.　　⌐She⌐ **will finish** it on Saturday.

3 We use the verb 'to do' with **Where** and **When** questions in this way:

Where/When + the verb 'to do' + noun/pronoun + base form of main verb

EXAMPLES:

Where **do** ⌐Mr and Mrs Lim⌐ **live**?　　　When **did** ⌐you⌐ **visit** Mrs Ross?

⌐They⌐ **live** in Murdoch Street.　　　⌐I⌐ **visited** her this morning.

PRACTICE ⌐A⌐　Tick the correct sentences.

1　Where did they have the barbecue?

2　When is the next bus to Milan?

3　Where are you hide?

4　When will we know the results of the election?

5　When did she phoned you?

6　Where the nearest clinic?

7　When is Steve coming?

8　Where do the children keep their toys?

9　Where will you being tomorrow?

10　When does Karen wants to see me?

YOUR SCORE

/10

PRACTICE ⌐B⌐　Complete the conversations. Use pronouns in subject position.

1　A: Where is your car?

　　B: _____ *It is* _____ at the Regency car park.

2　A: When did your brother buy that house?

　　B: _____ last week.

3　A: Where will you stay in New Delhi?

　　B: _____ at my uncle's house there.

4　A: When are we going on a picnic?

　　B: _____ next weekend.

5　A: Where do you buy your fruit and vegetables?

　　B: _____ at King's Supermarket.

6　A: When will the boys finish painting the boat?

　　B: _____ on Friday.

YOUR SCORE

/10

Use the notes to ask questions.

1 those musicians ---- will perform ---- where?
   Where will those musicians perform?
   _____

2 you ---- are going ---- for a medical check-up ---- when?
   _____

3 James ---- learn ---- all about house-building ---- when?
   _____

4 Stan and Shirley ---- usually go for lunch ---- where?
   _____

5 we ---- are hiding ---- the presents ---- where?
   _____

6 the election results ---- will be out ---- when?
   _____

YOUR SCORE
10

PRACTICE D Form questions from the answers. Use the words in capital letters to help you.

EXAMPLES:

Question: *Who moved to a new office in Baker Street last week?*

Answer: DAVID moved to a new office in Baker Street last week.

Question: *Where did David move to last week?*

Answer: He (David) moved to A NEW OFFICE IN BAKER STREET last week.

Question: *When did David move to a new office in Baker Street?*

Answer: He (David) moved to a new office in Baker Street LAST WEEK.

1 Question: _____
   Answer: He (Joe) is taking HIS NIECES to the museum tomorrow.

2 Question: _____
   Answer: He (Joe) is taking his nieces TO THE MUSEUM tomorrow.

3 Question: _____
   Answer: He (Joe) is taking his nieces to the museum TOMORROW.

4 Question: _____
   Answer: They (Carol and Pam) will TAKE PART IN A TENNIS TOURNAMENT
              at the Raintree Sports Club in August.

5 Question: _____
   Answer: They (Carol and Pam) will take part in a tennis tournament at the
              Raintree Sports Club IN AUGUST.

YOUR SCORE
10

148

Rearrange the words to form questions.

1 morning — this — were — where — you?
   Where were you this morning?

2 did — fall — John — over — where?

3 coming — doctor — is — the — when?

4 does — his — John — keep — medicine — where?

5 a — bring — Sheila — wheelchair — when — will?

6 children — do — fetch — have — to — the — when — you?

Read the announcement and answer the questions.

Dr Henry Conway, an American expert on how the elderly can stay healthy, will give a talk on 'How to lose weight permanently' at the Mayfair Hotel at 7.30 p.m. on 7th October.

Dr Conway has written many books on the subject of health and has appeared on radio and TV shows to encourage people to exercise and eat the right types of food. His latest book 'Eat and Be Happy' will hit the bookstands in December.

For further enquiries, please contact Anne at 013-4125554 or e-mail to *concare@healthfarm.com*.

1 When is Dr Conway's talk on 'How to lose weight permanently'?

2 Where will Dr Conway give his talk?

3 Who has written many books on health?

4 What is the title of Dr Conway's latest book?

5 When will Dr Conway's latest book be available to the public?

UNIT 11.7 WH-QUESTIONS

which and whose

Look at the **A** and **B** sentences below. Find out why **B** is correct and **A** is wrong in the **Grammar Points** section.

CHECKPOINT

			GRAMMAR POINTS
1A	Which **book interesting**?	✗	
1B	Which **book is interesting**?	✓	1
2A	Which department store **sell** Chinese silk?	✗	
2B	Which department store **sells** Chinese silk?	✓	2
3A	Whose bicycle **you are** using?	✗	
3B	Whose bicycle **are you** using?	✓	3
4A	Whose compass you **found** – Sam's or mine?	✗	
4B	Whose compass **did** you **find** – Sam's or mine?	✓	4

GRAMMAR POINTS

1 We use the verb 'to be' with **Which** and **Whose** questions in these ways:

(a) **Which/Whose** + the verb 'to be'

EXAMPLES: Which **is** the first event – the fireworks display or the lantern dance?
The lantern dance **is** the first event.

Whose **are** these files?
They **are** mine/ours/his/hers/theirs.

(b) **Which/Whose** + noun + the verb 'to be'

EXAMPLES: Which file **is** yours?   Whose essay **is** the best – yours, Sue's or Jessie's?
<u>possessive pronoun</u>   <u>adjective</u>

The blue file **is** mine.   Jessie's **is** the best.

REMEMBER!

■ **Which** is used to ask the listener to identify or choose a specific item from a list that is known to both the listener and the speaker.

Take note of the differences between **which**, and **what** or **who**.

EXAMPLES: **Who** is sick? (the possible answers are not known to the speaker)
Which girl is sick – Lina or Sue?

What dish is easy to prepare? (the possible answers are not known to the speaker)
Which dish is easy to prepare – spaghetti or pizza?

■ **Whose** is used to identify the person who owns something or the animal that has something.

■ When **Which** and **Whose** are used as the subjects in questions, they are followed by the verb 'to be'. When they are used as the objects in questions, they are followed by the verb 'to do'.

---

2 We use main verbs with **Which** and **Whose** questions in this way:

   Which/Whose + noun + main verb

   EXAMPLES: Which animal **runs** the fastest?
   The cheetah **runs** the fastest.

   Whose school **has** a chess club?
   Joe's school and my school **have** chess clubs.

3 We use the verb 'to be' together with the 'ing' form of the main verb in **Which** and **Whose** questions in this way:

   Which/Whose + noun + the verb 'to be' + noun/pronoun + base form of main verb + 'ing'

   EXAMPLES: Which paint **is** Dad **using** – oil or acrylic?
   He is using acrylic paint.

   Whose notes **are** they **borrowing** – yours or mine?
   They **are borrowing** mine.

4 We use the verb 'to do' in **Which** and **Whose** questions in these ways:

   (a)   **Which/Whose** + the verb 'to do' + noun/pronoun + base form of main verb

   EXAMPLES: Which **does** John **prefer** – a holiday in Spain or a holiday in the Maldives?
   He **prefers** a holiday in the Maldives.

   Whose **do** they **like** – your painting or mine?
   They **like** yours.

   (b)   **Which/Whose** + noun + the verb 'to do' + noun/pronoun + base form of main verb

   EXAMPLES: Which mirror **do** you **like**?
   I **like** the oval one.

   Whose telephone number **do** you **want**?
   I **want** Tina's telephone number.

PRACTICE _A_   Complete the questions with **Which** or **Whose**.

1 _____ colour suits me? (green)

2 _____ slogan is the most creative? (Mrs Simpson's)

3 _____ cap did you hide – Mike's or Janet's? (Mike's)

4 _____ uncle runs a farm? (Jim's)

5 _____ is Lily buying – the perfume or the cologne? (the perfume)

6 _____ brother is Joan marrying? (Larry's)

7 _____ bus goes to Zooland? (Bus No. 15)

8 _____ chess player is more experienced – Mike or David? (David)

9 _____ are the winning entries? (the ones over there)

10 _____ poster do you prefer – Tina's or Sue's? (Sue's)

YOUR SCORE

10

PRACTICE *B* Underline the correct words to complete the questions and answers.

1 Q: Which is your bedroom?

  A: The one at the end of the corridor is (my / your) bedroom.

2 Q: Whose computer has a virus?

  A: (Jean's computer / That computer) has a virus.

3 Q: Which bus (are we taking / we are taking)?

  A: We are taking bus No. 25.

4 Q: Whose binoculars did you (lose / lost) – Anne's or Sam's?

  A: I (lost / lose) Anne's binoculars.

5 Q: Which (is restaurant / restaurant is) the most expensive – Coco's, the Palms or Oasis?

  A: The Palms (is / is restaurant) the most expensive.

6 Q: Which (do / does) they (want / wants) to rent out – apartment 1J or apartment 3F?

  A: They (do want / want) to rent out apartment 3F.

YOUR SCORE
10

PRACTICE *C* Rewrite the answers correctly.

1 Q: Whose team lost in the netball finals?
  A: Sharon team lost in the netball finals.

  _____

2 Q: Which doctor do you go to?
  A: I do go to Dr Leo.

  _____

3 Q: Whose house is more suitable for the meetings?
  A: Our house is suitable for the meetings.

  _____

4 Q: Which washing machine is Bill buying?
  A: That washing machine is Bill buying.

  _____

5 Q: Whose did the judges like – Mary's or Jan's fruit cake?
  A: They did liked both Mary's and Jan's fruit cakes.

  _____

YOUR SCORE
10

Form **Which** or **Whose** questions from the answers. Use the words in capital letters to help you.

1 Question: *Which truck belongs to Mr Jones?*

   Answer: THAT truck belongs to Mr Jones.

2 Question: _____

   Answer: SUE'S uniform is torn.

3 Question: _____

   Answer: THE DINING room is messy.

4 Question: _____

   Answer: MY office caught fire last night.

5 Question: _____

   Answer: I shop at GOLDHILL department store.

6 Question: _____

   Answer: LISA'S uncle is the new manager.

YOUR SCORE
10

PRACTICE *E* Read the passage and answer the questions.

It was late at night and Joe could not sleep. He opened a book and began to read. Just then Rover, the dog belonging to his neighbour Mr Parry, began to bark angrily. Joe looked out of his bedroom window. He wanted to find out what was happening outside. He saw two men. They were climbing over the front gate of his house.

"Thieves!" thought Joe as he ran to his parents' room. He woke his father up and told him about the thieves. His father immediately telephoned the police. Then he quickly locked the bedroom door and asked Joe to help him place the heavy study table against the door.

The thieves tried to enter the room but they could not. They were very angry. They began to bang on the door.

Just then the police arrived. The thieves tried to leave by the back door but the police managed to catch them.

1 Whose dog began to bark fiercely?

_____

2 Which gate were the two men climbing over?

_____

3 Whose room did Joe run to?

_____

4 Which table did Joe and his father place against the door?

_____

5 Which door did the thieves try to use to escape?

_____

YOUR SCORE
10

UNIT 11.8 WH-QUESTIONS

how, how many, how much

Look at the **A** and **B** sentences below. Find out why **B** is correct and **A** is wrong in the **Grammar Points** section.

			GRAMMAR POINTS
1A	How tall **that building is**?	✗	
1B	How tall **is that building**?	✓	1
2A	How much money **we have**?	✗	
2B	How much money **do we have**?	✓	2
3A	How many **child needs** spectacles?	✗	
3B	How many **children need** spectacles?	✓	3
4A	How much **this computer costs**?	✗	
4B	How much **does this computer cost**?	✓	4

GRAMMAR POINTS

1 We use **How** with adjectives in this way:

How + adjective + the verb 'to be' + noun/pronoun

EXAMPLES:
How far is the supermarket from here? (**distance**)
It is about three kilometres from here.

How old is Sue's niece? (**age**)
She is 12 years old.

How big is his house? (**size**)
His house / It has four bedrooms
and three bathrooms.

How long is the programme? (**length of time**)
It is three hours long.

How tall is Henry? (**height**)
He is 1.7 metres tall.

> **REMEMBER!**
> - **How** is usually used with certain adjectives to ask for different types of information, for example, distance, age and size.

2 We use **How many** or **How much** with the verb 'to do' in these ways:

(a) **How many/How much** + noun + the verb 'to do' + noun/pronoun + base form of main verb

EXAMPLES: How many **paintings** did Tina sell?
She sold 10 paintings.

How much **time** do you need?
I need two hours.

(b) **How many/How much** + noun + the verb 'to be'

EXAMPLES: How many **students are** left-handed?
Eight students are left-handed.

> **REMEMBER!**
> - **How many** and **How much** are used to ask questions about quantity or amount.
> - **How many** is used with plural countable nouns, and **How much** with uncountable nouns.

How much **water is** there in the jug?
There is one litre of water in the jug.

3   We use **How many** with main verbs in this way:

     How many + plural noun + main verb

     EXAMPLES: How many athletes **have** four gold medals? (present tense)
                   Four athletes **have** four gold medals.

                   How many athletes **won** gold medals? (past tense)
                   Four athletes **won** gold medals.

4   We use **How much** with the verb 'to be' or the verb 'to do' to find out the cost of something in these ways:

     (a)   **How much** + the verb 'to be' + noun

          EXAMPLES: How much **is** this oven?   How much **are** these handphones?
                      It is 400 dollars.   They are between 400 and 1,000 dollars.

     (b)   **How much** + the verb 'to do' + noun + base form of main verb **cost**

          EXAMPLES: How much **does** this oven cost?   How much **do** these handphones cost?
                      It **costs** 400 dollars.   They **cost** between 400 and 1,000 dollars.

PRACTICE **A**   Underline the correct words in the brackets to complete the questions.

1   (How long / How tall) is that child?

2   (How many / How much) milk do you want?

3   (How many / How much) sisters do you have?

4   (How big / How much) do those shoes cost?

5   (How many / How much) people came to the wedding?

6   (How many / How much) is that hi-fi system over there?

7   (How many / How much) students walk to school?

8   (How many / How much) times do you eat out a week?

9   (How many / How much) information is there in this report?

10   (How many / How much) employees are there in this company?

YOUR SCORE

10

PRACTICE **B**   Fill in the blanks with the wh-words in the box. You may use each word more than once.

How far	How many	How much	How old

1   _____ people did you invite for dinner?

2   _____ guests asked for vegetarian food?

3   _____ vegetarian dishes did you prepare?

4   _____ did the birthday cake cost?

5   _____ candles do you want on the cake?

6   _____ rice do I have to cook?

7 _____ time is there before the guests arrive?

8 _____ is Mrs Hansen?

9 _____ is her house from here?

10 _____ is the cab fare from her house to our house?

PRACTICE $\boxed{C}$ Tick the correct questions and answers.

1 (a) ☐ **A** How high is that building?
      ☐ **B** How that building high?
      ☐ **C** How high that building?

   (b) ☐ **A** It high is 80 storeys.
       ☐ **B** 80 storeys is it high.
       ☐ **C** It is 80 storeys high.

2 (a) ☐ **A** How far the stadium is from your school?
      ☐ **B** How far from your school the stadium is?
      ☐ **C** How far is the stadium from your school?

   (b) ☐ **A** It is about five kilometres away.
       ☐ **B** About five kilometres it is from my school.
       ☐ **C** From my school about five kilometres away.

3 (a) ☐ **A** How much this table lamp costs?
      ☐ **B** How much is this table lamp?
      ☐ **C** How much do this table lamp cost?

   (b) ☐ **A** It is costing 20 dollars.
       ☐ **B** It is cost 20 dollars.
       ☐ **C** It is 20 dollars.

4 (a) ☐ **A** How many colleges provides photocopying facilities?
      ☐ **B** How many colleges provide photocopying facilities?
      ☐ **C** How many college provides photocopying facilities?

   (b) ☐ **A** Most colleges provides photocopying facilities.
       ☐ **B** Most colleges providing photocopying facilities.
       ☐ **C** Most colleges provide photocopying facilities.

5 (a) ☐ **A** How many roses did you order for Mum?
      ☐ **B** How many roses does you order for Mum?
      ☐ **C** How many roses did you ordered for Mum?

   (b) ☐ **A** I did ordered two dozen roses.
       ☐ **B** I ordered two dozen roses.
       ☐ **C** You ordered two dozen roses.

Rearrange the words to form questions.

1 how — is — journey — long — the?

_____

2 boots — cost — do — how — much — these?

_____

3 classical — how — like — many — music — people?

_____

4 far — from — how — is — London — Paris?

_____

5 did — how — James — many — postcards — receive?

_____

PRACTICE *E* Form questions from the answers. Use the words in capital letters to help you.

EXAMPLE: Question: *Who bought two bags of potatoes?*
Answer: JOE bought two bags of potatoes.

Question: *How many bags of potatoes did Joe buy?*
Answer: He (Joe) bought TWO bags of *potatoes*.

Question: *What did Joe buy?*
Answer: He (Joe) bought TWO BAGS OF POTATOES.

1 Question: _____
   Answer: She (Anita) broke NINE glasses just now.

2 Question: _____
   Answer: ANITA broke nine glasses just now.

3 Question: _____
   Answer: It (this brush) is TWO dollars.

4 Question: _____
   Answer: I want FOUR brushes.

5 Question: _____
   Answer: My dog Pinto is TEN YEARS old.

UNIT 11.9 WH-QUESTIONS

	why

Look at the **A** and **B** sentences below. Find out why **B** is correct and **A** is wrong in the **Grammar Points** section.

CH)ECKPOINT

				GRAMMAR POINTS
1A	Why **you are** sad?		✗	
1B	Why **are you** sad?		✓	1
2A	Why did Dad **worked** this Saturday?		✗	
2B	Why did Dad **work** this Saturday?		✓	2
3A	Why **the boy on** the roof?		✗	
3B	Why **is the boy on** the roof?		✓	3

GRAMMAR POINTS

1 We use the verb 'to be' with **Why** questions in these ways:

(a) **Why** + the verb 'to be' + noun/pronoun + adjective

EXAMPLES: Why **are** John and Liz worried?
They can't find their passports.

Why **aren't** you hungry?
I had a huge breakfast.

(b) **Why** + the verb 'to be' + noun/pronoun + base form of main verb + 'ing'

EXAMPLES: Why **isn't** the bus stopping?
It is already full of passengers.

Why **was** the baby howling just now?
She wanted to get out of the cot.

2 We use the verb 'to do' with **Why** questions in this way:

Why + the verb 'to do' + noun/pronoun + base form of main verb

EXAMPLES: Why **does** your grandfather want a caravan?
He wants to travel around the countryside.

Why **did** you resign from your job?
I had a better job offer at XL Computer Systems.

3 We use prepositions after the verb 'to be' in **Why** questions in these ways:

(a) **Why** + the verb 'to be' + noun/pronoun + preposition

EXAMPLES: Why **is** this room [in] a mess? The children had a pillow fight just now.

Why **are** you [under] the bed? I'm looking for my kitten.

REMEMBER!

- **Why** is used to ask questions about the cause, reason or purpose for something.

EXAMPLE:

A: Mr Daniels wants to see you immediately.
B: Why?

- **Why** questions can usually be answered by giving the reason straightaway. However, this is not acceptable in certain situations.

EXAMPLE:

Q: Why is he upset?

(in a conversation)
A: He failed his driving test.

(in a comprehension exercise)
A: **He is upset because** he failed his driving test.

158

(b) **Why** + the verb 'to be' + noun/pronoun + base form of main verb + 'ing'

    EXAMPLES: Why **is** John **hiding** behind the door? He wants to frighten Emily.

                    Why **were** you **shouting** at the children? They were playing with matches.

PRACTICE *A*   Complete the questions with some of the words in the box. Each word may be used more than once.

What	When	Where	Which	Who
Whose	Why	How	How many	How much

1 _____ prize is this? *It is Jeff's.*

2 _____ is Desmond so cheerful today? *He just got promoted.*

3 _____ tall is your sister? *She is five feet tall.*

4 _____ do they sleep so early? *They have to leave for work at 6 a.m.*

5 _____ bicycle is yours? *The black one is mine.*

6 _____ salt do you use for this chicken dish? *I use half a teaspoon of salt.*

7 _____ did Avana make these vases? *She made them yesterday.*

8 _____ is Mike in the ditch? *His puppy fell into it.*

9 _____ students visited the bakery? *Fifty students visited the bakery.*

10 _____ movie did you see – *Gangs of New York* or *Chicago*? *I saw Chicago.*

YOUR SCORE
/10

PRACTICE *B*   The underlined words are wrong. Write the correct words in the boxes provided.

1 Why <u>does</u> Mrs Lee laughing?

2 Why are the workers <u>grumble</u>?

3 Why <u>weren't</u> you come with us?

4 Why is Mrs Smith <u>runs</u> up the driveway?

5 Why <u>do</u> Anne always make a fuss?

6 Why <u>wasn't</u> Sam and Kim at the match yesterday?

7 Why don't you <u>answering</u> the phone? You're near it.

8 Why <u>John isn't</u> home? It's already 11 p.m.

9 Why <u>the children are</u> in bed? It's only 8 p.m.

10 Why <u>they wanted</u> a new alarm system for their house?

YOUR SCORE
/10

1 Why this letter is important?

_____

2 Why the policeman stopped that motorist?

_____

3 Why she is in such a good mood?

_____

4 Why are those men work in the rain?

_____

5 Why you are leave so soon?

_____

YOUR SCORE
10

PRACTICE $\boxed{D}$ Form **Why** questions with the verbs 'to be' or 'to do' using the words below.

1 Why ---- this cup ---- chipped?

_____

_____

2 Why ---- you ---- switch ---- the TV channel ---- just now?

_____

_____

3 Why ---- all the cupboards ---- empty?

_____

_____

4 Why ---- he ---- sleeping ---- in the spare bedroom?

_____

_____

5 Why ---- the police ---- want ---- us ---- to leave ---- the building now?

_____

_____

YOUR SCORE
10

PRACTICE *E* Form questions from the answers. Use the words in capital letters to help you.

1 Question: _Why are you late?_

Answer: I'm late BECAUSE THE MAP TO YOUR HOUSE IS CONFUSING.

2 Question: _____

Answer: They play badminton twice a week BECAUSE THEY WANT THE EXERCISE.

3 Question: _____

Answer: Tom is climbing up the tree TO RESCUE MY CAT.

4 Question: _____

Answer: The dogs are barking BECAUSE THERE'S A MAN AT THE GATE.

5 Question: _____

Answer: Eric's leg is in a plaster cast BECAUSE HE FELL OFF THE LADDER.

6 Question: _____

Answer: Mrs Lee asked the store to give her a refund BECAUSE THE DRESS SHE BOUGHT SHRANK.

YOUR SCORE

10

PRACTICE *F* Rearrange the words to form **Why** questions.

1 father — pleased — so — was — why — your?

_____

2 aren't — coming — they — us — why — with?

_____

3 disbelieve — does — Maureen — why — you?

_____

4 are — behind — clothes — door — kitchen — the — why — your?

_____

5 Gary's — gate — outside — policeman — standing — the — was — why?

_____

YOUR SCORE

10

161

UNIT 12.1 MODALS

can and may

Look at the **A** and **B** sentences below. Find out why **B** is correct and **A** is wrong in the **Grammar Points** section.

			GRAMMAR POINTS
1A	I can **swimming** quite far.	✗	
1B	I can **swim** quite far.	✓	1
2A	**Want** I get you a drink?	✗	
2B	**Can/May** I get you a drink?	✓	2

GRAMMAR POINTS

1 In a statement, we use **can** or **may** in this way:

Subject + **can/may** + base form of main verb/the verb 'to be'

EXAMPLES: You **can/may** leave tonight. They **can/may** be hostile if provoked.
(subject) (base form) (subject) (base form)

2 In a question, we use **can** or **may** at the beginning in this way:

Can/May + subject + base form of main verb/the verb 'to be'

EXAMPLES: **Can/May** I borrow your pencil? **Can/May** we be your partners?
(subject) (base form) (subject) (base form)

REMEMBER!

- Modals are a type of auxiliary verb. Examples of modals are **can**, **may**, **must**, **shall**, **will** and **ought**.

- **Can** and **may** are used to ask for permission and give permission. **May** is usually considered more formal and polite than **can**.
  EXAMPLES: **Can/May** I use your telephone, please?
  The class is over and you **can/may** go home.

- **Can** and **may** are also used to express the possibility of an action or event. **May** is usually used to refer to a less likely possibility than **can**.
  EXAMPLES: We **can** go for a holiday later this year.   (definite possibility)
  We **may** go for a holiday later this year.   (slight possibility)

  May is also used to suggest that the speaker or writer is not very certain about something.
  EXAMPLE: I **may** have the spare keys to the car in my bag.

- **Can** is used to refer to the ability to do something.
  EXAMPLES: Stella **can** speak Japanese.
  Can he cook?

- Do not confuse **may be** with **maybe**. **May be** is a verb. **Maybe** is an adverb meaning 'perhaps'. It can also be the answer we give when we don't want to say either 'yes' or 'no'.
  EXAMPLES: The teacher **may be** in the staff room. ✓
  The teacher **maybe** in the staff room. ✗

PRACTICE *A*   Underline the correct words in the brackets.

1 (Can / May) you tell me the way to the post office?

2 (We can / Can we) help you cook?

3 That building may (be / being) the university.

4 The little boy can (climb / climbs) trees very quickly.

5 You may (play / played) with Jeff this evening.

6 (Can / May) you run faster than Joanna?

7 May I (paid / pay) for our lunch?

8 (May we / We may) see your new kittens?

9 You can (rest / resting) now.

10 Can (be I / I be) your partner in the game?

PRACTICE *B*   Rearrange the words to form statements or questions.

1 can — home — take — we — you?

_____

2 may — park — there — you.

_____

3 help — I — may — sweep — you?

_____

4 aunt — can — clothes — make — my.

_____

5 be — can — I — partner — your?

_____

PRACTICE *C*   Fill in the blanks with some of the words in the box. Each word may be used more than once.

can	may
maybe	occupy
occupies	pass
past	shoot
shot	take
tape	taped

1 _____ your pet bird talk?

2 I won't promise you but I _____ see you tonight.

3 That player can _____ the ball right into the net.

4 He is so strong that he _____ bend an iron bar.

5 _____ they are planning a surprise.

6 May I _____ your voices?

7 I'm certain you _____ succeed.

8 You may _____ my room while I'm away.

9 _____ you lay the table, please?

10 May we _____ a short cut through your garden?

Tick the correct statements and questions.

1   May you lend me your pen?
2   Can I borrow a suitcase?
3   Richard can do well in a chess tournament.
4   I may helps you with that?
5   Juanita may join our art class.
6   He may be the new chairman of the company.
7   Can they may be the suspects?
8   May Douglas come with us?
9   Joyce can maybe post it for you.
10 We may fly off tomorrow?

YOUR SCORE

10

PRACTICE *E*   Circle the letters of the five underlined phrases which contain mistakes. Rewrite the phrases, correcting the mistakes.

Recorded Message : "Hi there. This is Jane. I'm not at home now. You can leaves your message after
                                                                            A
                    the beep and I'll call you back."

Caller's Message : "Hi, Jane. Can you stopped being out when I need to talk to you? I may ask why
                               B   **C**
                    you are always rushing around? Nobody can reach you at home. Can you call me
                                                    D   **E**
                    back as soon as possible? Oops! I maybe rushing around myself! You can try
                                                       F   **G**
                    calling me on my handphone but it may goes crazy any moment. Never mind,
                                                    H
                    I can call you again. Who knows? I may catch you the next time."
                    I   **J**

1 _____

2 _____

3 _____

4 _____

5 _____

YOUR SCORE

10

Fill in the blanks with suitable words.

1 Last year he was a Big Walk champion. Now he _____ walk even farther.

2 May _____ model my silk dress for you?

3 Can I _____ you on your marvellous results?

4 You may _____ lunch at my house any time you wish.

5 They may _____ leaving this country soon.

6 Grandpa has a new pair of spectacles so now he can _____ clearly.

7 She is thinking about her career. She _____ decide to become an engineer.

8 Can _____ go back to our seats now?

9 He is very quiet today. He _____ be unhappy about something.

10 That chimpanzee is very bright. It _____ understand more than a hundred words.

PRACTICE *G* Circle the letters of the sentences where **can** and **may** are used correctly. There may be more than one answer for each question.

1 To offer to do something
   A Can I go to Fay's fancy dress party?
   Ⓑ Can I bring you a souvenir from Indonesia?
   Ⓒ May we help you across the street?

2 To mean 'possibility'
   A That phone call may be from the hospital.
   B You may do as you wish.
   C The company may offer mc a trip to Sweden.

3 To give permission
   A You can change the decor of the house if you like.
   B You may take the day off on your birthday.
   C You can hold the baby for a while.

4 To make a request
   A May I have a word with you?
   B Can you run fast without panting?
   C Can you give me a room with a view of the sea?

5 To offer to do something
   A May I make some chicken soup for you?
   B Can we get you a snack from the canteen?
   C Can you give me change for fifty dollars?

6 To mean 'to be able to'
   A You can wear my jacket for the party.
   B Five people can fit into the car.
   C You can go to the dance but be back by 11 p.m.

165

UNIT 12.2 MODALS

must

Look at the **A** and **B** sentences below. Find out why **B** is correct and **A** is wrong in the **Grammar Points** section.

				GRAMMAR POINTS
1A	Everyone must **obeys** traffic lights.	✗		
1B	Everyone must **obey** traffic lights.	✓	1
2A	**We must** bring our own food **or not**?	✗		
2B	**Must we** bring our own food?	✓	2

GRAMMAR POINTS

1 In a statement, we use **must** in this way:

Subject + **must** + base form of main verb/the verb 'to be'

EXAMPLES: Soldiers **must keep** their hair short.
She **must be** Beth's mother.

2 In a question, we use **must** in this way:

Must + subject + base form of main verb/the verb 'to be'

EXAMPLES: **Must** prefects **wear** ties every day?
Must everyone **be** a member of a school society?

REMEMBER!

■ **Must** is used in these ways:

(a) to say that something is a law or a rule
  EXAMPLE: You **must** register the birth of a baby.

(b) to say that something is necessary
  EXAMPLE: You **must** take Mum to the clinic.

(c) to say that something is sure to be true
  EXAMPLE: You **must** be proud of your polite children.

(d) to ask if something has to be done
  EXAMPLE: **Must** I wear this dress to the dinner?

PRACTICE $\boxed{A}$ Tick the correct sentences.

1 We must wear evening dress or not to the party?

2 You must be happy with those good photographs.

3 Must everyone comes early tomorrow?

4 Must you be Anthony's sister.

5 I must go to the dentist.

6 Must we attend all the Saturday classes?

7 Must we water these plants every day?

8 I must be at the airport before eight.

9 In America, you must driving on the right side of the road.

10 Must we washed our own clothes at the hostel?

YOUR SCORE 10

PRACTICE $\boxed{B}$ Rearrange the words to make sentences.

1 go — must — now — you?

_____

2 call — I — mother — must — my.

_____

3 asleep — be — Grandpa — must.

_____

4 accidents — all — must — report — we?

_____

5 be — good — driving — must — instructor — your.

_____

YOUR SCORE 10

PRACTICE $\boxed{C}$ Rewrite the sentences and correct them.

1 She must listening to her mother's advice.

_____

2 Those children must uses the pedestrian crossing.

_____

3 The top student in this class must being Kellie.

_____

4 Must I finishes this work today?

_____

5 Must they talks about football all the time?

_____

YOUR SCORE 10

Underline the correct words in the brackets.

1 Children love him. He must (be / being) a wonderful man.

2 (I must / Must I) swallow these huge pills?

3 It's a formal dinner. You must (wear / worn) a coat.

4 (We must / Must we) be over 18 to watch that movie?

5 She bought the painting for $15,000. She must (admire / admires) it very much.

6 He must (hurried / hurry) or he'll miss the train.

7 The man talking to the footballers must (be / been) the new coach.

8 Must you (has / have) a special pass to enter the camp?

9 The contractor must (complete / completed) the project by June.

10 Must you (take / took) such a long time to dress?

PRACTICE *E* Fill in the blanks with some of the words in the box. Each word may be used more than once.

be	being	bow	bows	has	have	keep	kept	like	liked
made	make	pay	paying	take	took	walk	walks	wash	washing

1 We must _____ our hands before every meal.

2 Hi, I'm Winona. You must _____ Jane's brother, Danny.

3 Must they _____ their fees on the first of every month?

4 Everyone must _____ his own room clean.

5 Must you and your friends _____ so much noise?

6 He never loses his temper. He must _____ great self-control.

7 Must I _____ to the audience before and after playing the piano?

8 This patient must _____ his medicine now.

9 John is always in blue. He must _____ that colour a lot.

10 Must we _____ all the way there and back again?

PRACTICE $\boxed{F}$ Underline the incorrect sentences and rewrite them correctly.

Dear Mrs Boyle,

You must forgives me for writing this note. First, I must telling you that you are a good neighbour. You must understand that I don't want to quarrel with you. However, I must raise one issue. Must your son really practised his trumpet day and night? There's a regulation that the neighbourhood must being quiet at night. All of us must have enough sleep to be fresh in the morning. Besides, you must knew that the notes your son plays can't be called music yet. Please tell him not to play loudly even during the day.

Your neighbour,
Sally Chan

1 _____

_____

2 _____

_____

3 _____

_____

4 _____

_____

5 _____

_____

YOUR SCORE 10

PRACTICE $\boxed{G}$ Complete the conversation with suitable words.

Anna : *(in a sleepy voice)* Hello. Anna speaking.

Jeff : Sorry, Anna. Did I wake you up?

Anna : I knew that it must (1) _____*be*_____ you calling, Jeff. It's five o'clock in the morning. What do you want?

Jeff : I need help, Anna. You must (2) _____ me.

Anna : Sure. But first, you must (3) _____ me what it's all about.

Jeff : Okay. Must I (4) _____ on a necktie for the interview today?

Anna : Jeff, must you (5) _____ me that question at five o'clock in the morning?

Jeff : I must (6) _____ properly for the interview. Tell me, must I (7) _____ a jacket too?

Anna : You must (8) _____ that job very much to think of wearing a jacket! I thought you'd rather die than wear one.

Jeff : Must you (9) _____ fun of me when I need help?

Anna : I'm sorry, Jeff. You must (10) _____ very nervous. Okay, wear a suit. But most important, you must (11) _____ your brain during the interview.

YOUR SCORE 10

UNIT 13.1 PREPOSITIONS OF POSITION

Look at the **A** and **B** sentences below. Find out why **B** is correct and **A** is wrong in the **Grammar Points** section.

			GRAMMAR POINTS
1A	The police station is **beside** the market and the cinema.	✗	
1B	The police station is **between** the market and the cinema.	✓	1
2A	Jane's apartment is **under** mine.	✗	
2B	Jane's apartment is **below** mine.	✓	2
3A	The aeroplane flew **on** the clouds.	✗	
3B	The aeroplane flew **above** the clouds.	✓	3
4A	Sue sat **behind** the bus.	✗	
4B	Sue sat **at the back of** the bus	✓	4

GRAMMAR POINTS

1 **beside, between, among**

We use **beside** when there are only two persons or things involved. We use **between** when there are three persons or things involved. We use **among** when there are more than three persons or things involved and we think of them as a group.

EXAMPLES:

I stood **beside** John.

I stood **between** John and Mary.

I stood **among** my friends and told them a story.

REMEMBER!

■ The preposition **beside** has the same meaning as **next to**. It is not to be confused with **besides** which means **in addition to**.

EXAMPLES:
We sat **beside** the pool.
Jan owns another two pairs of boots **besides** this pair.

---

2 **below, under**

We use both **below** and **under** to show a person or thing is in a lower position than someone else or something else. They are different in this way:

below
lower than but not necessarily vertical

EXAMPLE:

Rick and James
were **below** me.

Rick James

under
lower than and covered by the thing in a higher position

EXAMPLE:

They sat
under a tree.

3 **above, on**

We use both **above** and **on** to show a person or thing is in a higher position than someone else or something else. They are different in this way:

above
higher than and not touching the surface of the thing below

EXAMPLE: She placed the clock **above** the piano.

on
higher than but touching the surface of the thing below

EXAMPLE: She placed the clock **on** the piano.

4 **behind, at the back of**

The prepositions **behind** and **at the back of** are different in this way:

behind the lorry

at the back of the lorry

REMEMBER!
■ A preposition can also consist of more than one word. EXAMPLES: at the back of in between on top of

EXAMPLES: Your suitcase is **behind** the door.
Your socks are **at the back of** the second shelf.

PRACTICE *A* Complete the sentences with the correct words in the boxes.

1 There's a spider above _____ .

the ceiling
your head

2 Grandma is sitting among _____ .

her favourite armchair
her grandchildren

3 Your hockey stick is behind _____ .

the door
the room

4 I kept the suitcase under _____ .

the bed
the pillow

5 Jeff's office is between _____ .

a clinic
a clinic and a cafe

6 We sat at the back of _____ during the concert.

the hall
the first row

7 I can see a lot of fish below _____ .

the surface of the water
the water

8 They hung the tapestry on _____ .

the floor
the wall

9 Rachel arranged the glasses beside _____ .

the plates
the tables

10 The men hid under _____ .

a bridge
a tunnel

PRACTICE *B* Fill in the blanks with the correct words in the box. Each word may be used more than once.

YOUR SCORE 10

above	among	at the back of	behind	
below	beside	between	on	under

1 _____ the cupboard

4 _____ the train

Sue

5 _____ Sue

2 _____ an umbrella

3 _____ the river

6 _____ the letters

172

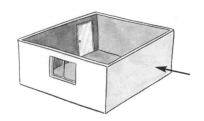

7 _____ the room

9 _____ the bridegroom

8 _____ the policemen

10 _____ the roof

YOUR SCORE
10

PRACTICE *C* Complete the passage with the correct prepositions.

GROUND FLOOR

TOP FLOOR

Farmer Grant's farmhouse is (1) _____ the road. The small houses (2) _____ the farmhouse are where the farmhands stay. The barn is (3) _____ the farmhands' houses. There is a vegetable garden (4) _____ the houses and the barn.

The barn is a two-storey building. The animal stalls are (5) _____ the ground floor. There is a staircase (6) _____ the barn. The farming tools are kept (7) _____ the staircase. There are hoes, rakes and shovels (8) _____ the many tools in the barn.

Hay is kept on the top floor of the barn. There are three shelves (9) _____ the hay. The top shelf has bags of animal feed such as oats. The shelf (10) _____ it has bags of fertiliser and seeds.

YOUR SCORE
10

UNIT 13.2 PREPOSITIONS OF TIME

Look at the **A** and **B** sentences below. Find out why **B** is correct and **A** is wrong in the **Grammar Points** section.

GRAMMAR POINTS

CHECKPOINT

1A	She finished her work **not yet at** noon.	✗	
1B	She finished her work **before** noon.	✓	1
2A	Now, 10 minutes **more** seven o'clock.	✗	
2B	It is now 10 minutes **to** seven.	✓	2
3A	You will get our reply **latest** April.	✗	
3B	You will get our reply **by** April.	✓	3
4A	**In** the holidays, we went scuba diving.	✗	
4B	**During** the holidays, we went scuba diving.	✓	4

GRAMMAR POINTS

1 **at, before, after**

We use **at** to point to exact times. We use **before** to point out that an action took place **earlier** than the time mentioned. We use **after** to point out that an action took place **later** than the time mentioned.

EXAMPLES:

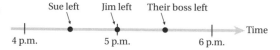

Jim left the office **at** 5 p.m.
Sue left the office **before** 5 p.m.
Their boss left the office **after** 5 p.m.

2 **to, past**

We use **to** when we want to point to an exact time before the stated hour. We use **past** when we want to point to an exact time after the stated hour.

EXAMPLES:

It is now 10 minutes **to** four.   It is now 10 minutes **past** four.

REMEMBER!

■ **Half past** is used to mean half an hour past the stated hour.

EXAMPLE: The matinee show starts at **half past three**. (3.30 p.m.)

■ **A quarter to** means 15 minutes before the stated hour.
A quarter past means 15 minutes after the stated hour.

EXAMPLES: He reached the bus stop at **a quarter to nine**. (8.45 a.m.)
He reached the bus stop at **a quarter past nine**. (9.15 a.m.)

---

3 **on, in, by**

We use **on** to point to a particular day or date. We use **in** to point to a year, a month or a period of time within a day. We use **by** to point to a period up to the time mentioned.

EXAMPLES: They'll complete the project **on** 21st July.

| ✗ | 19th July | ✗ | 20th July | ✓ | 21st July | ✗ | 22nd July |

They'll complete the project **in** July.

| ✗ | June | ✓ | July | ✗ | August | ✗ | September |

They'll complete the project **by** July.

| ✓ | May | ✓ | June | ✓ | July | ✗ | August |

4 **during**

We use **during** to point to a time between the start and the end of a period.

EXAMPLE:

One of the actors fainted **during** the play.

PRACTICE $\boxed{A}$ Circle the letters of the possible answers.

1 Our meetings always end before 6 p.m.

   A 6.15 p.m.   **B** 6.05 p.m.   **C** 5.50 p.m.   **D** 5.30 p.m.

2 The delivery van will be at your house by 11 a.m.

   A 10.25 a.m.   **B** 10.40 a.m.   **C** 11.00 a.m.   **D** 11.30 a.m.

3 The movie ended at 20 minutes past one.

   A 11.00 p.m.   **B** 1.20 p.m.   **C** 2.00 p.m.   **D** 2.20 p.m.

4 The storm began at 8 a.m. and ended three hours later.

   A 6.00 a.m.   **B** 8.00 a.m.   **C** 9.00 a.m.   **D** 11.00 a.m.

5 The plane from Chicago landed just after 7 p.m.

   A 7.01 p.m.   **B** 7.03 p.m.   **C** 7.05 p.m.   **D** 7.50 p.m.

YOUR SCORE
10

Match the sentences with the clocks by writing their numbers in the correct boxes.

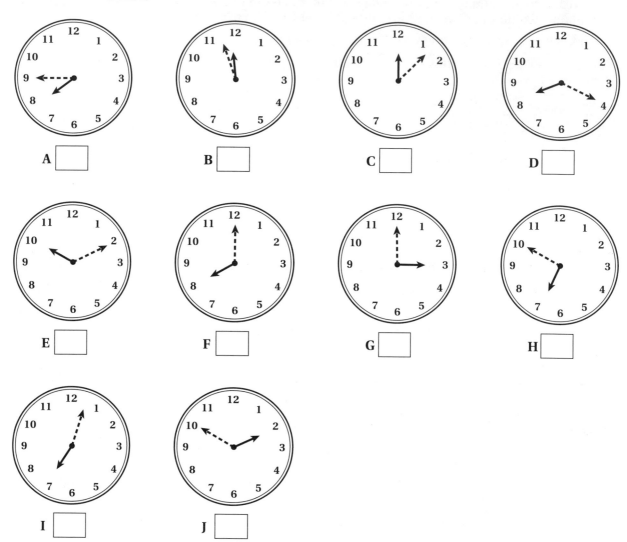

A ☐　　B ☐　　C ☐　　D ☐

E ☐　　F ☐　　G ☐　　H ☐

I ☐　　J ☐

1 Our train was due at 7 p.m. but it arrived a little after seven.

2 Sue said she would meet me in the lobby at a quarter to eight.

3 The conference was supposed to begin at 10 a.m. but there was a slight delay.

4 I am usually up before seven for my morning exercise at the park.

5 Mark phoned to say he would only be able to come for dinner after eight.

6 We lost our way several times and only got back to the hotel past midnight.

7 The tour guide told us to be on the bus by eight the next morning for our trip to the vineyards.

8 The film starts at 2 p.m. It's now 10 minutes to two so let's hurry.

9 The convicts broke out of prison early in the morning but the police managed to catch all of them just before noon of the same day.

10 I attend a bread-making class on Friday afternoons from 3 p.m. to 5 p.m. During that time, we learn how to make two different kinds of bread.

YOUR SCORE

10

PRACTICE *C* Rearrange the words to form correct sentences.

1 before — dinner — I — television — watch.

I watch television before dinner.

2 arrived — at — in — midnight — Paris — we.

_____

3 a — during — family — farm — my — on — stayed — summer.

_____

4 all — by — entries — must — office — our — reach — 20th May.

_____

5 arrived — it — minutes — past — police — the — two — was — when — 20.

_____

6 at — exactly — minutes — noon — seven — surrendered — terrorists — the — to.

_____

PRACTICE *D* Fill in the blanks with the correct prepositions in the box. Each word may be used more than once.

after	at	before	by	during
in	on	past	to	

1

Joe → airport → 9 a.m.
Sue → airport → 8.50 a.m.

(a) Joe arrived at the airport _____ Sue.

(b) Sue arrived at the airport _____ Joe.

2

House repairs:
✓ October
✓ November
✗ December

(a) The house repairs will be completed _____ November.

(b) The house repairs will be completed _____ December.

3

Dad fell asleep
├──────┼─────────┤
movie begaen   movie ended

(a) Dad fell asleep _____ the movie began.

(b) Dad fell asleep _____ the movie.

4

Nick and Julia – 20th May,1998

(a) I last saw Nick and Julia _____ 1998.

(b) I last saw Nick and Julia _____ 20th May, 1998.

5

5.55 → entering stadium
10:12 → leaving stadium

(a) It is now five minutes _____ six.
The first team is entering the stadium.

(b) It is now 12 minutes _____ ten.
The last few spectators are leaving the stadium.

UNIT 14 PUNCTUATION

> apostrophe, comma, exclamation mark, full stop, question mark

Look at the **A** and **B** sentences below. Find out why **B** is correct and **A** is wrong in the **Grammar Points** section.

CHECKPOINT

			GRAMMAR POINTS
1A	Who is in charge of this project**?.**	✗	
1B	Who is in charge of this project**?**	✓	1
2A	Julie **wont** go without her sister.	✗	
2B	Julie **won't** go without her sister.	✓	2
3A	Adam bought a pen **and** a book **and** a ruler and a sharpener.	✗	
3B	Adam bought a pen**,** a book**,** a ruler and a sharpener.	✓	3
4A	We saw a tiger in a cage, a monkey on a tree**,** a snake in a pit.	✗	
4B	We saw a tiger in a cage, a monkey on a tree **and** a snake in a pit.	✓	4

GRAMMAR POINTS

1 We use only **one** punctuation mark at the end of a sentence.

(a) We usually use a full stop (.) for a sentence that gives information and a question mark (?) for a sentence that asks for information.

   EXAMPLES: Kate missed the bus**.**
   Why is Kate late**?**

(b) We usually use an exclamation mark (!) after a word, phrase or sentence that expresses strong emotion such as surprise or anger.

   EXAMPLES: Wow**!** What an amazing car**!**
   He's 104 years old**!**

2 Besides using an apostrophe to show ownership or relationship (see **Possessives**, page 18), we use it to shorten certain words. We do it in these ways:

(a) <u>verb</u> + **not** = verb+n't (**'** takes the place of 'o' in **not**)

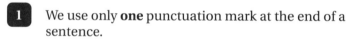

such verbs include **is, are, was, were, do, does, did, has, have, had, must, could, would**

> **REMEMBER!**
>
> ■ A sentence can take one of four forms:
>
> (a) a statement
>   **EXAMPLE:**
>   She is my neighbour.
>
> (b) a question
>   **EXAMPLE:**
>   Is she your neighbour?
>
> (c) an instruction or command
>   **EXAMPLES:**
>   Follow me.
>   Don't play with the fire extinguisher.
>
> (d) an exclamation
>   **EXAMPLE:**
>   He scored all five goals!

EXAMPLES: We **are not** leaving now.　→　We **aren't** leaving now.
You **do not** have the right answer. → You **don't** have the right answer.
He **could not** help me.　→　He **couldn't** help me.

(b) the verb **can/will** + **not** = **can't/won't**
EXAMPLES: He **cannot** miss the road sign.　→　He **can't** miss the road sign.
The store **will not** be open tomorrow. → The store **won't** be open tomorrow.

(c) pronoun + **is/are/am** = pronoun + shortened verb
EXAMPLES: **He is** at home. → **He's** at home.　(**is** becomes **'s**)
We are lost.　→　**We're** lost.　(**are** becomes **'re**)
I am Charles.　→　**I'm** Charles.　(**am** becomes **'m**)

(d) noun + **is** = noun + shortened verb
EXAMPLE: The **building is** on fire. → The **building's** on fire.

3 We use a comma (**,**) between each noun or adjective in a list. We use **and** and not a comma
before the last noun or adjective in the list.
EXAMPLES: Our canteen has many tables , chairs **and** benches .

Anna is a shy , quiet **and** thoughtful girl .

4 We use a comma to separate phrases in a list. We use **and** and not a comma before the last
phrase in the list.
EXAMPLE: Jane drew a small house , a tree beside the house **and** a bird in the tree .

PRACTICE | A | Tick the sentences that use punctuation marks correctly.

1 Are Mary and Victor in the attic.

2 Come into the house! There's lightning!

3 Our concert's on 14th July.

4 This dish needs a little more salt, pepper, tomato sauce.

5 I can't finish my homework on time.

6 Leon bought his wife a gold bracelet, a pair of pearl earrings and a diamond ring.

7 Theyre interested in renting out their house.

8 Where are my silver cufflinks?

9 He hasnt met her parents yet.

10 Could you pass me the hammer a nail and the screwdriver?

YOUR SCORE
10

PRACTICE B Mark with / where a punctuation mark or **and** is missing. Then write the answer in the box provided.

1 This lovely room is John/s.
2 Is Jenny good at cooking
3 I received a book a racquet and a kite for Christmas.
4 The museum is further down this road
5 Quick Use the fire extinguisher!
6 This apartment has good lighting, modern furniture a lovely view of the beach.

John's

YOUR SCORE
/10

PRACTICE C Rewrite the sentences and fill in the punctuation marks.

1 I wasn't at my grandfathers house yesterday

_____

_____

2 Her cars at the workshop

_____

_____

3 You dont have another dollar, do you

_____

_____

4 Peters brother wont be coming home this summer.

_____

_____

5 Hes ordering two cups of tea some scones and half a dozen sandwiches.

_____

_____

YOUR SCORE
/10

PRACTICE *D* Rewrite the sentences and shorten some words by using the apostrophe.

1 The train is late again as usual.
The train's late again as usual.

2 You must not enter the pool after 7 p.m.

3 Jane is the captain of our hockey team.

4 I have not got the keys to the store.

5 They are definitely worth more than 200 dollars.

6 Mrs Baker will not be discharged from hospital today.

YOUR SCORE
10

PRACTICE *E* There are five mistakes in the use of punctuation marks in the paragraphs below. Underline the words with the mistakes and write the answers in the boxes provided.

1 We were chatting in the kitchen when

Dad suddenly said, "This kitchens really

drab. I'm going to give it a new coat

of paint this weekend. I'll use blue beige and

5 white. It'll look great."

Mum wasnt pleased because Dad

could be messy. She wanted a professional

painter to do the job. "Why don't we

get Sue's painter to do it" she said. "You

10 should watch the football finals instead."

"My goodness I forgot. Yes, do

get Sue's painter," said Dad.

Mum smiled with relief.

YOUR SCORE
10

181

UNIT 15.1 **DIRECT SPEECH**

Look at the **A** and **B** sentences below. Find out why **B** is correct and **A** is wrong in the **Grammar Points** section.

GRAMMAR POINTS

CHECKPOINT

1A	Mother said to Alan, "What time will **Alan** return?"	✗	
1B	Mother said to Alan, "What time will **you** return?"	✓	1
2A	Mrs Ray said, **I** am your class **teacher**.	✗	
2B	Mrs Ray said, **"I** am your class **teacher."**	✓	2
3A	Mr Patten said to Mary, "**could** you close the window, please?"	✗	
3B	Mr Patten said to Mary, "**Could** you close the window, please?"	✓	3
4A	"I need to go to the post office**.**" said Julie.	✗	
4B	"I need to go to the post office**,**" said Julie.	✓	4

GRAMMAR POINTS

1 We use direct speech to state exactly what someone has said. We have to place the exact words of the speaker between quotation marks.

    EXAMPLE: Roy said, "I'm hungry." —⟨ exact words of Roy ⟩

> **REMEMBER!**
> - Direct speech consists of the exact words of the speaker.

2 We use quotation marks in pairs. To begin what a person says, we use **"**. To end what a person says, we use **"**.

    EXAMPLES: "Please carry my books," said Mrs Robertson.
                    Mr Lim said, "I'm going home."

3 When we begin a sentence with the speaker's name, we have to do the following:

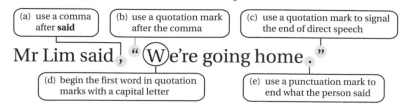

(a) use a comma after **said**
(b) use a quotation mark after the comma
(c) use a quotation mark to signal the end of direct speech
(d) begin the first word in quotation marks with a capital letter
(e) use a punctuation mark to end what the person said

Mr Lim said , " Ⓦe're going home . "

4 When we begin a sentence with the actual words of the speaker and end it with the speaker's name, we have to do the following:

(a) use a quotation mark to begin the sentence

(d) use a quotation mark to signal the end of direct speech

(e) end the sentence with a full stop

" Ⓟlease carry my books , " said Mrs Vaz .

(b) begin the first word in quotation marks with a capital letter

(c) use a comma, question mark or exclamation mark **but not** a full stop to end what the person said

---

PRACTICE *A*   Tick the correct sentences.

1 "This movie is boring," said Diana to her friends.

2 "The bus is here." said Mr Cook to Don.

3 "I have to go now, said Jackie, "it's getting dark."

4 "Do you know the way to the post office?" said the old lady.

5 "Martha," your cooking is delicious said Paul.

6 "Please come in," said Mr Shah's secretary.

7 Miss Hill said, "Please hand in your essays before you leave."

8 You were speeding" said the traffic policeman to Ned.

9 "Sit down said Irene sternly.

10 "Why is the baby crying?" said Peter to Nina.

YOUR SCORE

10

PRACTICE *B*   Rewrite the sentences and fill in the missing punctuation marks.

1 Mr Parkes said to Gwen Where do you live

Mr Parkes said to Gwen, "Where do you live?"

2 Gwen said I live in Milan

_____

3 The principal said to Mrs Ross Why are the students so noisy

_____

4 Mrs Ross answered There is a mouse under my table

_____

5 The manager asked his secretary Who called just now

_____

6 The secretary said the bank manager called to invite you for lunch

YOUR SCORE

10

_____

1 Mariam said her father is a dentist.
  A Mariam said, "Her father is a dentist".
  B Mariam said "My father is a dentist".
  C Mariam says "Her father is a dentist."
  D Mariam said, "My father is a dentist."

2 John asked me why I was sad.
  A John said, "Why are you sad?"
  B John said, "Why are you sad."
  C John said, 'Why are you sad?
  D John said "why are you sad?"

3 Peter said he did not like hockey.
  A "I don't like hockey?" said Peter.
  B "I don't like hockey," said Peter.
  C "I don't like hockey". said Peter.
  D "I don't like hockey" said Peter.

4 Mr Lee said Kim wasn't home.
  A Mr Lee said, "Kim isn't home.
  B Mr Lee said, "Kim isn't home."
  C Mr Lee said "Kim isn't home"
  D Mr Lee said "Kim isn't home.

5 Simon asked me what my favourite colour was.
  A Simon said, "Whats your favourite colour?"
  B Simon said, Whats your favourite colour."
  C Simon said, "What's your favourite colour?"
  D Simon said, "What's your favourite colour."

6 **A** Mrs Gan said, "You must be punctual this afternoon."
  B Mrs Gan said, You must be punctual this afternoon."
  C "You must be punctual this afternoon," said Mrs Gan.
  D "You must be punctual this afternoon." said Mrs Gan.

7 **A** Mr Brown said to his secretary, "Where are the minutes."
  B Mr Brown said to his secretary, "Where are the minutes?"
  C "Where are the minutes," said Mr Brown to his secretary.
  D "Where are the minutes?" said Mr Brown to his secretary.

8 **A** "What a beautiful painting? said Meg to her husband.
  B "What a beautiful painting" said Meg to her husband.
  C Meg said to her husband, "What a beautiful painting!"
  D Meg said to her husband "What a beautiful painting!"

YOUR SCORE

10

PRACTICE **D** Rewrite the sentences using the correct punctuation marks.

1 The cashier said to me "Are you paying cash."

_____

2 The director said to us, "our science exhibition is going to be in October,"

_____

3 The butcher said to Nelly, Which cut of lamb do you want?

_____

4 "Im not going to school today." said little Su Lin to her mother.

_____

5 The police officer said to my father, "You were driving at 120 km per hour

_____

PRACTICE **E** Rewrite the sentences and put in the missing punctuation marks.

1 Why is the bus so late today Lyn said to me.
we will be late for college if the bus doesn't come in another 10 minutes I said.

_____

_____

2 Mr Williams said to his personal secretary please cancel all my meetings today as I don't feel well.
Miss Cross said to him can I get some medication for you.

_____

_____

3 has anyone seen my house keys said Mum.
I saw them near the kitchen sink said my brother Kevin.

_____

_____

4 that man took my purse shouted the young woman.
Where did you put your purse Madam the security guard asked her.

_____

_____

5 Im very pleased with your term results said Dad to me.
Thanks Dad do you think I can have a raise in my allowance I said to him.

_____

_____

UNIT 15.2 **INDIRECT SPEECH**

Look at the **A** and **B** sentences below. Find out why **B** is correct and **A** is wrong in the **Grammar Points** section.

			GRAMMAR POINTS
1A	Jay and Alice said, "We **will** be at home."		
	Jay and Alice said that they **will** be at home.	✗	
1B	Jay and Alice said that they **would** be at home.	✓	1
2A	Maxine said, "I met Rita **yesterday**."		
	Maxine said that she had met Rita **yesterday.**	✗	
2B	Maxine said that she had met Rita the **previous day**.	✓	2
3A	The lecturer said, "The Earth **rotates** on its own axis."		
	The lecturer said that the Earth **rotated** on its own axis.	✗	
3B	The lecturer said that the Earth **rotates** on its own axis.	✓	3

GRAMMAR POINTS ───────────────────────────

1 We may state what someone has said by using **indirect speech**. When we change from direct to indirect speech, we keep the reporting verb **said** but we usually change the tense of the other verbs.

EXAMPLE:

Direct Speech	Indirect Speech
Rita **said**, "I **attend** dance classes on Fridays."	Rita **said that** she **attended** dance classes on Fridays.

2 When we change from direct to indirect speech, we also make changes to **pronouns**, **possessive adjectives**, **possessive pronouns** and **time** expressions.

EXAMPLES:

Direct Speech	Indirect Speech
They said, "**We went** to Korea **last week**."	They said that **they had gone** to Korea **the previous week**.

pronoun : We ⟶ they
verb : went ⟶ had gone
time : last week ⟶ the previous week

Direct Speech	Indirect Speech
Mr Steven said, "**I will take my** family to Disneyland **next year**."	Mr Steven said that **he would take his** family to Disneyland **the following year**.

pronoun : I ⟶ he   possessive adjective :   my ⟶ his
verb : will take ⟶ would take
time : next year ⟶ the following year

REMEMBER!

■ With indirect speech, not all the exact words of the speaker are used.

EXAMPLE:

Direct Speech	Indirect Speech
"**I am** the new manager," said Mr Brian Fraser.	Mr Brian Fraser said that **he was** the new manager.

■ The following changes are made to verbs in indirect speech.

Direct Speech	Indirect Speech
simple present – work simple past – worked simple future – will/shall + work	simple past – worked past perfect – had worked future – would + work
EXAMPLE: Sally said, "I **visited** the state park recently." The teacher said, "Monday **will be** a school holiday."	EXAMPLE: Sally said that she **had visited** the state park recently. The teacher said that Monday **would be** a school holiday.

---

3 We do not change the tenses of verbs in indirect speech if what we report is still true.

EXAMPLE: Our science teacher said, ⟶ Our science teacher said that
"Water **freezes** at 0˚C."   water **freezes** at 0˚C.

PRACTICE $\boxed{A}$ Change the sentences from direct speech to indirect speech.

1 Mr Lim said, "Vicky is at the dentist's."

Mr Lim said that Vicky was at the dentist's.

2 Mrs Pinto said, "I will be at a staff meeting tomorrow."

_____

3 Mrs Lea said, "Malaysia has a tropical climate."

_____

4 "Raj left for Singapore last week," said Mr Lopez.

_____

5 Lynn said, "I've already seen the movie."

_____

6 Adam and Aaron said, "We bought some new tapes at the sale."

_____

YOUR SCORE

10

PRACTICE **B** Change the sentences from indirect speech to direct speech.

1 Jean told me that she was not well.

Jean said to me, _____

2 Mr Clive said that he was flying back to England the following week.

Mr Clive said, _____

3 Mark said that he had a plan for our vacation.

Mark said, _____

4 I asked Dad where he was going.

I said to Dad, _____

5 Our neighbour told us that he had finished writing his first novel.

Our neighbour said to us, _____

PRACTICE **C** Underline the mistakes in the indirect speech sentences and write the correct words in the spaces provided.

1 John said to me, "I'm going for rugby practice
and I will come back late."
John told me that he is going for rugby practice   _____
and he would come back late.   _____

2 "I'm cooking your favourite chicken stew today,"
said Mum to me.
Mum told me that she was cooking your   _____
favourite chicken stew that day.   _____

3 "We have already watched this movie," said our
neighbours to us.
Our neighbours told us that they have already   _____
watched that movie.   _____

4 My friend Linda said to me, "I will be going to
Canada for further education."
My friend Linda told me that she will be going to   _____
Canada for further education.   _____

5 "You are all welcome to my party," said Gloria to
her friends.
Gloria told her friends that they are all welcome   _____
to her party.   _____

188

Change the sentences from indirect speech to direct speech.

1 Melissa told her boss Mr Lee that he had an appointment at 2.30 that afternoon.
Melissa said to Mr Lee, "You have an appointment at 2.30 this afternoon."

2 Sandra told her little boys not to disturb their father as he was tired.

3 We told Uncle Raj that we were unable to go to his house for dinner that night.

4 Ann told her mother that she had choir practice that day so she would be late.

5 The workmen told us that they were sorry but they couldn't complete the work that day.

6 Celine said that it was good to see us again.

YOUR SCORE
10

PRACTICE E The following are two messages for your mother. Write them down in indirect speech so that you can pass them to her.

(a) "This is Maggie Stewart. I won't be attending the club's fund-raising dinner on Saturday. My son is sick."

Maggie Stewart said

(b) "This is Aunt Nora. I'll meet your mother at the mall at 12.30 on Saturday. I'll wait for her at the florist's next to Macy's. She must not be late."

Aunt Nora said

YOUR SCORE
10

UNIT 16.1 **SENTENCE STRUCTURE**

joining two or more sentences with **and**, **but**, **or**

Look at the **A** and **B** sentences below. Find out why **B** is correct and **A** is wrong in the **Grammar Points** section.

GRAMMAR POINTS

				GRAMMAR POINTS
1A	Rachel plays the piano **but** her sister plays the flute.	✗		
1B	Rachel plays the piano **and** her sister plays the flute.	✓		1a
2A	I am untidy **and** my wife is neat.	✗		
2B	I am untidy **but** my wife is neat.	✓		1b
3A	We must leave now, we will be late.	✗		
3B	We must leave now **or** we will be late.	✓		1c
4A	This is my seat **and** this is yours and these are theirs.	✗		
4B	This is my seat**,** this is yours and these are theirs.	✓		2

**GRAMMAR POINTS**

1 (a) We use **and** to join sentences when their meanings go well together.

   EXAMPLE: Every evening Mum walks. Every evening Dad jogs.
   Every evening Mum walks **and** Dad jogs.

   (b) We use **but** to join sentences when their meanings contrast with each other.

   EXAMPLE: My brother enjoys playing hockey. I dislike games.
   My brother enjoys playing hockey **but** I dislike games.

   (c) We use **or** to join sentences to show that only one of the choices will take place.

   EXAMPLES: You must do some exercise. You will get fat.
   You must do some exercise **or** you will get fat.

   We can go to the zoo. We can visit the museum.
   We can go to the zoo **or** we can visit the museum.

2 When we use **and**/**or** to join three or more sentences, it is best to do the following:

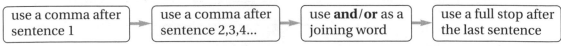

| use a comma after sentence 1 | → | use a comma after sentence 2,3,4... | → | use **and**/**or** as a joining word | → | use a full stop after the last sentence |

EXAMPLES: I'll sing. You'll dance. She'll play the piano. He'll tell jokes.

   I'll sing **,** you'll dance **,** she'll play the piano **and** he'll tell jokes **.**

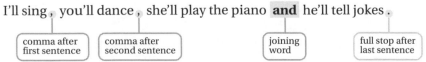

| comma after first sentence | comma after second sentence | joining word | full stop after last sentence |

We can also omit a repeated subject when we join two or more sentences.

subject   subject   subject

EXAMPLES: On Saturday afternoons **I** go fishing. **I** visit Grandpa. **I** stay at home.

On Saturday afternoons **I** go fishing **,** visit Grandpa **or** stay at home **.**

subject

| comma after first sentence | joining word | full stop after last sentence |

REMEMBER!

- It is also possible to use a combination of **and**, **but**, **or** to join sentences together.

    EXAMPLES: Dad is active **and** Mum is hardworking **but** I am lazy.

                I'll write **and** you'll draw **or** we'll chat **but** we must be quiet.

PRACTICE *A*   Circle the letters of the correct sentences. There may be more than one answer for each question.

1 A They are gentle and they will not hurt the butterfly.
  B They must be gentle or they will hurt the butterfly.
  C They must be gentle but they will hurt the butterfly.

2 A I play netball, she plays hockey but he plays badminton.
  B I play netball and she plays hockey but he doesn't play any games.
  C I play netball, she plays hockey and he plays badminton.

3 A You'll sweep and I'll mop or the floor will be dirty.
  B You'll sweep but I'll mop and the floor will be dirty.
  C You'll sweep, I'll mop and the floor will be clean.

4 A I like jasmines, you like lilies and she likes roses but he hates flowers.
  B I like jasmines, you like lilies, she likes roses and he likes orchids.
  C I like jasmines, you like lilies and she likes roses and he hates flowers.

5 A I'll swim, you'll fish, we'll go home early and Mum will not worry.
  B I'll swim or you'll fish but we'll go home early and Mum will worry.
  C I'll swim and you'll fish but we'll go home early or Mum will worry.

YOUR SCORE
10

PRACTICE *B*   Underline the correct words in the brackets to complete the paragraph.

Every Saturday, my family and I go to the seaside **1** (and / but / or) we all have fun. Dad, Pat and I swim in the sea **2** (and / but / or) Mum sits under a tree **3** (and / but / or) listens to music. Dad and Pat are strong swimmers **4** (and / but / or) I am not. Mum is afraid of the sea **5** (and / but / or) she still comes along **6** (and / but / or) soon, she joins in the fun. On a hot day I usually join Mum under the tree **7** (and / but / or) I will get sunburn **8** (and / but / or) my skin will peel. After lunch Dad takes out his fishing-rod **9** (and / but / or) fishes in his favourite place **10** (and / but / or) we all go for a boat ride.

YOUR SCORE
10

PRACTICE *C*   Rearrange the words in the boxes and mark their correct places in the sentences with ⋏ .

1 For me English is simple ⋏ but History is hard .

and – easy – Science – is – too –
and Science is easy too

2 This video game is exciting but I have to rest .

exhausted – I – be – or – tomorrow – will

3 The journey is long and they won't feel tired .

are – but – they – young

4 Jeff kicked it and it went into the goal .

ball – Jeff – Ken – passed – the – to,

5 I'll drive or I'll sit beside you .

alone – are – but – drive – not – to – you

6 If it doesn't belong to you , you will be in trouble .

have – it – or – return – to – you

YOUR SCORE
10

PRACTICE *D*   Join the sentences into one sentence. Use commas, **and**, **but**, or **or**.

1 Rover charged out of the house. He chased the neighbour's cat Cleo. She jumped onto the roof of a car. She just sat there.

_____

_____

2 Mrs Johnson gave her husband his lunch packet. She asked him to post a letter. He accidentally posted his lunch.

_____

_____

3 Janet painted the front door. Fiona painted the gate. Steve painted the upstairs windows. Little Harry painted himself.

_____

_____

4 You must be patient and speak gently to the children. They will not listen to you.

_____

_____

5 Kenneth wiped a mould. He mixed clay with sufficient water. He poured the clay mixture into the mould. He waited for the clay to harden into the shape of a vase.

_____

_____

YOUR SCORE
10

PRACTICE *E* Tick the correct sentences.

1 Sue gave him first aid and Joe helped, I called for an ambulance.

2 The course is tough but she is bright and she'll do well.

3 Mum bathed Jimmy and I dressed him but he looked smart.

4 The boy saw a squirrel and he tried to catch it but it ran away.

5 Skiing is fun and you have to take care or you'll get hurt.

6 She patted the lamb's head, it bleated and they became friends.

7 Tomorrow we'll swim or we'll rest but we won't shop again.

8 The weather was fine, the sea was polluted and the beach was dirty.

9 I'll go home now and take a nap or I'll fall asleep at your party.

10 Some were scared or others were angry but he kept calm.

YOUR SCORE
10

PRACTICE *F* Underline the incorrect sentences and rewrite them correctly. Use commas, **and**, **but**, or **or**.

It is 7.30 in the evening but I am watching a beautiful sunset. The sun is a red ball but the clouds have several colours. Some are red, others are golden or a few are purple. I love the sky at sunset and I sometimes try to paint it but I am not good at it yet. I have to keep trying and I will not improve. I want to try again now or I do not have my watercolours with me. Sunsets do not last long and there is no time to look for my paint box. Anyway, I hear my mother calling but I have to take a shower immediately or she will be upset. Soon she will finish cooking, she will call me again and I will set the table for dinner. Tomorrow evening I will be ready with my colour pencils or I will try to paint the sunset with watercolours.

1 _____

_____

2 _____

_____

3 _____

_____

4 _____

_____

5 _____

_____

YOUR SCORE
10

UNIT 16.2 SENTENCE STRUCTURE

relative clauses with **who**

Look at the **A** and **B** sentences below. Find out why **B** is correct and **A** is wrong in the **Grammar Points** section.

**CH**ECKPOINT

GRAMMAR POINTS

			GRAMMAR POINTS
1A	My brother is the little boy who **chasing** a hen.	✗	
1B	My brother is the little boy who **is chasing** a hen.	✓	1
2A	We paid the man painted our house.	✗	
2B	We paid the man **who** painted our house.	✓	2
3A	They are the athletes who my brother **admire**.	✗	
3B	They are the athletes who my brother **admires**.	✓	3

GRAMMAR POINTS

1 When we join two sentences, we can turn one into a main clause and the other into a subordinate clause. Each clause has a subject and a finite verb.

EXAMPLE: They greeted Mr Shan. He smiled at them.

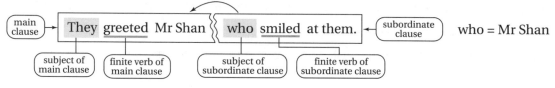

who = Mr Shan

2 A relative clause is a type of subordinate clause. It describes a noun. We use a relative clause beginning with **who** to describe a person or people.

EXAMPLE: I saw the thieves. They stole my bicycle.

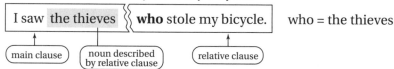

who = the thieves

REMEMBER!

- Simple and compound sentences do not contain subordinate clauses but complex sentences do.

  EXAMPLES: They greeted Mr Shan. He smiled at them. (two simple sentences)

  They greeted Mr Shan and he smiled at them. (compound sentence)

  They greeted Mr Shan who smiled at them. (complex sentence)

- A main clause can form a complete sentence on its own but a subordinate clause cannot.

  EXAMPLE: They greeted Mr Shan. ✓

  Who smiled at them. ✗

- Relative clauses are also known as adjectival clauses.

---

3 The finite verb of the relative clause must agree with its subject. The subject can be **who** or a noun/pronoun in the relative clause.

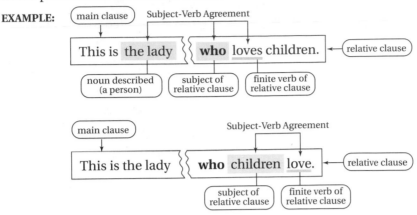

EXAMPLE:

PRACTICE _A_ Join the pairs of sentences to form sentences with **who**.

1 This is our friend Tasha. She was the best speaker at yesterday's debate.

_____

2 We like to spend weekends with Grandma. She is an excellent cook.

_____

3 Dad spoke to Mr and Mrs Tan. They are our new neighbours.

_____

4 The police officer stopped the young woman. She was speeding.

_____

5 Steve had an argument with the salesman. He tried to sell him a faulty electric shaver.

_____

PRACTICE _B_ Underline the correct words in the brackets.

1 He was a detective (solved / who solved) many difficult cases.

2 We trust people who (are / is) honest.

3 Each class has a monitor who the students (choose / chooses) themselves.

4 They are calling out the names of people who (are to report / to report) for duty at once.

5 The reporters are interviewing (a worker / workers) who was there at the time of the bombing.

6 Bobby was one of the children who the bigger boys (was / were) always bullying.

7 The company has a new manager (who / who is) very hard-working.

8 My grandfather is a person who every member of the family (respect / respects).

9 We are trying to guess who (going / is going) to drive to Sydney.

10 I would like to meet the foreign student who Terry and Jane (are / is) showing around the school.

195

PRACTICE *C*   Complete the sentences with relative clauses. Choose the correct answers in the boxes.

1   Alicia met an artist _____

wanted to paint her.
who wanted to paint her.
who he wanted to paint her.

2   Li Yen joined the students _____

who were reading magazines.
who's reading magazines.
were reading magazines.

3   We must thank the lady _____

so kind to us.
who was kind to us.
who she's kind to us.

4   Mr Lim is an entertainer _____

who all my friends enjoy.
who all my friends enjoys.
my friends enjoy him.

5   Animals like children _____

who is gentle and playful.
is gentle and playful.
who are gentle and playful.

YOUR SCORE

10

PRACTICE *D*   Fill in the blanks with suitable words in the box. Each word may only be used once.

has	helps	is	lived	tell
told	walked	want	was	were	will

Uncle Ben is a man who (1) _____ a very kind heart. One day, he caught a boy who (2) _____ trying to pick his pocket. He spoke firmly to the boy who (3) _____ him a sad story. He said he was an orphan who (4) _____ with foster parents. "Sir, they are lazy people who (5) _____ to get money without working," he said. "They want me to become a clever thief who (6) _____ make them rich." He said they were angry because the boy who they (7) _____ bringing up was not good at stealing. Uncle Ben took the boy into his own home. He grew fond of the boy who later (8) _____ off with some valuable things in the house. However, Uncle Ben is still helping people who (9) _____ him sad stories. Fortunately, some of the people who Uncle Ben (10) _____ do tell the truth.

YOUR SCORE

10

196

Rearrange the words to form sentences.

1 break — catch — people — rules — they — traffic — who.

_____

2 child — gang — kidnapped — rescue — the — the — we'll — who.

_____

3 counsels — get — he — into — trouble — who — youth.

_____

4 booing — pitied — player — she — the — they — were — who.

_____

5 after — is — looked — me — nurse — that — the — who.

_____

YOUR SCORE
10

PRACTICE *F* Underline the incorrect sentences and rewrite them correctly.

I like watching people who are waiting to board a plane. I am looking at a man and a little girl who is sitting side by side. The man looks like a wrestler who I often see on television. He seems to be a person is always cool and confident. He is speaking softly to the little girl who are sitting close to him. She seems to be a child who is rather shy and nervous. Then we all hear the conversation of two teenagers who are chatting loudly nearby. They are talking about people who afraid of flying. Suddenly a cry comes from the man who looks like a wrestler. He holds on to the hands of the little girl who say, "Don't be scared, Daddy. I'll be with you on the plane."

1 _____

_____

2 _____

_____

3 _____

_____

4 _____

_____

5 _____

_____

YOUR SCORE
10

UNIT 16.3 SENTENCE STRUCTURE

relative clauses with **which** and **that**

Look at the **A** and **B** sentences below. Find out why **B** is correct and **A** is wrong in the **Grammar Points** section.

			GRAMMAR POINTS
1A	He is the engineer **which** built that bridge.	✗	
1B	He is the engineer **who** built that bridge.	✓	1
2A	He wants the maps which/that **is** on the wall.	✗	
2B	He wants the maps which/that **are** on the wall.	✓	2

 GRAMMAR POINTS

1 We use a relative clause beginning with **which/that** to describe all nouns except people.

EXAMPLES:

main clause | noun described (animals) | relative clause

I see two tiger cubs ⟨⟨ ~~who~~/which are very cute.

main clause | noun described (person) | relative clause

This is the businessman ⟨⟨ who/~~which~~ is Dad's friend.

> **REMEMBER!**
> ■ Sometimes, **that** can be used instead of **who** in a relative clause to describe people.
> **EXAMPLES:**
> The teacher **who/that** taught us last year is leaving the school.
> The movie star **who/that** you like is coming to town.

2 A relative clause with **which/that** has a finite verb. The finite verb must agree with its subject.
EXAMPLES:

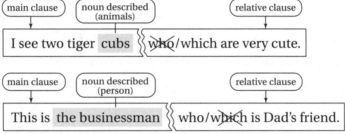

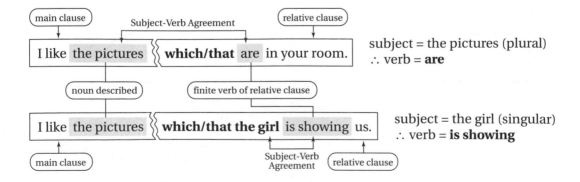

main clause | Subject-Verb Agreement | relative clause

I like the pictures ⟨⟨ **which/that are** in your room.

subject = the pictures (plural)
∴ verb = **are**

noun described | finite verb of relative clause

I like the pictures ⟨⟨ **which/that the girl is showing** us.

main clause | Subject-Verb Agreement | relative clause

subject = the girl (singular)
∴ verb = **is showing**

PRACTICE *A*   Tick the correct sentences.

1 She was listening to the frogs who were croaking loudly.
2 Those are the visitors which are part of the debating team.
3 The mechanic repaired the engine that making noise.
4 They ate all the oranges which were in the basket.
5 I remember the song which won the music award.
6 He likes the furniture that are in your sitting room.
7 He said something that made her laugh.
8 He is the footballer that Archie admires.
9 This is the horse who loves apples.
10 The little girl enjoys the stories which are in that book.

YOUR SCORE

10

PRACTICE *B*   Rearrange the words to make sentences.

1 any — food — he — is — likes — spicy — that.

_____

2 lost — here's — document — that — the — was.

_____

3 her — Jasmine — laugh — make — movies — watches — which.

_____

4 bit — he — him — killed — mosquito — the — which.

_____

5 are — I — people — like — that — they.

_____

YOUR SCORE

10

199

1   **A**   This is the statue which we saw from our hotel.
    B   This is the statue that we saw from our hotel.
    C   This is the statue who we saw from our hotel.

2   **A**   They sailed on a lake which were calm and lovely.
    B   They sailed on a lake which was calm and lovely.
    C   They sailed on a lake that was calm and lovely.

3   **A**   I go to a dentist that a friend recommended to me.
    B   I go to a dentist which a friend recommended to me.
    C   I go to a dentist who a friend recommended to me.

4   **A**   She was watching an ewe which was romping with its lambs.
    B   She was watching an ewe that was romping with its lambs.
    C   She was watching an ewe that romping with its lambs.

5   **A**   He is setting aside the clothes that are to be given away.
    B   He is setting aside the clothes which to be given away.
    C   He is setting aside the clothes which are to be given away.

YOUR SCORE
10

PRACTICE $\boxed{D}$ Underline the correct words in the brackets.

1   I am wearing the brooch (which / who) my mother gave me.

2   This is a city that (look / looks) beautiful at night.

3   My brother is stroking his kitten Whiskers (which / who) he rescued from a ditch.

4   You are not to touch the (newspaper / newpapers) that are on my table.

5   He will solve the problem which (is puzzling / puzzling) us.

6   She is signing the letters that (have to / to) go first.

7   These are trees which usually (grow / grows) in temperate climates.

8   They are the owners of the horses (which / who) we want to ride.

9   The boy is looking at the bow and arrows of his brother (which / who) won the archery prize.

10   He is telling stories that everyone already (know / knows).

YOUR SCORE
10

PRACTICE E Fill in the blanks with suitable words in the box. Each word may be used more than once.

are	beat	beats	charge	charges	is	look	looks
meet	meets	shine	understand	understood	which	who	

Switzerland is a country (1) _____ I dream of visiting one day. I will go with a friend (2) _____ also loves travelling. We will be able to see the mountains which (3) _____ awesome in pictures. We will go in winter which (4) _____ the most exciting season there. Of course, we will look for a skiing instructor who (5) _____ reasonable fees. I love to imagine my friend and me skiing down snowy slopes that (6) _____ brightly in the winter sunlight. We will make friends with interesting people that we (7) _____ there. We will speak to them in English which most people in the world (8) _____ . We will also learn a little French and German (9) _____ some of the Swiss people speak. It will be a holiday that (10) _____ all other holidays.

YOUR SCORE

10

PRACTICE F Underline the incorrect sentences in the poem and rewrite them correctly.

This is the room that I like best.
I love the view which I see from a window.
I feel like a bird that sitting in its nest.
I look at the city which lies far below.
I watch the car which pass along the street.
They look like toys that I loved as a boy.
I see a girl which I would like to meet.
She walks with a spring that full of joy.
They showed me rooms that face the sea.
But this is the room which always cheer me.

1 _____

_____

2 _____

_____

3 _____

_____

4 _____

_____

YOUR SCORE

5 _____

10

_____

UNIT 16.4 SENTENCE STRUCTURE

adverbial clauses with **because**

Look at the **A** and **B** sentences below. Find out why **B** is correct and **A** is wrong in the **Grammar Points** section.

GRAMMAR POINTS

1A	She comes from Zurich **because she speaks German.**	✗	
1B	She speaks German **because she comes from Zurich.**	✓	1
2A	He rested **it's because** he had a headache.	✗	
2B	He rested **because** he had a headache.	✓	2
3A	Everyone likes her **because of** she is friendly.	✗	
3B	Everyone likes her **because** she is friendly.	✓	3

GRAMMAR POINTS

1 We use an adverbial clause beginning with **because** when we want to give the reason for what is happening or what is stated in the main clause. An adverbial clause with **because** answers the question "Why?".

EXAMPLE:

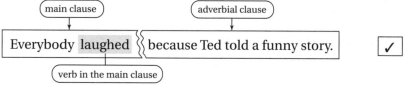

Everybody laughed ⟩⟩ because Ted told a funny story.   ✓

Why did everybody laugh? Because Ted told a funny story.   ✓

Ted told a funny story ⟩⟩ because everybody laughed.   ✗

Why did Ted tell a funny story? Because everybody laughed.   ✗

2 We do not use **it's** before an adverbial clause beginning with **because**.

EXAMPLE: They shouted **it's because** there was a fire.   ✗

They shouted **because** there was a fire.   ✓

> **REMEMBER!**
> - The adverbial clause is also a kind of subordinate clause.

3 We do not use **of** after **because** at the beginning of an adverbial clause.

EXAMPLE: We are playing **because of** there is no school today.   ✗

We are playing **because** there is no school today.   ✓

PRACTICE `A`   Tick the correct sentences.

1 Mr Gan felt hot because he took off his coat.

2 My mother is slim because she walks every day.

3 I needed a thick blanket because of the night was cold.

4 We are happy it's because we won the debate.

5 Sheena is angry because of her brother teased her.

6 We must leave because it will soon be dark.

7 She hates cockroaches because they look dirty.

8 The garden is pretty because we look after it.

9 Darren ate a lot it's because he was hungry.

10 We stopped because we saw a waterfall.

YOUR SCORE

10

PRACTICE `B`   Match Column A with Column B and write out the sentences.

Column A	**Column B**
1 The little girl ran	because it is beautiful.
2 I sent her flowers	because it's too expensive.
3 She is saving money	because a goose chased her.
4 Dad won't buy that shirt	because she wants to buy a car.
5 Many tourists visit Venice	because it's her birthday.

1 _____

2 _____

3 _____

4 _____

5 _____

YOUR SCORE

10

PRACTICE `C`   Underline the correct words in the brackets.

1 She takes in stray cats (because / because of) she feels sorry for them.

2 He asked me to be (noisy / quiet) because he wanted to sleep.

3 (Everybody / Nobody) trusts him because he is dishonest.

4 The bread smells nice because it is (fresh / stale).

5 The Arab boy loved his camel (because / it's because) it was loyal to him.

6 They read a lot because they (improved / wanted to improve) their vocabulary.

7 Sally (dislikes / likes) sailing because it makes her seasick.

8   We like him because he always speaks (gently / roughly).

9   Many accidents occur because people (disobey / obey) traffic rules.

10 They (accepted / rejected) her because she answered their questions well.

PRACTICE $\boxed{D}$ Fill in the blanks with suitable words in the box.

arrived	ate	because	but	clumsily	early	energetic
fear	gracefully	hurried	late	locked	love	midnight
noon	playful	recovering	serious	suffering	tired	

1   Her skin is good _____ she takes care of it.

2   He had to leave _____ because he had a meeting.

3   They _____ up all the food because it was delicious.

4   She feels _____ because she bathed in the cool spring.

5   I was sleepy because it was past _____ .

6   We are happy because she is _____ from her illness.

7   Many animals _____ the cheetah because it is fast and fierce.

8   Rose walks very _____ because she learnt ballet.

9   Young animals are fun to watch because they are _____ .

10 She _____ home because she wanted to tell her mother the good news.

PRACTICE $\boxed{E}$ Circle the right word in each box and mark with $\wedge$ where it should go in the sentence.

(brilliantly)	poorly
crowded	deserted
awkwardly	expertly
funny	scary
loudly	softly
jokes	news
new	old
lies	the truth
already	not
fast	slowly
much not	

1   The players performed $\wedge$ because their supporters cheered them.

2   We found the beach because it was a weekend.

3   I felt no pain because she injected me.

4   I am shivering because I am watching a movie.

5   You and I have to speak because the restaurant is noisy.

6   They exchanged because they wanted to amuse each other.

7   John is coming home because he misses his friends.

8   I believe them because they always tell.

9   She can't sleep soundly because she is used to the new house.

10 We are doing the work because we are afraid of making mistakes.

11 I can't get into Mum's clothes because she is smaller than me.

Rearrange the words in the brackets to complete the sentences.

1 Lina rushed to get dressed (because — for — late — she — was — work.)

   Lina rushed to get dressed _____

2 Dad bought me a racing bicycle (because — was — birthday — it — my.)

   Dad bought me a racing bicycle _____

3 The girls fled from the room (a — because — rat — saw — they.)

   The girls fled from the room _____

4 Norain drove slowly (because — heavily — it — raining — was.)

   Norain drove slowly _____

5 Everybody was pleased (because — became — champions — football — new — the — our — school — team.)

   Everybody was pleased _____

YOUR SCORE

/10

PRACTICE *G* Underline the incorrect sentences and rewrite them correctly.

Lisa is taking piano lessons because she wants to play at least one musical instrument. At first she tried learning the violin it's because she loved its sound. She soon realised her mistake because she was making the poor violin screech. Her brother begged her to stop because of she was hurting his eardrums. Her mother said nothing because she did not want to discourage Lisa. Then her father bought her a piano because her violin playing was driving him crazy. It was driving her crazy too because she was very thankful. Lisa much prefers the piano because it does not screech when played badly. She is improving fast it's because she practises every day. Her teacher is pleased with her because of she is such a keen pupil.

1 _____

   _____

2 _____

   _____

3 _____

   _____

4 _____

   _____

5 _____

   _____

YOUR SCORE

/10

205

UNIT 16.5 SENTENCE STRUCTURE

adverbial clauses with **when** and **while**

Look at the **A** and **B** sentences below. Find out why **B** is correct and **A** is wrong in the **Grammar Points** section.

				GRAMMAR POINTS
1A	We clapped **while** our team won.	✗		
1B	We clapped **when** our team won.	✓		1
2A	She was working while the others **played**.	✗		
2B	She was working while the others **were playing**.	✓		2

GRAMMAR POINTS

1 We often use an adverbial clause beginning with **when** to show two things happening one immediately after the other.

EXAMPLE:

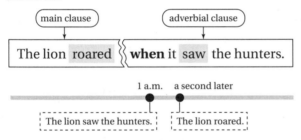

The lion roared **when** it saw the hunters.

2 We often use the same tense for the main clause and the adverbial clause beginning with **while**.

EXAMPLE:

Len was swimming **while** Andy was fishing.

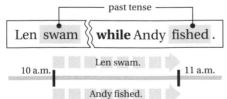

Len swam **while** Andy fished.

REMEMBER!
- An adverbial clause beginning with **while** is used to show two things happening at the same time.

206

PRACTICE *A*   Tick the correct sentences.

1   He smiled when he heard the good news.

2   The vase broke while it fell.

3   It rained heavily while you slept.

4   The little boy was singing when he took a shower.

5   The children were playing while their mothers were chatting.

6   I listen to music when I feel sad.

7   We welcomed him while he arrived.

8   He is just shaking his head when we ask him a question.

9   It was getting dark while they are walking home.

10   Cats often swish their tails when they see dogs.

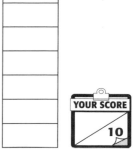

PRACTICE *B*   Underline the most suitable words in the brackets to complete the sentences.

1   They were laughing while the clowns (performed/ were performing).

2   We helped her when she (broke / was breaking) her leg.

3   Mum cooked (when / while) Dad mowed the lawn.

4   Everyone (screamed / was screaming) when the rope broke.

5   I (looked / was looking) after her baby while she rested.

6   Mrs Ravi always smiles (when / while) she sees us.

7   The boys are cooking while the girls (prepare / are preparing) the drinks.

8   Some people were talking while the president (spoke / was speaking).

9   We all cheered (when / while) Rita received the prize.

10   Lily stood up when we (asked / were asking) her to sing.

PRACTICE *C*   Rearrange the words in the brackets to complete the sentences.

1   My friend interviewed the players (I — pictures — their — took — while).

_____

2   She hugged her brother (he — her — luck — when — wished).

_____

3   We were telling ghost stories (howling — the — was — while — wind).

_____

4   Sheila always helps me (a — have — I — problem — when).

_____

5   We are wasting time (are — others — the — working — while).

_____

Circle the letters of the correct sentences. There may be more than one answer for each question.

1 A   Mum was working while Dad was studying at the university.
  B   Mum is working while Dad was studying at the university.
  C   Mum worked while Dad studied at the university.

2 A   She feels thankful when she thinks of her lucky escape.
  B   She felt thankful when she thought of her lucky escape.
  C   She is feeling thankful while she thinks of her lucky escape.

3 A   Bobby smeared his face with lipstick while his mother dresses.
  B   Bobby is smearing his face with lipstick while his mother is dressing.
  C   Bobby was smearing his face with lipstick while his mother was dressing.

4 A   He brought us little gifts when he returned from a trip.
  B   He was bringing us little gifts while he is returning from a trip.
  C   He brings us little gifts when he returns from a trip.

5 A   We packed our belongings while the water rose.
  B   We were packing our belongings while the water was rising.
  C   We pack our belongings while the water rose.

PRACTICE $\boxed{E}$ Join the adverbial clauses in Column B to the main clauses in Column A by writing the correct numbers in the boxes.

Column A	Column B
1 We were surprised	[ ] when he saw the soaring sales figures.
2 Ralph was painting the gate	[*1*] when we heard of Jackie's dismissal from the firm.
3 Julia was singing a lovely song	[ ] when he won the international squash tournament.
4 The manager was happy	[ ] when a snake slithered towards me.
5 Ravi's family was very pleased	[ ] while Tony was playing the saxaphone.
6 I shouted for help	[ ] while his wife was trimming the hedge.

Fill in the blanks with suitable words in the box.

am	are	argue	argued	is	mentioned	mentions
row	rowed	sleeps	sleeping	was	were	while	when

Dear Julie,

I was very pleased (1) _____ you phoned me last night. You know, my 12-year-old

brother Jimmy was listening on the extension phone while we (2) _____ chatting. I

(3)_____ rather amused when he does this sort of thing. He thinks my social life

(4)_____ more interesting than his. I'm sure he nearly died of boredom while we

(5)_____ about history. Jimmy's eyes droop when someone (6)_____

history. He is always (7) _____ in class while the history teacher is talking about people

and events in the past.

I did some dangerous things when I (8) _____ his age. I often (9) _____

my Dad's boat out to sea at midnight while the family was asleep. In fact, I am looking longingly at the

sea through my bedroom window (10) _____ I am writing this.

Bye now.

Ben

YOUR SCORE

10

PRACTICE G Underline the incorrect sentences and rewrite them correctly.

At this moment I am trying to keep calm while Auntie Kate drove me to school in her rickety old

car. She fell in love with this car when she looked after it for her neighbour 17 years ago. She was

caring for it tenderly while her neighbour was away. She hoped her neighbour would sell it to her

when he wanted to buy a new car. She saved carefully while she waited for that day. She was working

long hours while her friends were enjoying themselves. So she has enough savings to buy the car when

her neighbour offered it to her. She loves the car and just smiles when people tease her about its

cranky ways. Now too she is smiling while the car was threatening to stop. It does stop but started

again when she pats it playfully on its bonnet.

1 _____

_____

2 _____

_____

3 _____

_____

4 _____

_____

YOUR SCORE

5 _____

10

_____

UNIT 16.6 SENTENCE STRUCTURE

noun clauses with **who** and **what**

Look at the **A** and **B** sentences below. Find out why **B** is correct and **A** is wrong in the **Grammar Points** section.

				GRAMMAR POINTS
1A	I know **what** made you cry and I'll speak to him.	✗	
1B	I know **who** made you cry and I'll speak to him.	✓	1
2A	Tell us **who** her name is.	✗	
2B	Tell us **what** her name is.	✓	2
3A	Everyone is asking what **did you see**.	✗	
3B	Everyone is asking what **you saw**.	✓	3

GRAMMAR POINTS

1 We use a noun clause beginning with **who** to refer to people.

EXAMPLE:
Cheryl can guess **who** hid her shoes. (who = the person)

subject — verb — object (noun clause)

2 We use a noun clause beginning with **what** to refer to things.

EXAMPLE:
Cheryl can guess **what** she'll get for her birthday.

subject — verb — object (noun clause) (what = the things)

REMEMBER!

- The noun clause is a kind of subordinate clause that acts as a noun. It answers the question "What?".

- Unlike a relative clause (see page 194), the word **who** in a noun clause does not refer back to the subject in the main clause.

EXAMPLE:

(main clause) (noun clause)

| Cheryl can guess }} who hid her shoes. |

What can Cheryl guess? Who hid her shoes.
Who hid her shoes is the object of **can guess**.

---

3 In a noun clause with **who** or **what**, we use the word order for a statement, not a question.

EXAMPLES:	Question	:	**Who is she?**	✓
	Statement	:	We want to know **who is she**.	✗
	Statement	:	We want to know **who she is**.	✓
	Question	:	**What does he want?**	✓
	Statement	:	Tell me **what does he want?**	✗
	Statement	:	Tell me **what he wants**.	✓

PRACTICE *A* Underline the correct words in the brackets.

1 We did not understand what (he was / was he) saying.

2 We can guess who (they will / will they) want on the committee.

3 I have decided (what / who) I'm going to ask for help.

4 Please explain what (are you / you are) trying to do.

5 Diana wants to know who (did you visit / you visited) that day.

6 I know (who are you / who you are) waiting for.

7 Ask them (what / who) they have named their baby.

8 She doesn't care what (do we think / we think) about her idea.

9 Find out who (does she like / she likes) and invite them.

10 Tell me (what / who) makes you happy and I'll help you do it.

PRACTICE *B* Rearrange the words to make sentences.

1 are — knows — she — who — you.

_____

2 I — me — remember — taught — what — you.

_____

3 doing — guessed — he — what — were — you.

_____

4 me — met — tell — they — who.

_____

5 is — love — she — singing — we — what.

_____

PRACTICE *C* Tick the correct sentences.

1 I really appreciate what you did for me.

2 He told us who his father's rank was in the army.

3 She was surprised to learn what his occupation was.

4 Please write down who would you like as your partner.

5 They believe what they read in the newspapers.

6 The people can tell who will make good leaders.

7 The police will find out what caused the accident and they will charge him.

8 We are wondering what is he going to play at the concert.

9 You are not supposed to say who you voted for.

10 He is trying to remember what did he carve on that tree long ago.

1 Bill   : I can guess who did take my car keys.

I can guess who took my car keys.

2 Anna : Tell me who is the culprit?

_____

3 Bill   : Let me make sure who is it.

_____

4 Anna : Can you guess what did he or she do with the keys?

_____

5 Bill   : Tell me what are you thinking of?

_____

6 Anna : I can guess what is he doing with your keys now.

_____

_____

YOUR SCORE
/ 10

PRACTICE $\boxed{E}$ Complete the sentences by changing the questions into noun clauses.

1 Who did you see at the office?

Tell me _____

2 What does she do nowadays?

I don't know _____

3 What did Mother tell you to do yesterday?

I don't remember _____

4 Who did she dance with at the party last week?

I'm not sure _____

5 What did Sue buy at the sale on Monday?

I don't really know _____

YOUR SCORE
/ 10

Circle the correct words in the boxes and mark their places in the sentences with λ .

1 You must give them λ you promised them.

2 They are beginning to wonder who he working for.

3 I remember you advised me to do.

4 We don't know we can trust here.

5 She heard what were saying to each other.

6 He can't reveal donated that big sum.

7 I can guess what you dreaming of.

8 She tried to see what the delivery man carrying.

9 We realised who they cheering for. It was us.

10 He is wondering who is writing to.

11 I understood you said just now.

(what)	who
are	is
what	who
what	who
I	we
what	who
are	is
is	was
are	were
it	she
what	who

YOUR SCORE
10

Underline the incorrect sentences and rewrite them correctly.

My schooldays are coming to an end but I still can't decide what should I do. I wonder who can I ask for advice. The person has to know what I am good at. He or she also needs to understand what am I really interested in. I don't know who can help me.

Suddenly I realise who I must talk to about my future. My parents must be anxious to hear what do I feel about it. I must not forget who brought me up and always encouraged me. They can help me find out what am I best suited for.

1 _____

2 _____

3 _____

4 _____

5 _____

YOUR SCORE
10

UNIT 16.7 SENTENCE STRUCTURE

adjectival phrases with prepositions

Look at the **A** and **B** sentences below. Find out why **B** is correct and **A** is wrong in the **Grammar Points** section.

			GRAMMAR POINTS
1A	I want to buy the bird **is in** that cage.	✗	
1B	I want to buy the bird **in** that cage.	✓	1
2A	We like the houses **very much** near the beach.	✗	
2B	We like the houses near the beach **very much**.	✓	2
3A	My sister is the girl **who with** long black hair.	✗	
3B	My sister is the girl **with** long black hair.	✓	3

GRAMMAR POINTS

1 An adjectival clause (or a relative clause) has a finite verb.
An adjectival phrase does not have a finite verb.

EXAMPLE:
Sid took the guitar **which/that was on the sofa**.   (adjectival clause)
Sid took the guitar **on the sofa**.   (adjectival phrase)

> **REMEMBER!**
> ■ Relative clauses are also known as adjectival clauses.

2 Both an adjectival clause and an adjectival phrase describe a noun and come immediately after the noun they describe.

EXAMPLE:

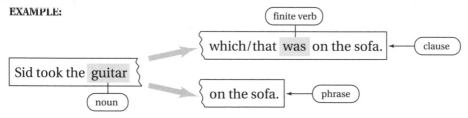

3 An adjectival phrase does not begin with **who**, **which** or **that**. It can begin with a preposition.
EXAMPLE: Sid took the guitar **on** the sofa.

Other examples of adjectival phrases beginning with prepositions are these:

| around the pool | next to me | by the sea |
| with curly hair | under the table | |

214

Which sentences have adjectival phrases? Tick them and underline the phrases.

1 ☐ **A** Mr Tan owns the building that is behind our house.
  ☐ **B** Mr Tan owns the building behind our house.

2 ☐ **A** My grandfather is that man with shining white hair.
  ☐ **B** My grandfather is that man who has shining white hair.

3 ☐ **A** We love the tomatoes from your garden.
  ☐ **B** We love the tomatoes which are from your garden.

4 ☐ **A** I feel sorry for the animals in the cage.
  ☐ **B** I feel sorry for the animals which are in the cage.

5 ☐ **A** I went to the supermarket which is opposite the library.
  ☐ **B** I went to the supermarket opposite the library.

YOUR SCORE
/10

PRACTICE B Rewrite the sentences using adjectival phrases.

1 Don't tease the kitten which is under the chair.

_____

2 He is looking for a house which is on a hill.

_____

3 I know a girl who has green eyes.

_____

4 Don't go into the hut which is beside the river.

_____

5 My mother has gone to the post office that is across the road.

_____

YOUR SCORE
/10

PRACTICE C Rearrange the words in the brackets to complete the sentences.

1 She rented a flat (city — in — middle — of — the — the).

_____

2 Aladdin could command the genie (inside — lamp — magic — the).

_____

3 I dreamt of a country (above — clouds — last — night — the).

_____

4 I don't mind a seat (emergency — exit — next — the — to).

_____

5 He honked at the lorry (front — him — in — loudly — of — very).

_____

YOUR SCORE
/10

PRACTICE *D* Join the sentences using adjectival phrases.

1 He sat in the chair. The chair was next to her.

   He sat in the chair next to her.

2 We play tennis at the club. The club is near our office.

   _____

3 The fox watched the hens. The hens were in the coop.

   _____

4 Sorry, I broke the spectacles. The spectacles were on the sofa.

   _____

5 We enjoyed the barbecue. The barbecue was at Jane's house.

   _____

6 I like the child. The child has big brown eyes.

   _____

PRACTICE *E* Circle the letters of the correct sentences. There may be more than one answer for each question.

1 **A** I knew the man in the grey suit.
   B I knew the man who was wearing a grey suit.
   C I knew the man who in the grey suit.

2 **A** They are hiding in the ditch which behind the school.
   B They are hiding in the ditch which is behind the school.
   C They are hiding in the ditch behind the school.

3 **A** We bought vegetables at the market across the river yesterday.
   B We bought vegetables at the market yesterday across the river.
   C Yesterday we bought vegetables at the market across the river.

4 **A** Be careful with the vase that on the piano.
   B Be careful with the vase that is on the piano.
   C Be careful with the vase on the piano.

5 **A** He sometimes photographs corals under the sea.
   B Sometimes he photographs corals under the sea.
   C He photographs corals sometimes under the sea.

PRACTICE _F_   Underline the correct words in the brackets.

1   Someone is dragging furniture around on the floor (above / which above) ours.

2   An accident took place in the street (outside / was outside) my office.

3   They are resting in the shed (now by the field / by the field now).

4   The water sank to a level (below / that below) the danger mark.

5   They often go to the shops (along / are along) Pine Street.

6   We waved to the girl (at / who at) the window.

7   He joined the kindergarten (last month near his house / near his house last month).

8   The baby sleeps in a cot (beside / which beside) my bed.

9   We'll meet in the restaurant (at noon opposite the station / opposite the station at noon).

10   She enjoyed novels (about / were about) adventure.

YOUR SCORE

/ 10

PRACTICE _G_   Underline the incorrect sentences and rewrite them correctly using adjectival phrases.

I'll take you into a cave that with a strange story. It has a rock formation in the shape of a ship with its captain and crew. According to the story, long ago the area used to be a village was by the sea. As a youth the captain sailed away to trade in many countries around the world. He made a lot of money and told everyone that he was a man from a rich family. One day, he had to take shelter in the harbour from a storm near his village. His mother came to the ship hoping to hear news of her son at sea. She recognised the well-dressed man who on the deck as her long-lost son. However, he was too proud to admit that the woman in faded old clothes was his mother. Her tears fell on the earth in torrents beneath her feet. The earth shook and the ship in the harbour turned into rock together with its captain and crew.

1   _____

_____

2   _____

_____

3   _____

_____

4   _____

_____

YOUR SCORE

5   _____

/ 10

_____

217

UNIT 16.8 SENTENCE STRUCTURE

adverbial phrases with **because of**

Look at the **A** and **B** sentences below. Find out why **B** is correct and **A** is wrong in the **Grammar Points** section.

GRAMMAR POINTS

1A	The actress has many fans because of she is **beautiful.**	✗	
1B	The actress has many fans because of her **beauty**.	✓	1
2A	I am sweating because of **hot**.	✗	
2B	I am sweating because of **the heat**.	✓	2

GRAMMAR POINTS

1 An adverbial clause has a finite verb. An adverbial phrase does not have a finite verb.
   EXAMPLE: She cried **because it was painful**.   (adverbial clause)

   finite verb

   She cried **because of the pain**.   (adverbial phrase)

> **REMEMBER!**
> ■ An adverbial clause with **because** and an adverbial phrase with **because of** answer the question "Why?".
> **EXAMPLE:**
>
>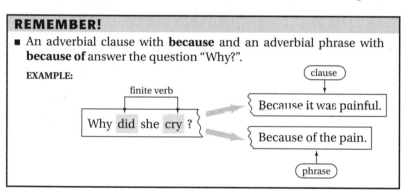

2 An adverbial phrase beginning with **because of** must be followed by a noun. The noun can have an article or a possessive pronoun before it.

   EXAMPLES: (clause)   They like Fay **because** she is kind.

   finite verb

   (phrase)   They like Fay **because of** her **kindness** .

   possessive pronoun   noun

   (clause)   I could not come **because it rained** .   finite verb

   (phrase)   I could not come **because of the rain** .

   article   noun

218

Underline the correct words in the brackets.

1 We like difficult problems because of (my / the) challenge.

2 Guy likes his neighbours because of (his / their) friendliness.

3 They respect Mrs Singh because of (her / the) integrity.

4 My ears ached because of (the / their) noise.

5 We stopped the game because of the (rain / raining).

6 Mum is upset because of my (ill / illness).

7 She lost her bicycle because of her (careless / carelessness).

8 Lamin loves elephants because of their (gentle / gentleness).

9 Everyone likes you because of your (honest / honesty).

10 The trees are swaying because of the (wind / windy).

PRACTICE *B* Complete the sentences with the noun forms of the words in the boxes.

1 Dad praised me because of my _____ .

| neat |

2 Everyone likes him because of his _____ .

| polite |

3 They chose Linda because of her _____ .

| intelligent |

4 He is famous because of his _____ .

| brave |

5 I like dogs because of their _____ .

| loyal |

6 Ants love sugar because of its _____ .

| sweet |

7 Jane is a good shooter in netball because of her _____ .

| high |

8 Rita looks graceful because of her _____ .

| slim |

9 You won the boxing match because of your _____ .

| strong |

10 I like watching young animals because of their _____ .

| playful |

Tick the correct sentences.

1 We like our neighbour because of his generosity.
2 The garden looks good because of your hardworking.
3 She lost her friends because of her pride.
4 The horse loves sugar because of its sweet.
5 He was able to succeed because of his wife's helping.
6 Kevin was jubilant because of his team victory.
7 The girl laughed loudly out of happy.
8 The animals fled the jungle because of the fire.
9 Bessy spoke loudly because of the noise around her.
10 The town bustled with cheerful people because of the celebrate.

YOUR SCORE
10

PRACTICE D Join the sentences with **because of**.

1 The university gave her a scholarship. She was brilliant.
   The university gave her a scholarship because of her brilliance.

2 I had three slices of cake. I was hungry.

3 Sometimes people get angry with him. He is frank.

4 Many cars are stuck in that area. It is flooded.

5 We will always honour him. He is courageous.

6 The department has a good name. It is efficient.

YOUR SCORE
10

220

1 A She makes mistakes because of her impatience.
  B She makes mistakes because of her impatient.
  C She makes mistakes because she is impatient.

2 A I felt scared because everything was silent.
  B I felt scared because of the silence.
  C I felt scared because the silence.

3 A The interviewers rejected him because of its rudeness.
  B The interviewers rejected him because of his rudeness.
  C The interviewers rejected him because he was rude.

4 A They acted fairly because of their wisdom.
  B They acted fairly because of their were wise.
  C They acted fairly because they were wise.

5 A We respect you because of our truthfulness.
  B We respect you because you are truthful.
  C We respect you because of your truthfulness.

PRACTICE *F* Underline the incorrect sentences. Rewrite them correctly, using adverbial phrases with **because of**.

Lee started writing in school and soon a newspaper published his stories because of their humour. He became famous because of his talented. He earned a lot from his stories because of their popularity. Many people invited him to parties because of he famous. They also wanted to be his friends because of their wealth. However, Lee avoided them because of insincere. He preferred his old friends because of their honesty. They liked him even more because of his loyalty. He asked them to help him set up a scholarship fund for students who could not go to university because of their poverty. Now many students have a bright future because of his generous.

1 _____

_____

2 _____

_____

3 _____

_____

4 _____

_____

5 _____

_____

UNIT 16.9 **SENTENCE STRUCTURE**

noun phrases with **to** and 'ing'

Look at the **A** and **B** sentences below. Find out why **B** is correct and **A** is wrong in the **Grammar Points** section.

			GRAMMAR POINTS
1A	I hate **is washing** dishes.	✗	
1B	I hate **washing** dishes. / I hate **to wash** dishes.	✓	1
2A	We enjoy **to watch** funny movies.	✗	
2B	We enjoy **watching** funny movies.	✓	2

GRAMMAR POINTS

1 A noun clause has a finite verb. A noun phrase does not have a finite verb.

EXAMPLE: I like **doing gymnastics**. (noun phrase)

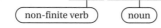

non-finite verb   noun

A noun phrase can be the **object** of the finite verb in a sentence.

EXAMPLE:

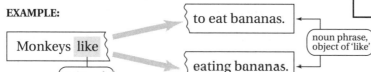

Monkeys like → to eat bananas.
finite verb → eating bananas.
noun phrase, object of 'like'

> **REMEMBER!**
> ■ A noun phrase answers the question "What?".
>
> **EXAMPLES:**
>
> He loves **playing** the guitar.
> He loves **to play** the guitar.
>
> What does he love?   Playing the guitar
>   To play the guitar.

2 Some finite verbs can have   (a) both **to** phrases and 'ing' phrases
                                     (b) **to** phrases, not 'ing' phrases
                                     (c) 'ing' phrases, not **to** phrases

EXAMPLES:

with 'to' and 'ing'	with 'to', not 'ing'	with 'ing', not 'to'
<u>Finite verb</u> begin hate like **to make** love cakes remember **making** start cakes try	<u>Finite verb</u> decide hope plan **to make** cakes promise want wish	<u>Finite verb</u> finish practise **making** cakes stop
EXAMPLE: I like **to make** cakes. I like **making** cakes.	**EXAMPLE:** I want **to make** cakes.	**EXAMPLE:** I practise **making** cakes every Sunday.

PRACTICE **A**   Tick the correct sentences.

1 I remember was staying by the sea.

2 Mei Ying decided to become a doctor.

3 He tried studying at the library.

4 Jill practises to play squash every day.

5 You promised coming to my party.

6 The cat began climbing the tree.

7 I will stop to get up late.

8 They started decorating their house.

9 All of us hope to be at the concert.

10 The girls wish going home.

YOUR SCORE

10

PRACTICE **B**   Rearrange the words to make sentences.

1 always — enjoys — them — visiting — she.

_____

2 all — hated — in — rain — the — walking — we.

_____

3 soon — they — to — away — go — plan.

_____

4 Christmas — finally — finished — her — she — shopping.

_____

5 come — everybody — here — to — wants.

_____

YOUR SCORE

10

PRACTICE **C**   Underline the correct words in the brackets.

1 We decided (to walk / walking) five miles a day.

2 My mother begins (prepared / preparing) for Christmas in October.

3 They hope (meeting / to meet) interesting people at the youth camp.

4 Jane remembers (seeing / to see) you at an art exhibition.

5 We enjoyed (skating / to skate) on the new ice rink.

6 I wish (reporting / to report) a burglary.

7 The bakery has stopped (making / to make) that special bread.

8 My father and I plan (going / to go) sailing next weekend.

9 I promise (being / to be) punctual from now on.

10 We finished (decorating / to decorate) the hall before noon.

YOUR SCORE

10

PRACTICE $\boxed{D}$ Rewrite the sentences by changing the **to** phrases to 'ing' phrases and vice versa.

1 Helen hates to tidy her room.
Helen hates tidying her room.

2 My uncle loves making pizza.

3 She tried to warn me but I didn't hear her.

4 We started to play tennis but then it rained.

5 I tried to swim two laps but I failed.

6 I like making traditional dishes.

YOUR SCORE
10

PRACTICE $\boxed{E}$ Rewrite the sentences correctly.

1 Mum always forgets locking the back door.
Mum always forgets to lock the back door.

2 Dylan promised taking care of our pet dalmation next week.

3 The girls practised to dance on the stage in their costumes.

4 Pamela plans marrying Ken next January.

5 George stopped to drive because of his accident.

6 The workers finished to load the oil palm fruit onto the lorries.

YOUR SCORE
10

Fill in the blanks with suitable words in the box. Each word may only be used once.

being	cheering	experiencing	having	living
to be	to cheer	to experience	had	lives
made	missed	mixing	sent	taking
to make	to miss	mixed	to send	takes

Lin was happy when her parents agreed (1) _____ her to a university in Hawaii. She wanted (2) _____ life in a foreign land. She loved (3) _____ with students from different countries. However, after a while she (4) _____ having her family around her. She hated (5) _____ so far away from home. She longed (6) _____ back in her own country. Luckily one of her new friends managed (7) _____ her up. The friend, called Kay, started (8) _____ Lin back to her house at weekends. Kay's family really tried (9) _____ Lin feel at home. Soon Lin stopped (10) _____ so homesick.

YOUR SCORE

10

PRACTICE *G*   Underline the incorrect sentences and rewrite them correctly.

Dear Mark,

You asked me when I decided becoming an artist. I don't remember deciding to make art my career. I never planned to study art. I didn't even hope doing well in the subject at school. Like other children, I liked drawing on walls. Next, I began sketching on paper. Then, I practised to daub paint on canvas. For years I refused letting anyone see my work. As soon as I finished to paint something, I would hide it. Finally, I did show a painting to my grandfather when he promised to keep my art a secret . . . .

1 _____

_____

2 _____

_____

3 _____

_____

4 _____

_____

5 _____

_____

YOUR SCORE

10

TEST 1

A Underline the correct items in the brackets.

1 (A / An) conference on **2** (the / –) women writers throughout **3** (the / –) world will be held at **4** (an / the) university in **5** (the / –) Kuala Lumpur on **6** (the / –) third of November this year.

The conference will be declared open by **7** (a / the) Vice-Chancellor of the university. **8** (An / The) Australian novelist will be presenting **9** (a / the) paper on **10** (a / an) innovative trend in modern literature.

YOUR SCORE

10

B Cross out the incorrect words to complete the sentences.

1 This vase has a crack in it. Take [that | this] one over there.

2 Marie, I like your costume but I don't like Lena's. Why is [her | hers] so plain?

3 I bought the groceries you wanted. I've put [it | them] on the kitchen table.

4 The packets are too expensive. We'll have to pack everything [ourselves | themselves].

5 Mr Shan doesn't eat at the office canteen. [He | She] brings sandwiches from home.

6 Aunty Mei, I'm making [me | myself] at home here.

7 These plates belong to our neighbour. [That | Those] are the caterer's.

8 A gazelle is an beautiful animal that is known for [its | it's] speed and grace.

9 The boys tried to get into Kate's car because it looked exactly like [hers | theirs].

10 You should cut [your | yours] hair before the sergeant sees it.

YOUR SCORE

10

C Circle the marks (⋀) to show the places where the adverbs in the boxes should go.

1 Cora ⋀ opens ⋀ her cake shop at 10 a.m.

2 Mrs Singh came ⋀ home ⋀ because her car had stalled at the traffic lights.

3 The families prayed ⋀ for ⋀ a good harvest.

4 Ben ⋀ looked for his missing book ⋀.

5 We have ⋀ spoken ⋀ to the principal about the anti-smoking campaign.

6 The rescue workers fought ⋀ to save ⋀ the accident victims.

7 I can't ⋀ find him ⋀. I don't know where he is.

8 Frankie ⋀ knows what to say ⋀ when he goes to a big party.

| usually |
| late |
| fervently |
| everywhere |
| already |
| desperately |
| upstairs |
| never |

9 The stewardess smiled at us as we boarded the plane .

10 I will be meeting Robin at the airport when he flies in .

D Read the passage and insert an apostrophe (') where necessary.

The female dancers appeared on stage. The audiences approval was clear from the loud   1
clapping. The lead dancers costume was beautiful. It was more glittering than the other dancers
costumes. Then the male dancers came on stage and the crowds cheers began again. The mens
constumes were simple, just black trousers and white shirts.

The guitarist at the side of the stage then introduced the dance troupes lead dancer Maria.   5
She curtsied and waved to her partner Carlos. He came forward and held Marias hand. When
Carlos heard the guitarists first note, he lifted Maria up into the air. The other men held their
partners hands and they moved in step with Carlos and Maria. The dancers movements were
very graceful. As the guitarist plucked the strings more and more quickly, the dancers too moved
swiftly to keep up with the rhythm.   10

E Circle the letters of the correct sentences.

1 A The prince was riding on an enormous grey African elephant.
  B The prince was riding on a enormous grey African elephant.
  C The prince was riding on an African enormous grey elephant.

2 A Alice is best at basketball than me.
  B Alice is more better at basketball than me.
  C Alice is better at basketball than me.

3 A I was so boring with the movie that I walked out.
  B I was so bored with the movie that I walked out.
  C I was so bore with the movie that I walked out.

4 A It was the most wonderfullest experience in my life.
  B It was the most wonderful experience in my life.
  C It was the wonderfullest experience in my life.

5 A Don't make so much noise. You're disturbing the others.
  B Don't make so much noises. You're disturbing the others.
  C Don't make so many noise. You're disturbing the others.

6 A The pink grey cushion covers look just right.
  B The pink, grey cushion covers look just right.
  C The pink and grey cushion covers look just right.

7 A He arrived home sooner than expected.
  B He arrived home more sooner than expected.
  C He arrived home most sooner than expected.

8 A A few chilli powder can make a big difference.
  B A little chilli powder can make a big difference.
  C A little chillies can make a big difference.

9 A This car runs more worse this year than last year.
  B This car runs worser this year than last year.
  C This car runs worse this year than last year.

10 A We gave Mum a small blue Persian rug for her birthday.
   B We gave Mum a blue small Persian rug for her birthday.
   C We gave Mum a Persian blue small rug for her birthday.

YOUR SCORE

10

TEST 2

Units 6 – 11

A Tick the correct words to complete the sentences.

1 Large crowds of teenagers [ ] was / [ ] were waiting impatiently outside the stadium.

2 [ ] The cows / [ ] The herd remains in the shelter of the barn during the long winter months.

3 The tourists [ ] don't like / [ ] doesn't like spicy food because they are not used to it.

4 [ ] Are / [ ] Is Brenda in charge of the entire project?

5 Does the [ ] antique furniture / [ ] antiques cost a lot of money?

YOUR SCORE / 5

B Fill in the blanks with suitable words in the box. Each word may only be used once.

already accepted	has already accepted	is taking	takes
are enjoying	enjoyed	cheers	cheered
has worked	have worked	mowed	were mowing
have queued	queued	returned	will be returning
is going to study	was going to study	set	will set

1 The crowd _____ excitedly each time the home team scored a goal.

2 The old lady always _____ her dog for a walk in the evenings.

3 Our neighbours _____ their lawn yesterday morning when we passed by.

4 Uncle Jack and his family _____ on the ranch for the last 10 years.

5 The supermarket was crowded and we _____ _____ up for quite a long time to pay the cashier.

6 Our Historical Society _____ off on a trip to the east coast next Friday.

7 She _____ the post of company secretary in a new firm.

8 After the hard work, we _____ a well-earned coffee break now.

9 Karen _____ in the United Kingdom next year.

10 My cousins _____ home next week after a two-week vacation.

YOUR SCORE / 10

C Cross out the incorrect words in the boxes.

1 Active Voice : Mr Wells tuned our piano.
   Passive Voice : Our piano | is | was | tuned by Mr Wells.

2 Passive Voice : New aeroplanes are tested by very skilled pilots.
   Active Voice : Very skilled pilots | are test | test | new aeroplanes.

3 Active Voice : Ken beat last year's squash champion.
   Passive Voice : Last year's squash champion was | beat | beaten | by Ken.

4 Active Voice : The little girl draws delightful pictures.
   Passive Voice : Delightful pictures | are | is | drawn by the little girl.

5 Passive Voice : My jacket was sewn by Kim's mother.
   Active Voice : Kim's mother | sewed | sewn | my jacket.

YOUR SCORE / 5

D Fill in the blanks with the correct question tags.

1 My sister and I look like our mother, _____ ?
2 Colombo is the capital of Sri Lanka, _____ ?
3 Miss Dale lives in that big house, _____ ?
4 I belong to your group, _____ ?
5 The three brothers are talented musicians, _____ ?

YOUR SCORE / 5

E Tick the correct words to complete the wh-questions.

1 When are you | | go | to the art gallery?
              | | going |

2 | | Who | passport is lost?
   | | Whose |

3 | | Why Bill | dislike chess?
   | | Why does Bill |

4 | | What | is Meredith's locker?
   | | Which |

5 How much | | sugar | do you want in your tea?
           | | sugar cubes |

YOUR SCORE / 5

230

F Read the newspaper extract and answer the questions.

Tuesday — Marissa Werner, Switzerland's latest singing sensation, is planning to tour Asia next month to promote her latest album 'Shadows in the day'. Her singing engagements will take her to Singapore, Kuala Lumpur, Bangkok and other Asian capitals.

"We expect thousands to turn up for her concerts," said Robert Newton her manager. "As part of the promotion, we will give each fan attending her concerts a copy of the photo taken when she won last year's 'Songbird of the year' award . . . . "

1 Where does Marissa Werner come from?

_____

_____

2 When is she planning to tour Asia?

_____

_____

3 Why does she want to tour Asia?

_____

_____

4 Who is Marissa's manager?

_____

_____

5 What will each fan at the concerts get?

_____

_____

YOUR SCORE
10

G Underline the correct words in the brackets to complete the passage.

In the 15th century, Malacca **1** (is / was) a busy trading centre. Traders from many countries exchanged **2** (their goods there / there their goods). The kingdom of Malacca **3** (became soon / soon became) rich and strong. **4** (Conquered / It conquered) weaker kingdoms nearby.

Some powerful nations in Europe, however, **5** (to / wanted to) conquer Malacca. Early in the 16th century, the Portuguese heard that Malacca **6** (getting / was getting) weaker because its people **7** (are fighting / were fighting) among themselves. The Portuguese **8** (decided to / to) attack the city. They managed to conquer **9** (in 1511 Malacca / Malacca in 1511). The Sultan of Malacca and his followers **10** (had to / to) retreat to the south.

YOUR SCORE
10

TEST 3

A Fill in the blanks with the correct prepositions in the box.

| above | at | before | behind | between | during | on | past | under |

It is now 4.30 p.m. The boat race began half an hour ago, (1) _____ 4 p.m. (2) _____ the race, two boats ran aground and one capsized. The only teams left in the race now are The Blue Fins and the Titans.

Many people are (3) _____ the bridge with me. They are cheering the teams on as they pass (4) _____ the bridge. Oh, the Blue Fins are moving much faster than the Titans. The Titans are far (5) _____ them . . . Yes, the champions this year are the Blue Fins.

YOUR SCORE
5

B Underline the correct words in the brackets.

1 You may (use / uses) this door to leave the building.
2 (May / Must) he speak so loudly?
3 Richard (can / may) play the saxophone as well as the flute.
4 I must (be / am) home by 6 p.m.
5 This (may be / maybe) the file you are looking for.

YOUR SCORE
5

C Rewrite the passage and put in the missing punctuation marks.

A : Dads silk shirt black jacket and trousers arent in the cupboard did Mum send them to the dry cleaner's.

B : No, theyre over there by the ironing board Sheilas ironing them

_____

_____

_____

_____

_____

_____

YOUR SCORE
5

D Rewrite the sentences in indirect speech.

1 "We didn't see you yesterday." they said to me.

_____

_____

2 I asked Peter, "Are you coming with us?"

_____

_____

3 The nurse said to me, "You have to wait for 10 minutes to see the doctor."

_____

_____

4 Ted said to Gary, "I am taking part in the elocution contest tomorrow."

_____

_____

5 Mum said, "Rita, your room is a mess!"

_____

_____

E Tick the words in the boxes that can fit into the sentences at the places marked 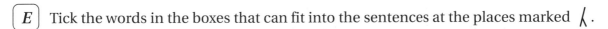.

1 Dad's ready, I'm ready too ⅄ Mum's almost ready but Fay is still dressing.

and		but	

2 The winner is the child ⅄ the spacesuit.
3 We liked Sam's story ⅄ made us laugh.
4 It's raining but I have to go there ⅄ I'll be in trouble.
5 He wants one of those watches that ⅄ funny faces.
6 I love the time ⅄ dawn and sunrise.
7 They live next to a man who ⅄ rabbits.
8 I'll cook or I'll wash the dishes ⅄ I won't do both.
9 He is the fastest runner ⅄ our country has produced.
10 They knew about the money ⅄ her mattress.

in		who in	
which		who	
and		or	
has		have	
between		is between	
rear		rears	
but		or	
that		who	
under		was under	

F Complete the passage with some of the words and phrases in the box. You may use a word or a phrase more than once.

acting	to act	joining	to join	putting	to put
being	to be	pretending	to pretend	what	who

My little brother Bobby enjoys (1) _____ . He enjoys (2) _____
on different costumes and (3) _____ to be different characters. He says he wants
(4) _____ a famous actor one day.

Every evening after dinner, he will ask (5) _____ would like to act with him.
One of us will quickly offer (6) _____ him in his play-acting because we don't want
to hurt his feelings.

Bobby always knows (7) _____ he wants to do. He decides (8) _____ is
to play the hero – he or I. However, Bobby seldom does (9) _____ you expect
him to do. It's hard to guess (10) _____ he considers the hero of the story.
We have taken turns playing some strange heroes!

YOUR SCORE

10

G Circle the letters of the correct sentences. There may be more than one answer for each question.

1 A The windscreen of our car broke while a stone hit it.
   B The windscreen of our car broke when a stone hit it.
   C The windscreen of our car broke because a stone hit it.

2 A My family laughed at me because of my stubbornness.
   B My family laughed at me because of my stubborn.
   C My family laughed at me because I was stubborn.

3 A Water was dripping on his face from a hole in the roof while he snored away.
   B Water was dripping on his face from a hole in the roof while he was snoring away.
   C Water dripped on his face from a hole in the roof while he snored away.

4 A Many people like her because of her wit.
   B Many people like her because she is witty.
   C She is witty because many people like her.

5 A He felt very happy when the plan succeeded.
   B He felt very depressed it's because the plan succeeded.
   C He felt very depressed because of the plan's success.

YOUR SCORE

10

234

TEST 4

A Fill each blank with the most suitable word.

Rowing is a sport that is popular in many parts (1) _____ the world. For some races, a single oar (2) _____ used by each oarsman. The oar has to (3) _____ grasped with both hands. For others, each oarsman (4) _____ two oars.

There are competitions where the crews (5) _____ eight in number and those where just two (6) _____ four oarsmen make up the team. Sometimes there (7) _____ an additional member on the team – a coxswain. (8) _____ duty is not to row but to direct (9) _____ strategy of the team. Seated at the stern (10) _____ the boat, he calls the stroke and tries to steer the team to victory.

YOUR SCORE
10

B Read the passage and answer the questions.

We use buttons to fasten shirts, blouses, jackets and other items of clothing by passing them through buttonholes made in those garments. Buttonholes were invented only in the 13th century. Before that people used buttons together with loops.

Within a century after their invention, buttons became not just useful but also decorative items. Gold, silver and ivory buttons were used to indicate wealth and position. The more common types of buttons were made of bone, pewter and wood. Some manufacturers used fabric to cover the bone and wood.

In the 18th century, Matthew Boulton, an English manufacturer, introduced steel in the production of buttons. In the 19th century, B. Sanders produced buttons made of two metal discs. Fabric covering one disc was held in place by the second disc around the edges.

In later years, other materials came into use as well such as glass, porcelain, papier-mâché and shell. Plastic buttons, so common today, came into use only in the twentieth century. They are produced on a large scale in factories through the use of moulds.

1 What do people use to fasten shirts?

_____

2 When did people use buttons with loops?

_____

3 Which type of buttons showed a person was wealthy or held a high position?

_____

4 Who introduced steel in the manufacture of buttons?

_____

5 Where are plastic buttons produced?

YOUR SCORE
10

_____

$\boxed{C}$ Circle the letters of the correct answers to complete the passage below.

Last week, Mike's class (1) _____ a shoe factory. The factory employs 40 workers (2) _____ do various jobs such as cutting, sewing, glueing and assembling. Working together, (3) _____ usually complete 300 pairs of shoes a day.

The students spent two hours at the factory learning how shoes (4) _____ . According to the factory manager, shoe-making (5) _____ with the design itself. He showed them an (6) _____ design of a woman's shoe and then gave it to a factory worker. (7) _____ worker pasted it on a wooden block (8) _____ was in the shape of a foot. He used the block (9) _____ cut-outs of the different parts of a shoe such as the insole and the upper section. Then he outlined the cut-outs (10) _____ hard paper to finalise their shapes.

Next, the children (11) _____ to a cutting machine. They could (12) _____ stacks of leather pieces beside the machine. A worker took 10 pieces (13) _____ placed a shape on them. The machine cut through the bundle to get 10 identical shapes and the worker smiled and said, "It's very fast, (14) _____ it?"

The factory manager then led the way to the sewing room where workers (15) _____ flowers, buckles or frills onto the shoe uppers. In another part of the factory, they (16) _____ workers glueing and nailing shapes to the insoles and outsoles, and a pressure machine pressing down on the parts of shoes to ensure they had (17) _____ compact shape.

The final part of the shoe-making process (18) _____ the attaching of the heels, and the glueing of the insole lining and label. Mike and his classmates enjoyed themselves tremendously (19) _____ the tour round the factory. The highlight of their visit, however, was when the factory manager got them to design a shoe each on a piece of paper and then got his designers to select (20) _____ design.

1 A visit	**5 A** begin	**9 A** to make
B visits	**B** begins	**B** made
C will visit	**C** began	**C** make
D visited	**D** beginning	**D** making
2 A what	**6 A** interest	**10 A** among
B which	**B** interests	**B** behind
C who	**C** interested	**C** on
D –	**D** interesting	**D** under
3 A they	**7 A** A	**11 A** was taken
B their	**B** An	**B** were taken
C theirs	**C** The	**C** taken
D them	**D** –	**D** taking
4 A are making	**8 A** what	**12 A** see
B made	**B** which	**B** sees
C make	**C** who	**C** saw
D are made	**D** –	**D** seen

13	A	and	16	A	watch	19	A	at
	B	but		B	watches		B	after
	C	because		C	watched		C	in
	D	of		D	watching		D	during

14	A	is	17	A	a	20	A	good
	B	isn't		B	an		B	the best
	C	are		C	the		C	the attractive
	D	aren't		D	–		D	most attractive

15	A	sew	18	A	is
	B	sews		B	are
	C	sewn		C	was
	D	were sewing		D	were

YOUR SCORE
20

D   Rearrange the words to form correct sentences.

1 bookcase — by — designed — grandfather — my — the — was.

_____

_____

2 had — Jim's — not — postcard — received — Ruth — said — she — that.

_____

_____

3 accident — I — man — spoke — the — the — to — who — witnessed.

_____

_____

4 along — coast — don't — old — route — take — the — the.

_____

_____

5 because — decided — employ — good — him — his — of — record — they — to.

_____

_____

YOUR SCORE
10

TEST 5

A Fill each blank with the most suitable word.

Sheep and goats are cud-chewing mammals. Sheep, however, (1) _____ stockier and the males do not have beards. (2) _____ sheep are called rams. Females are called ewes (3) _____ the little ones, lambs. A fully-grown sheep can (4) _____ up to 180 kg.

Sheep are reared for (5) _____ wool, meat and milk. Some breeds produce fine (6) _____ and so are bred for wool production. Sheep (7) _____ give coarse wool are usually raised for mutton (8) _____ milk. The Oxford breed is greatly valued for (9) _____ wool. The Shropshire and Merino breeds are kept (10) _____ their fine mutton and wool.

YOUR SCORE
10

B Read the passage and answer the questions.

It was about six in the morning when Steve and I set out for Wave Rock. It was a long journey for the rock is located about 340 km from Perth. When we arrived about six hours later, many busloads of tourists were already there to view this natural wonder.

Wave Rock is remarkable. Fourteen metres high and 110 metres long, it looks like a huge tidal wave about to crash down to the ground. Its vertical streaks of colour make it look even more like a giant wave.

Steve and I walked some distance along the rock and then Steve decided to climb to the top. He urged me to follow him but I refused because I am afraid of heights. Surprisingly, it didn't take him long to get to the top.

Just as Steve joined me again, we felt some gentle drops of rain. Soon after, there was a heavy downpour. Steve and I didn't run back to our car. Instead, we stood right in front of Wave Rock to watch the rain flow down the concave slope. It looked as if a great wave had come alive.

1 When did the writer and his friend leave for Wave Rock?

_____

_____

2 How far is Wave Rock from Perth?

_____

_____

3 What does Wave Rock look like?

_____

_____

238

4 Why didn't the writer climb to the top of Wave Rock?

_____

_____

5 Where were the writer and his friend when rain flowed down Wave Rock?

_____

_____

C Circle the letters of the correct answers to complete the conversation below.

Reporter : When (1) _____ you leave your banking job to start your own business?

Mr Hall : Six months ago.

Reporter : And in six months you (2) _____ to make your restaurant (3) _____ eatery in town. What is your (4) _____ ?

Mr Hall : I enjoy (5) _____ my customers (6) _____ they want. They come to my restaurant (7) _____ the fresh and nutritious food, the reasonable price and (8) _____ of our premises. In fact, they have my permission (9) _____ our kitchen at any time.

Reporter : I notice your employees work extremely hard (10) _____ they do not look unhappy.

Mr Hall : Well, that's because they _are_ happy. They each (11) _____ a certain percentage of the restaurant. They know that when they work hard for me, they're also helping (12) _____ . I treat them as my family. Whatever remains (13) _____ the buffet table after the lunch hour (14) _____ home by my workers. I make it a rule never (15) _____ leftover food. Our customers get food cooked that very day.

Reporter : You only open for lunch and yet you are able to make a sizeable profit each month. (16) _____ do you explain that?

Mr Hall : It's the variety we offer. We never (17) _____ a dish for a week. As you can (18) _____ , there are 10 varieties of salad here. Today is Tuesday. These salads (19) _____ again until next Tuesday. With such variety, the public (20) _____ to our restaurant every day.

1 A do	**3 A** popular	**5 A** give
B does	**B** popularising	**B** gives
C did	**C** more popular	**C** giving
D doing	**D** the most popular	**D** to give
2 A manage	**4 A** secret	**6 A** that
B manages	**B** secrets	**B** what
C will manage	**C** secretive	**C** which
D have managed	**D** secretively	**D** who

7	A	because	12	A	myself	17	A	repeat
	B	because of		B	ourselves		B	repeated
	C	is because of		C	themselves		C	has repeated
	D	it is because		D	himself		D	repeating

8	A	the cleanliness	13	A	after	18	A	seen
	B	cleanliness		B	among		B	sees
	C	cleaning		C	during		C	see
	D	cleaner		D	on		D	saw

9	A	check	14	A	is taken	19	A	is not served
	B	checks		B	is taking		B	are not served
	C	checked		C	take		C	was not served
	D	to check		D	takes		D	were not served

10	A	because	15	A	refrigerate	20	A	is drawing
	B	but		B	refrigerating		B	is drawn
	C	or		C	to refrigerate		C	draw
	D	–		D	refrigerated		D	draws

11	A	owning	16	A	How
	B	owned		B	What
	C	owns		C	Which
	D	own		D	Why

YOUR SCORE
20

D Rewrite the sentences correctly using the words in the brackets.

1 We watched the boys were carrying ice-skates. (who)

We _____

2 Those are the trucks we passed them on the road just now. (that)

Those _____

3 I'd like to buy the large picture it is in that corner. (which)

I'd _____

4 Tony's house was burgled he is careless. (because of)

Tony's house _____

5 Our great-aunt promising visiting us again in August. (to visit)

Our great-aunt _____

YOUR SCORE
10

TEST 6

A Fill each blank with the most suitable word.

Water can be used in different ways in the preparation of food. Boiling is one way (1) _____ cook food like rice, meat and vegetables. In (2) _____ United States, some communities like (3) _____ boil their vegetables to a soft consistency. It (4) _____ the same with Indian cooking. Vegetables like eggplant (5) _____ pumpkin are boiled till they are soft before (6) _____ are mashed and cooked with spices. In Chinese (7) _____ , however, the emphasis is on minimal boiling of (8) _____ in order to preserve their fresh colour, texture (9) _____ flavour. An added advantage of minimal boiling (10) _____ that less fuel is needed.

B Read the passage and answer the questions.

The Galapagos are a group of several hundred islands in the Pacific Ocean. The islands belong to Ecuador. They are special because of their location. Animals from different parts of the world have been able to find their way to the islands and have settled there, including birds from the Antarctic.

Long ago, when a person visited the islands, he would be able to see wildlife in all its wonderful variety. He would not need to search to find giant tortoises, iguanas and other reptiles, giant albatrosses, pelicans, flamingos and hosts of other birds.

Today, however, the scene is quite different. Much of the wildlife on the islands is in danger of extinction. This is because of the destructive activities of man. Some time back, for instance, hundreds of giant tortoises were taken on board ships by sailors because the reptiles could live for a year without food. They themselves became food for the sailors.

1   Where are the Galapagos islands?

_____

_____

2   Which country do the Galapagos islands belong to?

_____

_____

3   What is special about the Galapagos?

_____

_____

4 Why did sailors take hundreds of the giant tortoises from the islands onto their ships?

_____

_____

5 Who killed the giant tortoises for food?

_____

_____

YOUR SCORE

10

C Circle the letters of the correct answers to complete the letter below.

Dear Editor,

Thank you for (1) _____ article in your newspaper about a programme (2) _____ schoolchildren not to take drugs. I (3) _____ by the efforts of the Life Education Unit. (4) _____ you tell (5) _____ more about this unit, please? According to the article, (6) _____ is part of a worldwide network of centres that (7) _____ preventive drug abuse programmes to children between the ages of five and 15.

I am a teacher (8) _____ I teach children between the ages of 12 and 15. Could you give me the address of the teacher (9) _____ conducted the lesson (10) _____ reporter observed? Her lesson was (11) _____ . She (12) _____ not focus on drugs (13) _____ emphasised how unique each child (14) _____ . She taught the children about the organs of the body and (15) _____ functions. She (16) _____ interesting teaching aids like films and a talking brain! She helped them (17) _____ why they should value their own bodies.

What was truly marvellous was that by the end of the lesson, the children decided that people who took drugs (18) _____ out of their minds. They also made (19) _____ important decision as a group – "We (20) _____ 'NO' to drugs."

1 A a
  B an
  C the
  D –

2 A teach
  B teaches
  C taught
  D to teach

3 A is fascinated
  B was fascinated
  C is fascinating
  D was fascinating

4 A Can
  B Do
  C May
  D Must

5 A I
  B me
  C my
  D mine

6 A its
  B it
  C it's
  D –

7 A has provided
  B are provided
  C is providing
  D provide

8 A and
  B but
  C or
  D –

9 A what
  B which
  C who
  D –

10	A	its	14	A	is	18	A	is
	B	my		B	am		B	are
	C	our		C	are		C	was
	D	your		D	being		D	were

11	A	wonder	15	A	them	19	A	an
	B	wonderful		B	theirs		B	a
	C	more wonderful		C	their		C	the
	D	the most wonderful		D	they		D	–

12	A	do	16	A	had	20	A	saying
	B	doing		B	has		B	says
	C	does		C	having		C	will say
	D	did		D	will have		D	said

13	A	and	17	A	understands
	B	but		B	understanding
	C	because		C	to understand
	D	or		D	were undertood

YOUR SCORE 20

D Rewrite the sentences correctly using the words in the brackets.

1 Rita's ambition becoming a concert pianist. (to become)

_____

_____

2 She practises to play the piano every evening. (playing)

_____

_____

3 She is only 14 years old, has already passed her Grade 8 exam, hope to continue her music education abroad. (and, but)

_____

_____

4 Yesterday, Rita's parents met principal Mr Mark Davies of a music college in Britain. (who)

_____

_____

5 Mr Davies was impressed of Rita had scored distinctions in all her theory and practical exams. (because)

_____

_____

YOUR SCORE 10

ANSWERS

1.1 ARTICLES
Practice A

a

1 conductor
2 flute
3 musician
4 pianist
5 violin

an

1 audience
2 entrance
3 instrument
4 orchestra
5 usher

Practice B

1 an	6 an
2 a	7 an
3 a	8 an
4 an	9 a
5 an	10 a

Practice C

2 We gave Mum an anklet and a bracelet for her birthday.
3 This is an egg, not a ping-pong ball.
4 My cousin is an engineer and his wife is an architect.
5 A pilot flies an aeroplane or a helicopter.
6 Marina lives in a village and Shan lives in a city.

Practice D

1 efficient	5 honourable	8 simple
2 oval	6 orange	9 beautiful
3 unique	7 huge	10 excellent
4 fascinating		

Practice E

1 opal ring	5 explosion	8 attic
2 large octagon	6 express train	9 patient editor
3 meal	7 club	10 address
4 quiet area		

Practice F

1 an	2 a	3 an	4 –	5 a
6 –	7 an	8 a	9 –	10 an

1.2 ARTICLES
Practice A

1 an, The	2 a, The	3 the
4 the, a	5 the, an	6 the

Practice B

1 The wind is blowing gently. [1 mark]
2 Our Sports Day is on the fourth of May. [1 mark]
3 Patrick chopped some firewood with a big axe. He piled the firewood behind his house. [2 marks]
4 I need a taxi because I am going to the train station now. [2 marks]
5 Dina has pictures of an ape and a panda. She likes the picture of the panda. [4 marks]

Practice C

1 a	2 an	3 the	4 a	5 a
6 a	7 a	8 the	9 the	10 the

Practice D

1 a	2 an	3 the	4 The	5 The
6 a	7 the	8 an	9 the	10 the

Practice E

I brought in a contractor to renovate /\ house. He walked around /\ place and turned me down. /\ Second contractor began work on /\ house but never returned after /\ first day. Fortunately for me, /\ third contractor stayed and finished /\ job. He pulled down several walls, he redid /\ staircase and turned /\ patio into an office for me. He was expensive but excellent. As he stood at /\ gleaming white gate he had fixed for me, ready to leave, he waved /\ cheque in his hand and said, "Enjoy your castle."

Practice F

You can make a food cover for picnics using an empty ice-cream container without its lid. You just need to buy a door knob, a washer and a screw. Turn the container upside down and make a small hole in the base of the container. The hole should be at the centre of the base. Place the door knob above the hole and fix it using the washer and the screw. The food cover is ready.

Practice G

1 A	2 B, D	3 B, C	4 A, C	5 B
6 C	7 D			

1.3 ARTICLES
Practice A

1 The Chongqing Tower
2 The Mississippi, America
3 The Republic of Pakistan
4 The Berlin Wall
5 the Prime Minister of Japan
6 Fleet Street
7 The Carribean Sea, the Atlantic Ocean
8 the United Nations

Practice B

1 the, –	2 The, –	3 the, –
4 –, –	5 The, the	

Practice C

/\ Canary Islands, also called /\ Canaries, are part of Spain. They have a mild climate, beautiful scenery and were once called /\ Fortunate Islands. Today holiday makers love to view /\ Maspalomas Dunes, which resemble /\ Sahara Desert. They also visit /\ Canary Islands Museum and learn about /\ history of /\ Canary Islands. There are exhibitions featuring /\ Guanches, who were pre-Spanish inhabitants of /\ islands.

Practice D

1 The manager of the Westin Hotel is an uncle of mine.
2 The River Ganges is in India.
3 The Prime Minister of Australia will visit the Republic of China next year.

244

4 The National Theatre is opposite the fire station on Stamford Road.

5 The Golden Gate Bridge in San Francisco is a popular tourist attraction.

Practice E

1 The	**2** –	**3** the	**4** the	**5** the
6 –	**7** –	**8** –	**9** –	**10** the

Practice F

1 C	**2** C	**3** B, C	**4** C	**5** B
6 A	**7** C	**8** C	**9** A	

1.4 ARTICLES

Practice A

Countable Noun	Uncountable Noun
1 a diskette	**1** aluminium
2 an envelope	**2** cloth
3 a hamburger	**3** music
4 a raincoat	**4** smoke
5 an umbrella	**5** wool

Practice B

1 –	**4** the	**7** an / the	**9** –
2 a	**5** the	**8** a	**10** –
3 –	**6** the		

Practice C

1 paint
2 the furniture, the furniture
3 –, –
4 soup, the soup
5 jam, the jam, a jar of jam

Practice D

2 a, –   **3** –, the   **4** –, The   **5** –, the   **6** an, –

Practice E

As a child, I loved going with my mother to the Indian grocery store in our neighbourhood. There were so many fascinating things in Mr Pandian's shop. There was the flour, the green peas, the red kidney beans, and the chickpeas in open gunny sacks. There was the white sugar in a metal container with the glass in front for easy viewing. On the floor were also large tins of the oil. Containers of the margarine and the ghee filled the lowest shelves.

I do believe Mr Pandian was fond of me for he never said anything whenever I picked up a handful of the rice, held it up in mid-air and let it drizzle back into the sack.

Practice F

2 a bottle of ketchup   **5** a can / tin of milk powder
3 a bowl of porridge   **6** a packet of salt
4 a pail of water

Practice G

Kaolin is a type of clay. It is also known as china clay. It is an essential item in the manufacture of porcelain. We use porcelain to make cups, plates and decorative objects such as figurines.

Kaolin is also used when making paper. The paper is coated with kaolin to make it shiny and more opaque.

2 POSSESSIVES

Practice A

1   3   4   6   8

Practice B

2 Amy's painting won the first prize.
3 My cousin's wife visited me at the hospital.

4 This sheep's tail is very short.
5 These ladies' watches are expensive.
6 The workmen's tools are in the shed.

Practice C

2 the umpire's decision
3 The rooms of this house
4 the brakes of my bicycle
5 my brothers' favourite team
6 the end of the movie
7 Sheila's mother-in-law
8 The soles of my sandals
9 the manager's report
10 The title of your essay
11 my parents' advice

Practice D

(line 1)	Emmas → Emma's
(line 2)	the river's edge → the edge of the river
(line 5)	Bettys → Betty's
(lines 6 – 7)	the huge raintree's trunk → the trunk of the huge raintree
(line 8)	Sam → Sam's
(line 10)	boys → boys'
(line 12)	mens → men's
(line 14)	girls → girls'
(line 15)	Nicks → Nick's
(line 17)	dogs → dog's

Practice E

1 C	**2** B	**3** A, D	**4** B, C	**5** B, C	**6** A, B

3.1 PERSONAL PRONOUNS AS SUBJECTS AND OBJECTS

Practice A

1 it	**2** You	**3** I	**4** She	**5** them
6 her	**7** I	**8** us	**9** We	**10** me

Practice B

1 They are watching him.
2 We saw him there.
3 You and I are late.
4 Dad took her and me swimming.
5 He and I will help them.

Practice C

2 him	**3** She	**4** it	**5** he	**6** her
7 us	**8** We	**9** us	**10** we	**11** them

Practice D

1 Please give George and me your address.
2 Kay ordered roast lamb. It was delicious.
3 Doris and I want to join the Adventure Club.
4 I asked them to finish the work. They refused.
5 She helped me once so now I will help her.

Practice E

1 He	**2** I	**3** it	**4** him	**5** I
6 me / us	**7** you	**8** me	**9** They	**10** I / We

Practice F

1 He	**2** they	**3** them	**4** him	**5** It
6 They	**7** He	**8** we	**9** you	**10** us

3.2 POSSESSIVE ADJECTIVES AND POSSESSIVE PRONOUNS

Practice A

2   3   6   7   10

Practice B
1 The pictures are hers.
2 It's wagging its tail.
3 Your jeans are like his.
4 Their mechanic knows ours.
5 Your kite is flying higher than mine.

Practice C
1	my	**2**	your	**3**	yours	**4**	mine	**5**	its
6	your	**7**	our	**8**	her	**9**	their	**10**	ours

Practice D
1 hers
2 his, mine
3 my, your, hers
4 our, ours, theirs, their

Practice E
1	his	**2**	her	**3**	his	**4**	ours	**5**	his
6	ours	**7**	his	**8**	his	**9**	mine	**10**	Her

Practice F
1	our	**2**	his	**3**	mine	**4**	ours	**5**	my
6	Their	**7**	theirs	**8**	Its	**9**	her	**10**	hers

3.3 DEMONSTRATIVE ADJECTIVES AND DEMONSTRATIVE PRONOUNS
Practice A
1	C	**2**	A	**3**	C	**4**	B	**5**	B
6	A	**7**	B	**8**	C	**9**	A	**10**	B

Practice B
1	Those, This	**2**	that, this	**3**	This, that
4	that, these	**5**	this	**6**	these

Practice C
2 that → those   8 those → these
3 Those → That   10 these → this
6 This → These

Practice D
1	these	**4**	this	**7**	this	**9**	those
2	Those	**5**	That	**8**	these	**10**	Those
3	Those	**6**	that				

3.4 REFLEXIVE PRONOUNS AS OBJECTS
Practice A
1	yourself	**5**	yourselves	**8**	himself
2	himself	**6**	themselves	**9**	ourselves
3	yourself	**7**	itself	**10**	yourselves
4	herself				

Practice B
1 Please make ⁁ comfortable.

2 Mr Morris bought ⁁ a caravan.

3 The elderly woman drove ⁁ to the hospital.

4 I made ⁁ a cup of tea.

5 We served ⁁ at the cafe.

6 They arranged ⁁ in a circle.

7 Help ⁁ to some of the cakes on the tray.

8 The little tiger cub forced ⁁ through the narrow opening in the cave.

9 She made ⁁ ill by forgetting to eat.

10 The boys told ⁁ that they must get up early the next morning.

Practice C
3   4   5   9   10

Practice D
1 He always talks about himself.
2 Enjoy yourselves at the seaside.
3 Challenge yourself to finish the task early.
4 The kitten is cleaning itself.
5 The little girl fed herself.

Practice E
1 Yesterday, the kids dressed themselves for the party. / The kids dressed themselves for the party yesterday.
2 Surprisingly, he behaved himself at the wedding.
3 We made ourselves at home and enjoyed our stay.
4 She told herself not to give up hope.
5 The horse injured itself when it stumbled and fell.

Practice F
1 ourselves → themselves   7 myself → yourself
2 herself → himself   9 themselves → ourselves
3 himself → herself

Practice G
1	ourselves	**5**	itself	**8**	myself
2	herself	**6**	yourself	**9**	yourselves
3	himself	**7**	themselves	**10**	themselves
4	herself				

3.5 REFLEXIVE PRONOUNS FOR EMPHASIS
Practice A
1	B	**2**	C	**3**	A	**4**	B	**5**	C
6	A	**7**	C	**8**	B	**9**	A	**10**	C

Practice B
1	himself	**5**	himself	**8**	myself
2	yourself	**6**	ourselves	**9**	yourselves
3	herself	**7**	herself	**10**	ourselves
4	themselves				

Practice C
1	himself	**5**	herself	**8**	themselves
2	itself	**6**	herself	**9**	herself
3	herself	**7**	ourselves	**10**	themselves
4	ourselves				

Practice D
1	herself	**5**	itself	**8**	yourselves
2	himself	**6**	ourselves	**9**	themselves
3	yourself	**7**	myself	**10**	herself
4	himself				

Practice E
1	ourselves	**5**	himself	**8**	myself
2	himself	**6**	myself	**9**	myself
3	herself	**7**	myself	**10**	ourselves
4	themselves				

Practice F
2 Jennifer ⁁ wrote the story ⁁.

3 They ⁁ built the wall ⁁.

4 Steve ⁁ laid the tiles for the patio ⁁.

5 We ⁁ washed all the curtains ⁁.

6 The children ⁁ grew these vegetables ⁁.

4.1 ADJECTIVES
Practice A
1 special   4 long   6 kind, old
2 heavy   5 bright, spacious 7 hot, cold
3 unusual

Practice B
2 The thirsty horse drank some water.
3 The detective walked into the smoky room.
4 That fearless man saved the baby from the fire.
5 This triangular road sign is new.
6 The naughty puppies chewed our slippers.

Practice C
1 ~~Thrifty~~ James is a thrifty man.
2 I dislike her because ~~bossy~~ she is bossy.
3 I enjoy walking in the ~~quiet~~ park when it is quiet.
4 You ~~busy~~ are always too busy to see me.
5 Tina is cheerful and therefore I enjoy ~~cheerful~~ her company.
6 Please put your dirty clothes into the ~~dirty~~ washing machine.
7 The children ~~impatient~~ were impatient to leave for the picnic.
8 Tony is going to play the ~~jealous~~ role of a jealous character.
9 That inquisitive squirrel is always watching us from its ~~inquisitive~~ tree.
10 The ~~successful~~ police were successful in tracking the robbers to their hideout.

Practice D
1 B   2 B   3 C   4 A   5 C
6 A   7 C   8 B   9 A   10 C

Practice E
1 late   5 bright   8 muddy
2 strong   6 excellent   9 shady
3 thick   7 angry   10 innocent
4 tired

Practice F
2 This report is incomplete.
3 His watch is expensive.
4 That story was awful.
5 My tutor's advice was sound.
6 That chef's apple pies are delicious.

4.2 ADJECTIVES
Practice A
2 N   3 A-N   4 A-S   5 A-N   6 A-S
7 A-C   8 N   9 A-C   10 A-S   11 N

Practice B
1 We need a ∧ cupboard for all these toys.
2 Ruth has to leave for the ∧ embassy now.
3 These tiny ∧ flowers are from my garden.
4 Our ∧ Nepalese guide waved frantically to get Mr Lee's attention.
5 I found a ∧ photo of myself when I was two years old.
6 Tina's Mum bought her a red and black ∧ shawl when she was abroad.
7 I love those miniature ∧ bowls in the shop window.

8 The workers damaged Grandma's ∧ orange sofa while they were moving it onto the lorry.
9 Those ∧ engineers over there are the ones who designed this bridge.
10 That ∧ yellow building is the city's main shopping centre.

Practice C
2   3   5   7   8

Practice D
2 Vicky wants those pink and white / white and pink carnations.
3 Look at this tiny green beetle.
4 I have a huge collection of storybooks.
5 A tall German man came to my school.
6 My friend loves big blue balloons.

Practice E
2 There was a yellow and green / green and yellow snake at the zoo.
3 My neighbour has a big white Swiss clock.
4 The blue and red / red and blue taxis here are very efficient.
5 That tall grey building changed the skyline.
6 We saw some gigantic red apples as big as melons at the trade fair.

Practice F
1 present   5 unusual   8 triangular
2 good   6 cheap   9 tune
3 expensive   7 musical   10 fine
4 bracelet

4.3 ADJECTIVES OF COMPARISON
Practice A
1 heavier   6 faster
2 loveliest   7 slower
3 prettier   8 smarter
4 tastiest   9 most experienced
5 shortest   10 messier

Practice B
2 bigger   7 more patient
3 the most enthusiastic   8 older
4 juicier   9 the loudest
5 the most practical   10 the sweetest
6 taller   11 more delicious

Practice C
2 the shortest   7 plainer than
3 older than   8 curlier than
4 taller than   9 the largest
5 thinner than   10 more fashionable than
6 longer than   11 more cheerful than

Practice D
2 Raoul is the fittest among the athletes.
3 My handwriting is smaller than Mariah's.
4 Mario is more patient than me.
5 Helen is the most creative artist among them.
6 That is the most beautiful fish in the aquarium.

Practice E
1 attractive → more attractive
3 moderner → more modern
4 tastefuller → more tasteful

6 <u>comfortablest</u> → most comfortable

9 <u>lovelier</u> → loveliest

4.4 ADJECTIVES
Practice A
1	moving	5	exciting
2	frightening	6	boring
3	less	7	the best
4	terrified		

8 more
9 pleased
10 thrilling

Practice B
1 worse than 5 worse 8 less
2 the worst 6 the most 9 better than
3 more than 7 the least 10 better than
4 good

Practice C
1 (a) confusing (b) confused
2 (a) tiring (b) tired
3 (a) satisfying (b) satisfied
4 (a) better (b) best
5 (a) worse (b) worst

Practice D
2 <u>terrified</u> → terrifying
3 <u>humiliating</u> → humiliated
5 <u>exhausting</u> → exhausted
7 <u>touched</u> → touching
9 <u>pleased</u> → pleasing

Practice E
1 A, C 2 A, B, C 3 B, C 4 A 5 A, B

Practice F
1 relaxing 5 photocopied 8 damaged
2 completed 6 rented 9 amusing
3 tiring 7 pressed 10 refreshing
4 interesting

4.5 ADJECTIVES OF QUANTITY
Practice A
1 a few 4 A few 7 A little 9 many
2 much 5 many 8 Many 10 A little
3 Much 6 a few

Practice B
1 Many 4 a little 7 much 9 a few
2 some 5 Much 8 some 10 a little
3 many 6 some

Practice C
1 a little 4 some 7 are 9 laughter
2 Many 5 much 8 is 10 dishes
3 a few 6 a little

Practice D
1 errors   6 copper sheets
2 cheese   7 kindness
3 time   8 types of perfume
4 damage   9 clothes
5 oranges   10 cooperation

Practice E
2 5 7 8 9

Practice F
2 They borrowed some equipment from us.
3 A little money is enough to make her happy.

---

4 Please give me some / a little advice on how to study .
5 In November much rain falls in the east coast.
6 There are many mushroom farms on those highlands.

Practice G
1 Some chairs in the hall are broken.
2 There is much traffic on the road.
4 A little baking powder is what you need for the batter.

5.1 ADVERBS OF MANNER
Practice A
1 B 2 A 3 B 4 B 5 A
6 B 7 A 8 B 9 A 10 B

Practice B
1 dangerously 5 confident 8 hard
2 joyful 6 stubbornly 9 tearfully
3 sternly 7 elegant 10 well
4 tired

Practice C
1 The young executive dresses. (beautifully)

2 The firemen dashed into the burning hotel to rescue the trapped children. (bravely)

3 The little girls smiled at us as we entered the house. (cheerfully)

4 The tourist guide spoke and therefore many of us could not hear her. (softly)

5 They danced to welcome the Prime Minister to their village. (gracefully)

6 Mum hugged us when we returned home from our school camp. (lovingly)

7 She gazed at the painting. (admiringly)

8 The hungry children grabbed the cakes. (eagerly)

9 Mark sat in the doctor's waiting room. (listlessly)

10 The archaeologists guarded the entrance to the ruins of an ancient city. (zealously)

Practice D
1 <u>curious</u> → curiously 5 <u>charming</u> → charmingly
2 <u>hardly</u> → hard 7 <u>hopeful</u> → hopefully
3 <u>straightly</u> → straight

Practice E
1 confidently 5 steadily 8 thunderously
2 unexpectedly 6 painfully 9 violently
3 tightly 7 deep 10 fearfully
4 fast

5.2 ADVERBS OF TIME AND PLACE
Practice A
2 3 5 7 9

Practice B
1 I will be in Morocco tomorrow. / Tomorrow I will be in Morocco.
2 Mary played in the badminton finals today. / Today Mary played in the badminton finals.
3 The children stayed indoors during the rain.

4 The repairmen were here an hour ago.

5 Mike and his father left for Singapore yesterday. / Yesterday Mike and his father left for Singapore.

Practice C

1 ⟨The alarm went off⟨.

2 I have ⟨finished my report⟨.

3 The strange man was standing⟨.

4 Please write your name⟨.

5 I'll deliver the parcel⟨.

6 Steve ran⟨and turned off the tap.

7 ⟨I have to go to the dentist's⟨.

Practice D

2 The lioness sleeps beside her cubs ~~beside~~ to protect them against any danger.

3 The rescue helicopter flew over the canyon ~~over~~ to search for the hikers.

4 Cora was recently offered ~~recently~~ a scholarship to study in the UK.

5 The doctor said that Henry's injury ~~yet~~ has not healed yet.

6 I will be meeting ~~tomorrow~~ Robin at the airport tomorrow.

7 Mrs Hall ~~anywhere~~ can't find her dog anywhere.

8 ~~Nowadays~~ Grandma nowadays doesn't travel a lot .

9 ~~Everywhere~~ Ben looked everywhere for his missing wallet.

10 They parked ~~nearby~~ the car nearby and walked to the restaurant.

11 We ~~already~~ have already spoken to the manager about the anti-smoking campaign.

Practice E

1 I am going to the bank to cash my cheque today. / I am going to the bank today to cash my cheque.

2 Nina came here last night to return my book. / Last night Nina came here to return my book.

3 She just called me at home to discuss the committee meeting. / She called me at home just to discuss the committee meeting.

4 We drove downtown to look in the shops there yesterday. / We drove downtown yesterday to look in the shops there.

5 The game is about to begin so the spectators are going inside now.

Practice F

2 We reached the village soon. / Soon we reached the village. / We soon reached the village.

3 Uncle Bob lives in an apartment now. / Now Uncle Bob lives in an apartment. / Uncle Bob now lives in an apartment.

4 I searched the room but my diary was not there.

5 Kevin has already booked the tickets for the show.

6 A hot-air balloon flew overhead.

Practice G

2 everywhere	**6** nowhere	**9** Soon
3 downstairs	**7** late	**10** Suddenly
4 upstairs	**8** there	**11** Immediately
5 out		

5.3 ADVERBS OF COMPARISON

Practice A

2 soonest
3 most courteously
4 more widely
5 more badly
6 most sweetly
7 most briskly
8 more
9 more cautiously
10 less
11 most easily

Practice B

1 the most dearly
2 thoroughly
3 well
4 more often
5 the hardest
6 the best
7 patiently
8 gently
9 remarkably
10 the most terribly

Practice C

1 earliest
2 prettiest
3 more gracefully
4 least nervous
5 radiantly
6 calmer / more composed
7 better
8 more dearly
9 more emotional
10 more composed / calmer

Practice D

2 less → least
3 badly → worse
4 the most → more
5 harder → the hardest
6 efficient → efficiently

Practice E

2 Among his classmates, Johan speaks the most clearly. / Johan speaks the most clearly among his classmates.

3 Susan dresses more smartly than her sister.

4 Richard runs the most swiftly among us. / Among us, Richard runs the most swiftly.

5 Mimi goes to school earlier than me. / Mimi goes earlier than me to school.

6 Celine exercises more regularly than her husband.

6.1 SUBJECT–VERB AGREEMENT

Practice A

2 3 6 7 8

Practice B

1 exercises **4** likes **7** visit **9** grow
2 rains **5** are **8** works **10** play
3 is **6** need

Practice C

1 is **5** were **8** returns
2 participates **6** intend **9** causes
3 is **7** does **10** works
4 have

Practice D

2 require → requires **9** are → is
4 roams → roam **10** was → were
5 make → makes

Practice E

1 B **2** A **3** B, C **4** A, C **5** B, C **6** A, C

Practice F

Strong winds and rain wear down rocks and reduce them to gravel. When rain falls on the bare earth, it carries the gravel into streams and rivers. As a river meanders, the gravel cuts the sides of the riverbank. This causes the river to widen. We call this process 'Erosion'.

6.2 SUBJECT–VERB AGREEMENT

Practice A

1	weren't	5	don't carry	8	doesn't speak
2	don't live	6	wasn't	9	aren't
3	doesn't watch	7	isn't	10	don't have
4	aren't				

Practice B

2 They aren't / are not working on the project now.
3 I / We don't / do not know that the concert is on tonight.
4 Bill doesn't / does not like the way she sings.
5 The players don't / do not need more refreshments.
6 The secretaries aren't / are not interested in the lunchtime fashion show.

Practice C

2	weren't	7	isn't
3	don't like	8	don't have
4	isn't	9	wasn't
5	doesn't want	10	isn't conducting
6	aren't	11	doesn't drive

Practice D

2 He isn't.
3 He doesn't like to take part in tournaments.
4 I'm not good in competitions.
5 They aren't better than you. / They're not better than you.
6 They're confident but I'm not.

Practice E

1	isn't	6	doesn't believe
2	doesn't have	7	aren't
3	doesn't play	8	don't understand
4	doesn't have	9	aren't
5	doesn't like	10	don't worry

Practice F

1 aren't → isn't
2 isn't → aren't
6 doesn't have → don't have
9 doesn't remembered → doesn't remember
10 were → was

6.3 SUBJECT–VERB AGREEMENT

Practice A

1	Does, enjoy	2	Are	3	Does, have
4	Is	5	Do, have	6	Do, have

Practice B

1	Eric and Paul	6	your brother
2	you	7	the committee members
3	that band	8	these suitcases
4	it	9	we
5	I	10	the parade

Practice C

2 Do your cousins have pets?
3 Does Joe cut the grass himself?
4 Is Jerry a member of the chess club?
5 Do Harry and Vanessa like fruit cake?
6 Are the children in the park?

Practice D

1	Do	2	Do	3	Do	4	Is	5	Am
6	Do	7	Are	8	Are	9	Is	10	Does

Practice E

2 Is this their first visit to Paris?
3 Are there many good restaurants in this area?
4 Do Ken and Eva own a bakery?
5 Does Anita have a college degree?
6 Do those factories observe laws on the environment?

Practice F

1	Do, know	5	Are	8	Am
2	Is	6	Do, think	9	Do, realise
3	Does, treat	7	Is	10	Are
4	Do, watch				

7.1 PRESENT TENSE

Practice A

1	is waiting	6	are chasing
2	is baking	7	is celebrating
3	are flying	8	produce
4	visits	9	listen
5	goes	10	comes

Practice B

2	is	7	is sitting
3	are	8	are watching
4	wake	9	are learning
5	jog	10	are swimming
6	am sitting	11	think

Practice C

1	use	4	go	7	traps	9	provides
2	occur	5	absorbs	8	make	10	escape
3	takes	6	obtain				

Practice D

1	need	6	require
2	am typing	7	have
3	is	8	are coming
4	are organising	9	think
5	is finishing	10	have

Practice E

1 is working → works
3 is driving → drives
6 go → am going
8 talk → talks
10 are hurry → are hurrying

Practice F

1	leads	6	tell
2	takes	7	is attending
3	records	8	is flying
4	puts	9	is covering
5	sees	10	hopes

7.2 SIMPLE PAST TENSE

Practice A

2	cut	6	heard	9	assembled
3	slipped	7	listen	10	goes
4	live	8	put	11	were
5	dried				

Practice B

2	left	6	piled	9	were
3	unpacked	7	built	10	caught
4	pitched	8	spent	11	grilled
5	trekked				

Practice C

1	woke	5	knew	8	tied
2	jumped	6	threw	9	grabbed
3	ran	7	caught	10	managed
4	saw				

Practice D

1	forgot	5	brings	8	lets
2	scrub	6	springs	9	sinks
3	glitters	7	spoke	10	are weeping
4	have				

Practice E

He <u>stretched</u> his arms sideways, <u>pulled</u> his shoulders straight and <u>breathed</u> in deeply. He <u>raised</u> himself up on his toes and <u>lowered</u> his body slowly. Then he <u>moved</u> his arms to a vertical position and <u>squatted</u> down as he <u>exhaled</u>. Dad <u>continued</u> this routine for 15 minutes before he <u>came</u> in for a cup of hot coffee.

Practice F

1	tidied	6	had
2	refuse	7	am begging
3	are	8	am typing
4	spent	9	try
5	didn't / did not bother	10	succeed

7.3 PAST CONTINUOUS TENSE

Practice A

2	walked	7	tied
3	went	8	were trembling
4	was counting	9	were waiting
5	shouted	10	were leaving
6	pointed	11	came

Practice B

1	was working	5	was baking
2	was sewing	6	were painting
3	forgot	7	fried
4	was sleeping, broke	8	was getting, knocked

Practice C

1 was getting
2 was muttering / muttered
3 was searching / searched
4 strolled
5 was rummaging / rummaged
6 offered
7 was stirring / stirred
8 was chopping / chopped
9 was simmering
10 laid

Practice D

2 <u>was coming</u> → came
4 <u>shopped</u> → was shopping
6 <u>waited</u> → were waiting
8 <u>get</u> → got
9 <u>roamed</u> → were roaming

Practice E

1 B, D	2 A, C	3 B, D	4 C, D	5 A, B

7.4 PRESENT PERFECT TENSE

Practice A

1 4 5 7 9

Practice B

2	has hung	7	have invited
3	washed	8	has baked
4	polished	9	have bought
5	decorated	10	has tied
6	drew	11	have even made

Practice C

1	faced	6	had
2	enrolled	7	were always
3	were	8	already discovered
4	experienced	9	had
5	do	10	never wake up

Practice D

1 Adam has already completed his 'A' levels.
2 Joyce has enrolled in a college.
3 Tina has applied for several jobs.
4 I have seen some interesting advertisements.
5 Tim has decided to work in a bank.

Practice E

2	have been	6	went	9	dared
3	have visited	7	sailed	10	screamed
4	have met	8	realised	11	rode
5	have seen				

Practice F

1 <u>has joined</u> → joined
2 <u>has announcing</u> → has announced
3 <u>already contributed</u> → has already contributed
4 <u>gets</u> → has got
5 <u>have fell</u> → have fallen

7.5 SIMPLE FUTURE TENSE

Practice A

1	is going to visit	6	will join
2	drew	7	has taken
3	are going to donate	8	are going to attend
4	will build	9	migrate
5	has bought	10	is learning

Practice B

2	ended	7	have been
3	shall / will clean	8	prepared
4	took	9	washes
5	has met	10	attacked
6	arrived	11	will be

Practice C

1	will	4	are going	7	cleaning	9	put
2	helped	5	sweeping	8	will	10	collecting
3	carry	6	use				

Practice D

1	will be	5	will hire	8	will have
2	have got	6	will look	9	will ask
3	will make	7	have come	10	has managed
4	will remember				

Practice E

3 <u>will followed</u> → will follow
4 <u>will being</u> → will be
5 <u>will angry</u> → will be angry
8 <u>talk</u> → will talk
10 <u>are going to fallen</u> → are going to fall

Practice F

2 I am going to exercise at the gym.
3 I will take Grandpa to the dental clinic.
4 Yes, Sandra, I am going to post a parcel today.
5 I will leave for New York on 24th May.
6 I will give you a lift to the train station.

7.6 FUTURE CONTINUOUS TENSE

Practice A

1	will be sitting	6	will believe
2	chopped	7	will be getting married
3	will be touring	8	will be enrolling
4	will be moving	9	will know
5	wish	10	will be cheering

Practice B

1	will be	4	will be	7	will be	9	will
2	will	5	will	8	will be	10	will
3	will	6	will be				

Practice C

2 They will be disappointed to hear that we are not going fishing with them.
3 She will be arranging accommodation for the team in Sydney.
4 The girls will be decorating the stage at 5 p.m. today.
5 The pub will be holding a karaoke contest on Saturday night.
6 We will remember to call you tomorrow regarding the schedule.

Practice D

2 will be staying
3 has already made
4 will contact / will be contacting
5 have checked
6 will be
7 have not seen
8 will have
9 will be
10 will fly / will be flying
11 will be

Practice E

1	will be sponsoring	6	will be
2	are going to leave	7	have already cleared
3	has struggled	8	has drawn
4	will be interviewing	9	will be setting up
5	were going to reveal	10	will be thronging

Practice F

2	will be staying	7	will be shopping
3	will join	8	will relax
4	will be sitting	9	will participate
5	will go	10	will have
6	will be touring	11	will watch

8.1 ACTIVE AND PASSIVE VOICE

Practice A

1	loves	5	was taken	8	flew
2	fed	6	was looked after	9	are heard
3	found	7	encouraged	10	joins
4	carried				

Practice B

1 The driver locked the car.
2 The door was opened by Jill.
3 Mr Lim's dog chased me.

4 The floor is mopped by the maid.
5 Many diseases are caused by germs.

Practice C

1	were	5	missed	8	attend
2	worn	6	saw	9	fear
3	rocked	7	forgot	10	weaves
4	are				

Practice D

3 5 6 8 9

Practice E

1 My father received a letter yesterday.
2 A treasure hunt is organised by the Rotary Club twice a year.
3 Your torn sock was mended by Mum this morning.
4 The little boy's nails are trimmed by his sister every month.
5 The rice was fried by the chef himself.

Practice F

1	joined	5	exchanged	8	entertained
2	borrows	6	thrilled	9	acted
3	are	7	am	10	is
4	enjoy				

8.2 ACTIVE AND PASSIVE VOICE

Practice A

1	C	2	A	3	B	4	A	5	C
6	B	7	A	8	C	9	A	10	B

Practice B

3 4 7 9 10

Practice C

1 Those words were said by a wise man.
2 The boys spun their tops on the ground.
3 The couple was robbed by two armed men.
4 The freshest fish is sold by the fishermen themselves.
5 She knows the scientific names of many flowers.

Practice D

1 The rules are ~~explain by the discipline master very clearly.~~ → The rules are explained by the discipline master very clearly.
2 Once in a while a rule is ~~broke by a novice.~~ → Once in a while a rule is broken by a novice.
3 A novice who keeps breaking rules ~~are punished by the discipline master.~~ → A novice who keeps breaking rules is punished by the discipline master.
4 Some years ago two monks ~~are sent by the monastery to attend a counselling course.~~ → Some years ago two monks were sent by the monastery to attend a counselling course.
5 In this way the novices ~~were given a chance to learn self-discipline.~~ → In this way the novices are given a chance to learn self-discipline.

Practice E

1 I was stung by a bee this morning.
2 That pedestrian crossing is used by commuters every day.
3 Three concerts are held by the music centre every year.
4 Adam was chosen by the players to be their captain.
5 Asian art is enjoyed by many Europeans.

252

9 SUBJECT AND PREDICATE

Practice A
2 is too expensive.
3 can return to our rooms.
4 like to grow flowers.
5 are going to a party tonight.
6 is to be a pilot.
7 prepares his own breakfast every day.
8 shed their leaves in autumn.
9 was last Saturday.
10 may win the spelling competition.
11 always make us laugh with your stories.

Practice B
1 B, C   2 A, C   3 A, C   4 B, C   5 A, B

Practice C
1 The teachers are marking our test papers in the staffroom.
2 Grandpa was a fine athlete in his youth.
3 All employees are to assemble in front of the building at once.
4 The children decorated their kindergarten beautifully.
5 She will be our guide on this tour.
6 One of the scenes in the movie is very frightening.
7 The little boy greeted his aunt with a cheeky smile.
8 He will be attending a meeting in Hawaii.
9 Mrs Lee made pineapple jam for her family.
10 Good managers have to be firm and fair to everyone.

Practice D
1 Christine is drinking green tea.
2 You have to come now.
3 She is a very good doctor.
4 The pupils cleaned the classroom.
5 She may take her sister there.

Practice E
1 is raining
2 rained yesterday
3 its banks soon
4 need to
5 to
6 a problem here
7 rises
8 have to
9 our crops badly
10 want to

Practice F
1 I sitting quietly on the beach. → I am sitting quietly on the beach.
2 Offered to wash our car. → They offered to wash our car.
3 He does twice a week his laundry. → He does his laundry twice a week.
4 Driving me crazy the noise. → The noise is driving me crazy.
5 We plan hold a party next Saturday. → We plan to hold a party next Saturday.

10 QUESTIONS TAGS

Practice A
1 aren't you
2 don't we
3 isn't it
4 doesn't he
5 aren't they
6 don't you
7 isn't it
8 doesn't she
9 don't they
10 aren't I

Practice B
1 B, C   2 B, C   3 A, B   4 A, C   5 A, C

Practice C
1 It's hot, isn't it?

2 Cats like fish, don't they?
3 Tim works here, doesn't he?
4 You and I are going, aren't we?
5 This piano costs a lot, doesn't it?

Practice D
2 don't → doesn't
3 lives → live
4 that → it
5 am → are
6 aren't → don't

Practice E
1 Monaco is just 1.5 square km in area, isn't it?
2 Canada and the United States grow wheat, don't they?
3 Raisins and currants are dried grapes, aren't they?
4 You do have my book 'Robinson Crusoe', don't you?
5 Your brother likes the cartoon character in this book, doesn't he?

Practice F
1 She, isn't
2 I, aren't
3 she, they
4 doesn't it
5 are, they
6 don't I
7 He, doesn't
8 is, isn't
9 don't they
10 are, you

Practice G
1 This party is really enjoyable, isn't it?
2 The desserts are delicious, aren't they?
3 You know how to spoil my fun, don't you?
4 He is wearing your favourite shirt, isn't he?
5 But it looks even better on me, doesn't it?
6 You and I argue a lot, don't we?
7 Our arguments make life interesting, don't they?
8 You are staying till the end of the party, aren't you?
9 Our hostess wants you to play the piano for the dance, doesn't she?
10 I am important, aren't I?

11.1 WH-QUESTIONS

Practice A
2 Why is your brother so happy today?
3 What is Kim's occupation?
4 How is your backache now?
5 When is Anne's flight?
6 Which is your suitcase?

Practice B
2 How fast does that fighter jet ⌃?
3 Where ⌃ the headquarters of the United Nations?
4 What ⌃ the old name for Istanbul?
5 Who ⌃ helping you with the housework?
6 Why ⌃ Steve look so pleased?
7 How many seats ⌃ there in this auditorium?
8 Which country ⌃ that tourist come from?
9 How much money did the thief ⌃?
10 When ⌃ Nelson Mandela become the President of South Africa?
11 Why did the Europeans ⌃ to the Americas in the fifteenth century?

Practice C

1 want	4 know	7 read	9 ask
2 take	5 find	8 get	10 have
3 chew	6 leave		

Practice D

1 A	2 A	3 B	4 A	5 B
6 B	7 A	8 B	9 A	10 B

Practice E

1 Which is	6 is going
2 How did you go	7 Why didn't, tell
3 Why was Kevin	8 When are
4 Whose house has	9 didn't sit
5 What didn't, bring	10 are you cooking

Practice F

3 Where did Joe buy that shirt?
5 Which classes are decorating the hall now?
6 How does this machine work?

11.2 WH-QUESTIONS

Practice A

1 is	6 requires
2 are	7 was delivering
3 were	8 is using
4 was	9 wishes
5 doesn't study	10 didn't understand

Practice B

1 is, was
2 are, were
3 thinks, doesn't think
4 wore, was wearing
5 locks, didn't lock

Practice C

2 has	7 were
3 is burning	8 doesn't know
4 are	9 collects
5 intends	10 is helping
6 didn't attempt	11 needs

Practice D

2 Who was the person you spoke to just now?
3 Who prefers tennis to badminton?
4 Who doesn't like to travel anywhere by train?
5 Who is coaching the boys now for the football tournament?
6 Who doesn't take take sugar in her coffee?

Practice E

1 B	2 B	3 A	4 A	5 A
6 B	7 A	8 B	9 A	10 B

Practice F

2 Who are those children?
3 Who does not have a sheet of drawing paper?
4 Who is using my camera?
5 Who doesn't need a dictionary?
6 Who has the box of slides?

11.3 WH-QUESTIONS

Practice A

1 What	2 What	3 Who	4 What	5 Who
6 Who	7 What	8 What	9 Who	10 Who

Practice B

1 are	2 does	3 keeps	4 play	5 are
6 were	7 is	8 grows	9 was	10 do

Practice C

1 A: What goes	B: What do
2 A: What are	B: What do
3 A: What does	B: What is
4 A: What soap is	B: What soap does
5 A: What makes	B: What is

Practice D

1 causes
2 are these?
3 is
4 does Sheila want?
5 were you saying
6 do they grow?
7 has legs
8 does Jenny use?
9 is Anne serving for dessert?
10 instrument measures the temperature of our bodies?

Practice E

2 What is the baby drinking?
3 What irritates your sister?
4 What films do you like?
5 What colour is your room?
6 What did Bill hide behind that cupboard?

Practice F

2 What gives my grandfather a headache?
3 Who is going to the airport to meet Aunt Ruth?
4 What sandwiches does Sheila recommend?
5 Who informed the landlord about the rodent problem?
6 What did Clarence use to remove paint from the brushes?

11.4 WH-QUESTIONS

Practice A

1 has	6 They
2 are	7 gets
3 He	8 us
4 were helping	9 They are making
5 me	10 Heavy rain caused the landslide

Practice B

1 My core subjects are Science and English. / They are Science and English. / Science and English are my core subjects.
2 Mrs Tanner brought me home.
3 They are children's magazines.
4 Anna and Laila were practising with me.
5 He is pointing to something strange in the sky.

Practice C

2 Mrs Rama works in a hospital.
3 He is Mr Watson.
4 My favourite game is soccer. / Soccer is my favourite game.
5 He is drawing a village scene.
6 Joe is printing the cards.

Practice D

1 B	2 B	3 B, C	4 C
5 A	6 A, C	7 B	8 A

11.5 WH-QUESTIONS

Practice A

1 does, do	2 What, He	3 like, I
4 don't, don't	5 Who, don't	

Practice B

1 I keep	2 He employed	3 don't know
4 She likes	5 We, want	

Practice C

1 does, me	4 refuse, refused
2 does, has	5 vote, They
3 play, don't	

Practice D

2 Susan doesn't play hockey.
3 It doesn't like sardines.
4 They want a two-storey house.
5 I want to speak to Trisha.
6 My uncle did the landscaping of my garden.

Practice E

3 Who didn't understand the instructions?
4 What didn't Steve understand?
5 What don't they have?
6 What did you hand over to the police?
7 Who did you hand over the wallet to?

Practice F

1 Michiyo does the cooking.
2 She speaks English, French and Hindi.
3 Indra and Carol do the cleaning and washing up.
4 They don't have a car. / cars.
5 Indra and Michiyo don't speak Italian.

11.6 WH-QUESTIONS

Practice A

1   2   4   7   8

Practice B

2 He bought it
3 I will stay
4 We are going on a picnic
5 I buy them
6 They will finish painting the boat / it

Practice C

2 When are you going for a medical check-up?
3 When did James learn all about house-building?
4 Where do Stan and Shirley usually go for lunch?
5 Where are we hiding the presents?
6 When will the elections results be out?

Practice D

1 Who is Joe taking to the museum tomorrow?
2 Where is Joe taking his nieces tomorrow?
3 When is Joe taking his nieces to the museum?
4 What will Carol and Pam do at the Raintree Sports Club in August?
5 When will Carol and Pam take part in a tennis tournament at the Raintree Sports Club?

Practice E

2 Where did John fall over?
3 When is the doctor coming?
4 Where does John keep his medicine?
5 When will Sheila bring a wheelchair?
6 When do you have to fetch the children?

Practice F

1 Dr Conway's talk on 'How to lose weight permanently' is on 7th October. / It is at 7.30 p.m. on 7th October.
2 He will give his talk at the Mayfair Hotel.
3 Dr Conway has written many books on health.
4 The title of Dr Conway's latest book / It is 'Eat and Be Happy'.
5 Dr Conway's latest book / His latest book / It will be available to the public in December.

11.7 WH-QUESTIONS

Practice A

1 Which	4 Whose	7 Which	9 Which
2 Whose	5 Which	8 Which	10 Whose
3 Whose	6 Whose		

Practice B

1 my	4 lose, lost
2 Jean's computer	5 restaurant is, is
3 are we taking	6 do, want, want

Practice C

1 Sharon's team lost in the netball finals.
2 I go to Dr Leo.
3 Our house is more suitable for the meetings.
4 Bill / He is buying that washing machine.
5 They liked both Mary's and Jan's fruit cakes.

Practice D

2 Whose uniform is torn?
3 Which room is messy?
4 Whose office caught fire last night?
5 Which department store do you shop at?
6 Whose uncle is the new manager?

Practice E

1 Mr Parry's dog began to bark fiercely.
2 They were climbing over the front gate.
3 He ran to his parents' room.
4 They placed the heavy study table against the door.
5 They tried to use the back door to escape.

11.8 WH-QUESTIONS

Practice A

1 How tall	5 How many	8 How many
2 How much	6 How much	9 How much
3 How many	7 How many	10 How many
4 How much		

Practice B

1 How many	5 How many	8 How old
2 How many	6 How much	9 How far
3 How many	7 How much	10 How much
4 How much		

Practice C

1 (a) A	2 (a) C	3 (a) B	4 (a) B	5 (a) A
(b) C	(b) A	(b) C	(b) C	(b) B

Practice D

1 How long is the journey?
2 How much do these boots cost?
3 How many people like classical music?
4 How far is Paris / London from London / Paris?
5 How many postcards did James receive?

Practice E

1 How many glasses did Anita break just now?
2 Who broke nine glasses just now?
3 How much is this brush?
4 How many brushes do you want?
5 How old is your dog Pinto?

11.9 WH-QUESTIONS

Practice A

1 Whose	5 Which	8 Why
2 Why	6 How much	9 How many
3 How	7 When	10 Which
4 Why		

Practice B

1	is	5	does	8	isn't John
2	grumbling	6	weren't	9	are the children
3	didn't	7	answer	10	did they want
4	running				

Practice C

1 Why is this letter important?
2 Why did the policeman stop that motorist?
3 Why is she in such a good mood?
4 Why are those men working in the rain?
5 Why are you leaving so soon?

Practice D

1 Why is this cup chipped?
2 Why did you switch the TV channel just now?
3 Why are / were all the cupboards empty?
4 Why is / was he sleeping in the spare bed room?
5 Why do the police want us to leave the building now?

Practice E

2 Why do they play badminton twice a week?
3 Why is Tom climbing up the tree?
4 Why are the dogs barking?
5 Why is Eric's leg in a plaster cast?
6 Why did Mrs Lee ask the store to give her a refund?

Practice F

1 Why was your father so pleased?
2 Why aren't they coming with us?
3 Why does Maureen disbelieve you?
4 Why are your clothes behind the kitchen door?
5 Why was the policeman standing outside Gary's gate?

12.1 MODALS

Practice A

1	Can	4	climb	7	pay	9	rest
2	Can we	5	play	8	May we	10	I be
3	be	6	Can				

Practice B

1 Can we take you home?
2 You may park there.
3 May I help you sweep?
4 My aunt can make clothes.
5 Can I be your partner?

Practice C

1	Can	4	can	7	can	9	Can
2	may	5	Maybe	8	occupy	10	take
3	shoot	6	tape				

Practice D

2   3   5   6   8

Practice E

A   B   C   F   H

1 – You can leave	2 – Can you stop
3 – May I ask	4 – I may be rushing
5 – it may go	

Practice F

1	can	6	see
2	I	7	may
3	commend / congratulate	8	we
4	have	9	may / could
5	be	10	can

Practice G

2 A, C   3 A, B, C   4 A, C   5 A, B   6 B

12.2 MODALS

Practice A

2   5   6   7   8

Practice B

1 Must you go now?
2 I must call my mother.
3 Grandpa must be asleep.
4 Must we report all accidents?
5 Your driving instructor must be good.

Practice C

1 She must listen to her mother's advice.
2 Those children must use the pedestrian crossing.
3 The top student in this class must be Kellie.
4 Must I finish this work today?
5 Must they talk about football all the time?

Practice D

1	be	4	Must we	7	be	9	complete
2	Must I	5	admire	8	have	10	take
3	wear	6	hurry				

Practice E

1	wash	4	keep	7	bow	9	like
2	be	5	make	8	take	10	walk
3	pay	6	have				

Practice F

1 You must forgives me for writing this note. → You must forgive me for writing this note.

2 First, I must telling you that you are a good neighbour. → First, I must tell you that you are a good neighbour.

3 Must your son really practised his trumpet day and night? → Must your son really practise his trumpet day and night?

4 There's a regulation that the neighbourhood must being quite at night. → There's a regulation that the neighbourhood must be quite at night.

5 Besides, you must knew that the notes your son plays can't be called music yet. → Besides, you must know that the notes your son plays can't be called music yet.

Practice G

2	help	5	ask	8	want	10	be
3	tell	6	dress	9	make	11	use
4	put	7	wear				

13.1 PREPOSITIONS OF POSITION

Practice A

1	your head	6	the hall
2	her grandchildren	7	the surface of the water
3	the door	8	the wall
4	the bed	9	the plates
5	a clinic and a cafe	10	a bridge

Practice B

1	behind	5	below	8	between
2	under	6	among	9	beside
3	above	7	at the back of	10	on
4	at the back of				

Practice C

1	beside	5	on	8	among
2	behind	6	at the back of	9	above
3	behind	7	under	10	below
4	between				

13.2 PREPOSITIONS OF TIME
Practice A
1 C, D   **2** A, B, C   **3** B   **4** D   **5** A, B, C

Practice B
A 2   B 9   C 6   D 5   E 3
F 7   G 10   H 4   I 1   J 8

Practice C
2 We arrived in Paris at midnight.
3 My family stayed on a farm during summer. / A family stayed on my farm during summer.
4 All entries must reach our office by 20th May.
5 It was 20 minutes past two when the police arrived.
6 The terrorists surrendered at exactly seven minutes to noon.

Practice D
1 (a) after   (b) before
2 (a) by   (b) before
3 (a) after   (b) during
4 (a) in   (b) on
5 (a) to   (b) past

14 PUNCTUATION
Practice A
2   3   5   6   8

Practice B
1 Is Jenny good at cooking ⁄   ` ? `
2 I received a book ⁄ a racquet and a kite for Christmas.   ` , `
3 The museum is further down this road ⁄   ` . `
4 Quick ⁄ Use the fire extinguisher!   ` ! `
5 This apartment has good lighting, modern furniture ⁄ a lovely view of the beach.   ` and `

Practice C
1 I wasn't at my grandfather's house yesterday.
2 Her car's at the workshop.
3 You don't have another dollar, do you?
4 Peter's brother won't be coming home this summer.
5 He's ordering two cups of tea, some scones and half a dozen sandwiches.

Practice D
2 You mustn't enter the pool after 7 p.m.
3 Jane's the captain of our hockey team.
4 I haven't got the keys to the store.
5 They're definitely worth more than 200 dollars.
6 Mrs Baker won't be discharged from hospital today.

Practice E
(line 2)   kitchens → kitchen's
(line 4)   blue → blue,
(line 6)   wasn't → wasn't
(line 9)   it → it?
(line 11)   goodness → goodness!

15.1 DIRECT SPEECH
Practice A
1   4   6   7   10

Practice B
2 Gwen said, "I live in Milan."
3 The principal said to Mrs Ross, "Why are the students so noisy?"

4 Mrs Ross answered, "There is a mouse under my table!" / ."
5 The manager asked his secretary, "Who called just now?"
6 The secretary said, "The bank manager called to invite you for lunch."

Practice C
1 D   **2** A   **3** B   **4** B
5 C   **6** A, C   **7** B, D   **8** C

Practice D
1 The cashier said to me, "Are you paying cash?"
2 The director said to us, "Our science exhibition is going to be in October."
3 The butcher said to Nelly, "Which cut of lamb do you want?"
4 "I'm not going to school today," said little Su Lin to her mother.
5 The police officer said to my father, "You were driving at 120 km per hour."

Practice E
1 "Why is the bus so late today?" Lyn said to me.
"We will be late for college if the bus doesn't come in another 10 minutes," I said.
2 Mr Williams said to his personal secretary, "Please cancel all my meetings today as I don't feel well."
Miss Cross said to him, "Can I get some medication for you?"
3 "Has anyone seen my house keys?" said Mum.
"I saw them near the kitchen sink," said my brother Kevin.
4 "That man took my purse!" shouted the young woman.
"Where did you put your purse, Madam?" the security guard asked her.
5 "I'm very pleased with your term results," said Dad to me.
"Thanks, Dad. Do you think I can have a raise in my allowance?" I said to him.

15.2 INDIRECT SPEECH
Practice A
2 Mrs Pinto said that she would be at a staff meeting the following day.
3 Mrs Lea said that Malaysia has a tropical climate.
4 Mr Lopez said that Raj had left for Singapore the previous week.
5 Lynn said that she had already seen the movie.
6 Adam and Aaron said that they had bought some new tapes at the sale.

Practice B
1 Jean said to me, "I am not well."
2 Mr Clive said, "I am flying back to England next week."
3 Mark said, "I have a plan for our vacation."
4 I said to Dad, "Where are you going?"
5 Our neighbour said to us, "I have finished writing my first novel."

Practice C
1 John told me that he is going for rugby practice and he would come back late. → was
2 Mum told me that she was cooking your favourite chicken stew that day. → my
3 Our neighbours told us that they have already watched that movie. → had
4 My friend Linda told me that she will be going to Canada for further education. → would
5 Gloria told her friends that they are all welcome to her party. → were

Practice D

2 Sandra said to her little boys, "Don't / Do not disturb your father as he is tired."

3 We said, "Uncle Raj, we are unable to go to your house for dinner tonight." / We said to Uncle Raj, "We are unable to go to your house for dinner tonight."

4 Ann said, "Mother / Mum, I have choir practice today so I will be late." / Ann said to her mother, "I have choir practice today so I will be late."

5 The workmen said to us, "We are sorry but we can't complete the work today."

6 Celine said, "It is / It's good to see you again."

Practice E

(a) Maggie Stewart said that she wouldn't be attending the club's fund-raising dinner on Saturday. She said that her son is / was sick.

(b) Aunt Nora said that she would meet you at the mall at 12.30 on Saturday. She said that she would wait for you at the florist's next to Macy's. She said that you must not be late.

16.1 SENTENCE STRUCTURE

Practice A

1 A, B   2 B, C   3 A, C   4 A, B   5 A, C

Practice B

1 and   2 but   3 and   4 but   5 but
6 and   7 or   8 and   9 and   10 or

Practice C

2 This video game is exciting but I have to rest ⋀.

| or I will be exhausted tomorrow |

3 The journey is long ⋀ and they won't feel tired.

| but they are young |

4 ⋀ Jeff kicked it and it went into the goal.

| Ken passed the ball to Jeff, |

5 I'll drive or I'll sit beside you ⋀.

| but you are not to drive alone |

6 If it doesn't belong to you, ⋀ you will be in trouble

| you have to return it or |

Practice D

1 Rover charged out of the house and chased the neighbour's cat Cleo but she jumped onto the roof of a car and just sat there.

2 Mrs Johnson gave her husband his lunch packet and asked him to post a letter but he accidentally posted his lunch.

3 Janet painted the front door, Fiona painted the gate, Steve painted the upstairs windows and Little Harry painted himself.

4 You must be patient and speak gently to the children or they will not listen to you.

5 Kenneth wiped a mould, mixed clay with sufficient water, poured the clay mixture into the mould and waited for the clay to harden into the shape of a vase.

Practice E

2   4   6   7   9

Practice F

1 It is 7.30 in the evening but I am watching a beautiful sunset. → It is 7.30 in the evening and I am watching a beautiful sunset.

2 Some are red, others are golden or a few are purple. → Some are red, others are golden and a few are purple.

3 I have to keep trying and I will not improve. → I have to keep trying or I will not improve.

4 I want to try again now or I do not have my watercolours with me. → I want to try again now but I do not have my watercolours with me.

5 Anyway, I hear my mother calling but I have to take a shower immediately or she will be upset. → Anyway, I hear my mother calling and I have to take a shower immediately or she will be upset.

16.2 SENTENCE STRUCTURE

Practice A

1 This is our friend Tasha who was the best speaker at yesterday's debate.

2 We like to spend weekends with Grandma who is an excellent cook.

3 Dad spoke to Mr and Mrs Tan who are our new neighbours.

4 The police officer stopped the young woman who was speeding.

5 Steve had an argument with the salesman who tried to sell him a faulty electric shaver.

Practice B

1 who solved   5 a worker   8 respects
2 are   6 were   9 is going
3 choose   7 who is   10 are
4 are to report

Practice C

1 who wanted to paint her.
2 who were reading magazines.
3 who was kind to us.
4 who all my friends enjoy.
5 who are gentle and playful.

Practice D

1 has   4 lived   7 were   9 tell
2 was   5 want   8 walked   10 helps
3 told   6 will

Practice E

1 They catch people who break traffic rules.
2 We'll rescue the child who the gang kidnapped.
3 He counsels youth who get into trouble.
4 She pitied the player who they were booing.
5 That is the nurse who looked after me.

Practice F

1 I am looking at a man and a little girl who is sitting side by side. → I am looking at a man and a little girl who are sitting side by side.

2 He seems to be a person is always cool and confident. → He seems to be a person who is always cool and confident.

3 He is speaking softly to the little girl who are sitting close to him. → He is speaking softly to the little girl who is sitting close to him.

4 They are talking about people who afraid of flying. →
They are talking about people who are afraid of flying.

5 He holds on to the hands of the little girl who say, "Don't be scared, Daddy. I'll be with you on the plane." → He holds on to the hands of the little girl who says, "Don't be scared, Daddy. I'll be with you on the plane."

16.3 SENTENCE STRUCTURE
Practice A
4   5   7   8   10

Practice B
1 He likes any food that is spicy.
2 Here's the document that was lost.
3 Jasmine watches movies which make her laugh.
4 He killed the mosquito which bit him.
5 They are people that I like.

Practice C
1 A, B	2 B, C	3 A, C	4 A, B	5 A, C

Practice D
1 which	5 is puzzling	8 which
2 looks	6 have to	9 who
3 which	7 grow	10 knows
4 newspapers		

Practice E
1 which	5 charges	8 understand
2 who	6 shine	9 which
3 look	7 meet	10 beats
4 is		

Practice F
1 I feel like a bird that sitting in its nest. → I feel like a bird that is sitting in its nest.

2 I watch the car which pass along the street. → I watch the cars which pass along the street.

3 I see a girl which I would like to meet. → I see a girl who / that I would like to meet.

4 She walks with a spring that full of joy. → She walks with a spring that is full of joy.

5 But this is the room which always cheer me. → But this is the room which always cheers me.

16.4 SENTENCE STRUCTURE
Practice A
2   6   7   8   10

Practice B
1 The little girl ran because a goose chased her.
2 I sent her flowers because it's her birthday.
3 She is saving money because she wants to buy a car.
4 Dad won't buy that shirt because it's too expensive.
5 Many tourists visit Venice because it is beautiful.

Practice C
1 because	6	wanted to improve
2 quiet	7	dislikes
3 Nobody	8	gently
4 fresh	9	disobey
5 because	10	accepted

Practice D
1 because	5 midnight	8 gracefully
2 early	6 recovering	9 playful
3 ate	7 fear	10 hurried
4 energetic		

Practice E
2 We found the beach ⟨because it was a weekend. | crowded |

3 I felt no pain because she injected me ⟨. | expertly |

4 I am shivering because I am watching a ⟨movie. | scary |

5 You and I have to speak ⟨because the restaurant is noisy. | loudly |

6 They exchanged ⟨because they wanted to amuse each other. | jokes |

7 John is coming home because he misses his ⟨friends. | old |

8 I believe them because they always tell ⟨. | the truth |

9 She can't sleep soundly because she is ⟨ used to the new house. | not |

10 We are doing the work ⟨because we are afraid of making mistakes. | slowly |

11 I can't get into Mum's clothes because she is ⟨smaller than me. | much |

Practice F
1 because she was late for work.
2 because it was my birthday.
3 because they saw a rat.
4 because it was raining heavily.
5 because our school team became the new football champions.

Practice G
1 At first she tried learning the violin it's because she loved its sound. → At first she tried learning the violin because she loved its sound.

2 Her brother begged her to stop because of she was hurting his eardrums. → Her brother begged her to stop because she was hurting his eardrums.

3 It was driving her crazy too because she was very thankful. → She was very thankful because it was driving her crazy too.

4 She is improving fast it's because she practises every day. → She is improving fast because she practises every day.

5 Her teacher is pleased with her because of she is such a keen pupil. → Her teacher is pleased with her because she is such a keen pupil.

16.5 SENTENCE STRUCTURE
Practice A
1   3   5   6   10

Practice B
1 were performing	5 looked	8 was speaking
2 broke	6 when	9 when
3 while	7 are preparing	10 asked
4 screamed		

Practice C
1 My friend interviewed the players while I took their pictures.
2 She hugged her brother when he wished her luck.
3 We were telling ghost stories while the wind was howling.
4 Sheila always helps me when I have a problem.
5 We are wasting time while the others are working.

Practice D
1 A, C 2 A, B 3 B, C 4 A, C 5 A, B

Practice E
4 1 5 6 3 2

Practice F
1 when	5 argued	8 was
2 were	6 mentions	9 rowed
3 am	7 sleeping	10 while
4 is		

Practice G
1 At this moment I am trying to keep calm while Auntie Kate drives me to school in her rickety old car. → At this moment I am trying to keep calm while Auntie Kate is driving me to school in her rickety old car.
2 She was caring for it tenderly while her neighbour was away. → She cared for it tenderly while her neighbour was away.
3 So she has enough savings to buy the car when her neighbour offered it to her. → So she had enough savings to buy the car when her neighbour offered it to her.
4 Now too she is smiling while the car was threatening to stop. → Now too she is smiling while the car is threatening to stop.
5 It does stop but started again when she pats it playfully on its bonnet. → It does stop but starts again when she pats it playfully on its bonnet.

16.6 SENTENCE STRUCTURE
Practice A
1 he was	4 you are	7 what	9 she likes
2 they will	5 you visited	8 we think	10 what
3 who	6 who you are		

Practice B
1 She knows who you are.
2 I remember what you taught me.
3 He guessed what you were doing.
4 Tell me who they met.
5 We love what she is singing.

Practice C
1 3 5 6 9

Practice D
2 Tell me who the culprit is.
3 Let me make sure who it is.
4 Can you guess what he or she did with the keys?
5 Tell me what you are thinking of.
6 I can guess what he is doing with your keys now.

Practice E
1 Tell me who you saw at the office.
2 I don't know what she does nowadays.
3 I don't remember what Mother told me to do yesterday.
4 I'm not sure who she danced with at the party last week.

5 I don't really know what Sue bought at the sale on Monday.

Practice F
2 They are beginning to wonder who he / working for. [is]
3 I remember / you advised me not to do. [what]
4 We don't know / we can trust here. [who]
5 She heard what / were saying to each other. [we]
6 He can't reveal / donated that big sum. [who]
7 I can guess what you / dreaming of. [are]
8 She tried to see what the delivery man / carrying. [was]
9 We realised who they / cheering for. It was us. [were]
10 He is wondering who / is writing to. [she]
11 I understood / you said just now. [what]

Practice G
1 My schooldays are coming to an end but I still can't decide what should I do. → My schooldays are coming to an end but I still can't decide what I should do.
2 I wonder who can I ask for advice. → I wonder who I can ask for advice.
3 He or she also needs to understand what am I really interested in. → He or she also needs to understand what I am really interested in.
4 My parents must be anxious to hear what do I feel about it. → My parents must be anxious to hear what I feel about it.
5 They can help me find out what am I best suited for. → They can help me find out what I am best suited for.

16.7 SENTENCE STRUCTURE
Practice A
1 B : Mr Tan owns the building behind our house.
2 A : My grandfather is that man with shining white hair.
3 A : We love the tomatoes from your garden.
4 A : I feel sorry for the animals in the cage.
5 B : I went to the supermarket opposite the library.

Practice B
1 Don't tease the kitten under the chair.
2 He is looking for a house on a hill.
3 I know a girl with green eyes.
4 Don't go into the hut beside the river.
5 My mother has gone to the post office across the road.

Practice C
1 in the middle of the city.
2 inside the magic lamp.
3 above the clouds last night.
4 next to the emergency exit.
5 in front of him very loudly.

Practice D
2 We play tennis at the club near our office.
3 The fox watched the hens in the coop.

4 Sorry, I broke the spectacles on the sofa.
5 We enjoyed the barbecue at Jane's house.
6 I like the child with big brown eyes.

Practice E
1 A, B   2 B, C   3 A, C   4 B, C   5 A, B

Practice F
1 above
2 outside
3 by the field now
4 below
5 along
6 at
7 near his house last month
8 beside
9 opposite the station at noon
10 about

Practice G
1 I'll take you into a cave that with a strange story. → I'll take you into a cave with a strange story.
2 According to the story, long ago the area used to be a village was by the sea. → According to the story, long ago the area used to be a village by the sea.
3 One day, he had to take shelter in the harbour from a storm near his village. → One day, he had to take shelter from a storm in the harbour near his village.
4 She recognised the well-dressed man who on the deck as her long-lost son. → She recognised the well-dressed man on the deck as her long-lost son.
5 Her tears fell on the earth in torrents beneath her feet. → Her tears fell in torrents on the earth beneath her feet.

16.8 SENTENCE STRUCTURE
Practice A
1 the   5 rain   8 gentleness
2 their   6 illness   9 honesty
3 her   7 carelessness   10 wind
4 the

Practice B
1 neatness   5 loyalty   8 slimness
2 politeness   6 sweetness   9 strength
3 intelligence   7 height   10 playfulness
4 bravery

Practice C
1   3   6   8   9

Practice D
2 I had three slices of cake because of my hunger.
3 Sometimes people get angry with him because of his frankness.
4 Many cars are stuck in that area because of the flood.
5 We will always honour him because of his courage.
6 The department has a good name because of its efficiency..

Practice E
1 A, C   2 A, B   3 B, C   4 A, C   5 B, C

Practice F
1 He became famous because of his talented. → He became famous because of his talent.

2 Many people invited him to parties because of he famous. → Many people invited him to parties because of his fame.
3 They also wanted to be his friends because of their wealth. → They also wanted to be his friends because of his wealth.
4 However, Lee avoided them because of insincere. → However, Lee avoided them because of their insincerity.
5 Now many students have a bright future because of his generous. → Now many students have a bright future because of his generosity.

16.9 SENTENCE STRUCTURE
Practice A
2   3   6   8   9

Practice B
1 She always enjoys visiting them.
2 We all hated walking in the rain.
3 They plan to go away soon.
4 She finally finished her Christmas shopping.
5 Everybody wants to come here.

Practice C
1 to walk   5 skating   8 to go
2 preparing   6 to report   9 to be
3 to meet   7 making   10 decorating
4 seeing

Practice D
2 My uncle loves to make pizza.
3 She tried warning me but I didn't hear her.
4 We started playing tennis but then it rained.
5 I tried swimming two laps but I failed.
6 I like to make traditional dishes.

Practice E
2 Dylan promised to take care of our pet dalmation next week.
3 The girls practised dancing on the stage in their costumes.
4 Pamela plans to marry Ken next January.
5 George stopped driving because of his accident.
6 The workers finished loading the fruit onto the lorries.

Practice F
1 to send   5 living   8 taking
2 to experience   6 to be   9 to make
3 mixing   7 to cheer   10 being
4 missed

Practice G
1 You asked me when I decided becoming an artist. → You asked me when I decided to become an artist.
2 I didn't even hope doing well in the subject at school. → I didn't even hope to do well in the subject at school.
3 Then, I practised to daub paint on canvas. → Then, I practised daubing paint on canvas.
4 For years I refused letting anyone see my work. → For years I refused to let anyone see my work.
5 As soon as I finished to paint something, I would hide it. → As soon as I finished painting something, I would hide it.

TEST 1

A
1 A	2 –	3 the	4 the	5 –
6 the	7 the	8 An	9 a	10 an

B
1 this	4 themselves	7 That	9 hers
2 her	5 She	8 it's	10 yours
3 it	6 me		

C

1 Cora / opens / her cake shop at 10 a.m.

2 Mrs Singh came / home / because her car had stalled at the traffic lights.

3 The families prayed / for / a good harvest.

4 Ben / looked for his missing book / .

5 We have / spoken / to the principal about the anti-smoking campaign.

6 The rescue workers fought / to save / the accident victims.

7 I can't / find him / . I don't know where he is.

8 Frankie / knows what to say / when he goes to a big party.

9 The stewardess smiled at us / as we boarded the plane / .

10 I will be meeting / Robin at the airport when he flies in / .

D
1 line 1: audience's	6 line 5: troupe's
2 line 2: dancer's	7 line 6: Maria's
3 line 2: dancers'	8 line 7: guitarist's
4 line 3: crowd's	9 line 8: partners'
5 line 4: men's	10 line 8: dancers'

E
1 A	2 C	3 B	4 B	5 A
6 C	7 A	8 B	9 C	10 A

TEST 2

A
1 were	4 Is
2 The herd	5 antique furniture
3 don't like	

B
1 cheered	6 will set
2 takes	7 has already accepted
3 were mowing	8 are enjoying
4 have worked	9 is going to study
5 queued	10 will be returning

C

1 is   2 are test   3 beat   4 is   5 sewn

D
1 don't we	2 isn't it	3 doesn't she
4 don't I	5 aren't they	

E
1 going	2 Whose	3 Why does Bill
4 Which	5 sugar	

F

1 She comes from Switzerland.

2 She is planning to tour Asia next month. / the following month.

3 She wants to promote her latest album. / her latest album 'Shadows in the day'.

4 Robert Newton is Marissa's manager. / Her manager is Robert Newton.

5 Each fan at the concerts will get a copy of the photo taken when Marissa won last year's 'Songbird of the year' award.

G
1 was	6 was getting
2 their goods there	7 were fighting
3 soon became	8 decided to
4 It conquered	9 Malacca in 1511
5 wanted to	10 had to

TEST 3

A
1 at	2 During	3 on
4 under	5 behind	

B
1 use	2 Must	3 can
4 be	5 may be	

C

A : Dad's silk shirt, black jacket and trousers aren't in the cupboard. Did Mum send them to the dry cleaner's?

B : No, they're over there by the ironing board. Sheila's ironing them.

D

1 They told me that they didn't see me the day before.

2 I asked Peter if he was coming with us.

3 The nurse told me that I had to wait for 10 minutes to see the doctor.

4 Ted told Gary that he was taking part in the elocution contest the next day.

5 Mum told Rita that her room was a mess.

E
1 and	5 have	8 but
2 in	6 between	9 that
3 which	7 rears	10 under
4 or		

F
1 acting	5 who	8 who
2 putting	6 to join	9 what
3 pretending	7 what	10 who
4 to be		

262

G

1 B, C 2 A, C 3 B, C 4 A, B 5 A, C

TEST 4

A

1	of	2	is	3	be	4	has / uses	5	are
6	or	7	is	8	His	9	the	10	of

B

1 They use buttons (to fasten shirts).
2 They used buttons with loops before the 13th century / before buttonholes were invented.
3 Gold, silver and ivory buttons showed (that) a person was wealthy or held a high position.
4 Matthew Boulton introduced steel in the manufacture of buttons.
5 They are produced in factories.

C

1	D	5	B	9	A	13	A	17	A
2	C	6	D	10	C	14	B	18	C
3	A	7	C	11	B	15	D	19	D
4	D	8	B	12	A	16	C	20	B

D

1 The bookcase was designed by my grandfather.
2 Ruth said that she had not received Jim's postcard.
3 I spoke to the man who witnessed the accident.
4 Don't take the old route along the coast.
5 They decided to employ him because of his good record.

TEST 5

A

1	are	5	their	8	and / or
2	Male	6	wool	9	its
3	and	7	that / which	10	for
4	weigh				

B

1 They left for Wave Rock at about six in the morning.
2 It is about 340 km from Perth.
3 It looks like a huge tidal wave. / a giant wave.
4 He didn't climb to the top of Wave Rock because he is afraid of heights.
5 They were / were standing in front of the rock.

C

1	C	5	C	9	D	13	D	17	A
2	D	6	B	10	B	14	A	18	C
3	D	7	B	11	D	15	C	19	B
4	A	8	A	12	C	16	A	20	B

D

1 We watched the boys who were carrying ice-skates.
2 Those are the trucks that we passed on the road just now.
3 I'd like to buy the large picture which is in that corner.
4 Tony's house was burgled because of his carelessness.
5 Our grand-aunt promised to visit us again in August.

TEST 6

A

1	to	5	and	8	vegetables
2	the	6	they	9	and
3	to	7	cooking	10	is
4	is				

B

1 They are in the Pacific Ocean.
2 They belong to Ecuador.
3 Their location is special. / Animals from different parts of the world have been able to find their way to the islands and have settled there.
4 They took hundreds of the giant tortoises onto their ships because the reptiles could live for a year without food.
5 The sailors killed the giant tortoises for food.

C

1	C	5	B	9	C	13	B	17	C
2	D	6	B	10	D	14	A	18	D
3	B	7	D	11	B	15	C	19	A
4	A	8	A	12	D	16	A	20	C

D

1 Rita's ambition is to become a concert pianist.
2 She practises playing the piano every evening.
3 She is only 14 years old but she has already passed her Grade 8 exam and hopes to continue her music education abroad.
4 Yesterday, Rita's parents met Mr Mark Davies who is the principal of a music college in Britain.
5 Mr Davies was impressed because Rita had scored distinctions in all her theory and practical exams.